A Farming Legacy 1910-2010
Celebrating the centenary of the Felix Thornley Cobbold Agricultural Trust

Felix Thornley Cobbold, from a painting by John Collier, now hanging in Christchurch Mansion. This was commissioned by Ipswich Borough Council and presented to Felix at the end of his mayoral year in 1897, which was also the year of Queen Victoria's Diamond Jubilee. Felix had paid for many of the town's celebrations out of his own pocket. (Courtesy of Colchester and Ipswich Museum Service)

A Farming Legacy 1910-2010
Celebrating the centenary of the Felix Thornley Cobbold Agricultural Trust

Rosalind Thomas

OLD POND PUBLISHING

ISBN 978-1-908397-14-0

A catalogue record for this book is available from the British Library

Published by
Old Pond Publishing
Dencora Business Centre
36 White House Road
Ipswich IP1 5LT
United Kingdom
www.oldpond.com

Cover design by Liz Whatling
Cover photograph of Quadtrac ploughing by Chris Lockwood
Typeset by Galleon Typesetting
Printed in China

ACKNOWLEDGEMENTS

Many people have helped me with the writing of this book. Among them, Dr Frank Grace, Andrew Phillips, Colin Smith, Bruce Hinton, Nicholas Fiske, Brian Bell MBE, Steve Coghill, Arthur Hicks, Robin Graham, Kenneth Wilding, Joan Prowse, Mr and Mrs Golding, John Pearson, Mrs Susan Bethell (Mrs Susan Doran), Sir Edward Greenwell, Sue Andrews and Jan Byrne of the Hadleigh Society, Ron Stobart, and the staff at the Suffolk Record Office.

Contents

Foreword

The History of the Felix Thornley Cobbold Agricultural Trust (FTCAT)

This book is more, much more, than an account of the development and progress of an agricultural charity; it amounts to a hundred years of the history of farming in Suffolk, and indeed of the major arable areas of England, from 1910.

Ros Thomas records the foundation of the Trust from a bequest of Felix Thornley Cobbold during the difficult days of the early twentieth century, through the deprivation of the Great Depression, the shortages of the Second World War and the security of farm commodity price support into the new millennium. She shows how political and social change has affected farming, and how the Trust has responded and changed to meet its founder's vision of a better rural economy. From providing self-employment opportunities for a few labourers in a handful of parishes in East Suffolk, the Trust's influence on agricultural improvement has evolved to supporting important projects at some of the major research institutions in the country. Through her painstaking research she has identified the people who have shaped the Trust through the years. We are grateful for her sensitive and detailed analysis of events.

The Trust is only able to make a difference in the farming scene through the generous dedication of time and expertise by trustees who have been selected for their specialist knowledge. They have the responsibility of deciding how resources should be invested for overall benefit; they build on the work of trustees past; they are responsible for looking ahead, and for making those decisions which ensure that the Trust continues to contribute to agricultural development in the future.

Stephen Cobbald
Chairman

Introduction

The History of the Felix Thornley Cobbold Agricultural Trust

In 1992 I began work in the library of Otley College, and became curious about Felix Thornley Cobbold and the Trust which bears his name. I discovered that little was known about him, and started doing my own research. There were few personal documents – two letters in St John's College Library, a notebook in the Lloyds Bank archives, and a book of obituaries owned by the Cobbold family. My research progressed slowly as I spent weekends reading the Ipswich newspaper archives stored in the University of Essex library. I was able to build a picture of an extraordinary man – cultured, sensitive, intelligent and unassuming.

The Cobbold Family Trust, run by Anthony Cobbold, agreed to publish my book to coincide with the centenary of his death in 2009, and a memorable evening was held at Christchurch Mansion, Ipswich – a site that Felix had donated to the town.

Following this evening the Felix Thornley Cobbold Agricultural Trust asked me to write a history of the centenary of the Trust, which I was delighted to do, as it meant that I could continue to research Felix's legacy. I soon discovered that the Trust in its three incarnations – as a provider of smallholdings and allotments, as the owner of a demonstration farm at Otley and landlord of Otley College, and finally as a provider of grants to support local agriculture – was at all times shaped by a wider history. Thus, a history of the Trust lands had to include a history of East Anglian agriculture – indeed, the Trust history becomes incomprehensible if the wider picture is not explored as it forms a microcosm within the local agricultural scene.

I also discovered that there are few such alternative accounts of twentieth century farming. Agricultural colleges are concerned with the task of equipping their students for the challenges of present-day farming, and farmers themselves are engaged in the day-to-day battle to survive and adapt to modern farming demands. Just as *To Suffolk with Love* was written almost entirely from primary sources, this history has relied on the minute books made available to me by the trustees, and I have then moved outside the Trust papers to look at the wider scene when prompted by their content.

This has presented a problem: modern official sites for the European Union or the British Government quote current farm subsidies and regulations, but to glean information about a slightly more distant era has proved more difficult. For some aspects of modern farming I have consulted Wikipedia, although some articles are insufficiently referenced and their accuracy may be suspect. Wherever possible my facts have been verified from other sources, and the effects of EU and government regulations were clearly mirrored in the actions of the Trust and its tenants.

During the last century, Britain has fought two world wars, become involved in the European community, and faced several periods of financial hardship. Similarly, British agriculture, and Suffolk agriculture in particular, has been shaped by extraordinary changes in agricultural research and mechanisation. The drive for increased food production has now become tempered by a similarly powerful drive to maintain the environment and to preserve the beauty of the countryside.

During the year of writing this book, Otley College celebrated its 40th birthday, and the trustees asked me to include a separate chapter on college history; the first draft was produced for use at the 'birthday bash'. The account of the college in that chapter presents at times an alternative view of the college than that which appears in the Trust chapters – not least because I was part of the staff for some years and I experienced the extraordinary environment that was Otley in the early 1990s.

For the last chapters of this Trust history I have not even had the benefit of hindsight, but have had to form an assessment that may be proved wrong. Nevertheless, it presents a view of farming as at the beginning of 2011, and this in itself is of value.

Felix Thornley Cobbold was one of a group of remarkable philanthropists of his time, and I know that he would be happy that his legacy is continuing to support local agriculture. The work of the trustees in these uncertain times carries forward his vision of helping those struggling to enter the industry.

Chapter One

January to October 1910
The First Phase: Idealism and Expediency

This book was commissioned by the Felix Thornley Cobbold Agricultural Trust to commemorate the centenary of the formation of the Trust in 1910, and forms a history of the Trust throughout its first hundred years. It also describes the turbulent progress of agriculture in the eastern counties during this period.

Felix Thornley Cobbold (1841–1909) was the youngest son of John Chevallier Cobbold, brewer, of Holywells Mansion, Ipswich. After leaving university, Felix became bursar of King's College, Cambridge, and then returned to Ipswich to enter the family bank. In later years, he became Mayor of Ipswich, a Liberal Member of Parliament for Stowmarket and then Ipswich, a landowner and a philanthropist. He died in his rooms at Westminster while still serving as the MP for Ipswich and by his will he gave land and money to East Suffolk County Council to provide allotments and smallholdings. (See Appendix 1 for a list of donated property.)

This chapter describes the background to the bequest and the process by which East Suffolk Council formed the Felix Thornley Cobbold Agricultural Trust in order to administer the property.

Felix Thornley Cobbold had for some years prior to his death had a vision of providing smallholdings and allotments in Suffolk to provide employment for unemployed agricultural labourers. Throughout the nineteenth century, there existed poor conditions for the labourers with low wages, abysmal living conditions in tied cottages, and farm closures which resulted in widespread unemployment. Also in the nineteenth century, the long process of enclosing common fields, moors, wasteland, and even roadside verges, came to an end with a series of General Enclosure Acts 1801, 1836 and 1845 – which replaced the custom of passing thousands of individual acts that had preceded them. Country dwellers lost their rights to graze common land and wastes, and even to gather firewood. This meant that their living standards fell even further.

Eastern Anglian Agricultural Lockout 1874

Some attempt at self-help led to the formation of the National Agricultural Workers' Union in 1872 under the leadership of Joseph Arch. In 1874, Arch organised a strike in Suffolk and North Essex seeking higher wages for labourers. By the beginning of April, over 6,000 men were on strike.

The strike was broken by a lockout of union members by farmers who formed the Essex and Suffolk Farmers' Defence Association, who declared that they would not pay more than 2s for a 12-hour day, and would sack workers who would not agree to leave the union.[1] Over 150 employers held a meeting at the Bull in Woodbridge to discuss the extra cost that would be involved, and they resolved not to allow themselves to be controlled by the union.

In May, the *Ipswich Journal* reported that 1,250 men were being paid strike pay by the union: 341 in Saxmundham, 576 in Woodbridge, 117 in Botesdale, 150 in Stowmarket, 44 in Westhorpe and 22 in Elmswell – extraordinary numbers of men for such small communities. In addition, around Exning there were 2,085 being paid strike pay – 412 in the Eye district and also 359 children.[2] In the two next editions, figures were also quoted for Wickham Market, Shottisham, Tunstall, Bredfield, Clopton, Great Bealings, Eyke, Alderton, Butley and Grundisburgh.

The lockout gradually ended with the coming of harvest time when some men drifted back into work as union funds for strike pay ran low, but Arch says that at the end of the dispute over 4,000 men had been thrown out of work leaving a legacy of poverty, unemployment, migration to industrial towns, or emigration to the colonies for the ex-strikers.[3]

One further consequence of the strike and lockout was the growing realisation that the labourers had a genuine grievance, which attracted sympathy not only from Liberal politicians, but also from some landowners. The second Earl of Stradbroke, for example, convened a meeting in Ipswich in April 1874 to create a Suffolk Provident Society, which gave practical help to poor agricultural workers.

The Liberal Party and Land Reform

One solution to preventing the gradual drift away from the land appeared to Liberals to be the provision of smallholdings by sympathetic landlords, private or public. However, throughout the nineteenth century there had been fierce controversy about the position of smallholdings, not least because earlier in the century the acquisition of small parcels of land by Chartists had been a way to obtain suffrage. Even after the labourers finally gained the right to vote in 1884 considerable hostility remained towards allowing labourers to become landowners and somehow step out of their class. Smallholdings were thus an ideological target for attack, not just one for agricultural debate.

The most prominent campaigners for land reform were Joseph Chamberlain and Jesse Collings in the Liberal Party. Jesse had been MP for Ipswich from 1880 to 1886, and had been a supporter of Joseph Arch for many years. In the ensuing election of 1886, 'three acres and a cow' had been the slogan which swept the Liberals to power under Gladstone, together with Liberal support for the extension of suffrage to agricultural labourers.[4] Jesse and Joseph argued that local authorities should be given the power to buy land and offer it out in small parcels to poor tenants to provide a living on the land, either as an allotment or as a smallholding. They argued that three acres and a cow would provide a subsistence income for an agricultural worker, although this was hotly contested in the correspondence columns of the Suffolk press. The first act to permit such land purchases was the Allotment Act of 1887, but the first Small Holdings and Allotment Act was only passed in 1907 and amended in 1908, the year before Felix's death.

Felix probably first came into contact with Jesse Collings at a Liberal Conference held in Ipswich in 1885, and he became an admirer of Jesse's work. During his time as an MP for Stowmarket and throughout his life as a banker, Felix had been made aware of the grinding poverty in the countryside at first hand. Felix also supported the work of Arch, even recommending unionisation in his speeches, although

many of his bank clients were probably the very landowners that were intent on breaking the union. Although born of a Tory family, Felix, whose father and eldest brother had been Tory MPs for Ipswich, became increasingly radical in his views, so much so that one of his final speeches was to a Trade Union Conference and it was said that he often sat with the Labour MPs in the House of Commons.

During the years from 1885 to 1909, Felix became convinced that one contribution he could make to aid social conditions in Suffolk – both in the countryside and the town – was to use his considerable wealth to purchase land that could be divided into allotments and smallholdings. He had acquired his own hobby farm at Felixstowe on the death of his father, and worked hard to understand current good practice under the tutelage of his farm manager, George Harrison. He became chairman of the Suffolk Agricultural Association and even held a meeting at the farm. One committee member commented that Felix clearly did not know much about farming, but was nevertheless an excellent chairman and was willing to learn.

In 1900, when he stood for election again, this time in the Woodbridge constituency, he placed an advertisement in the *East Anglian Daily Times* seeking tenants for land he owned in Sproughton. The advertisement promised that not only would the tenants be able to rent land at a fair rent but, if they paid a little extra, in due course they would be able to purchase the land and become small farmers rather than tenants. Felix's radicalism hardly endeared him to the farmers around Woodbridge and he lost the seat.

A second estate was also purchased by Felix around the turn of the century at Pond Hall outside Hadleigh. An advertisement for the letting of Valley Farm and Ramsey Farm had appeared in the *Ipswich Journal* in 1893, apparently without takers, because the following year, on 20 January 1894, the advertisement appeared again, this time with the addition of Pond Hall Farm. The advert said that the land was being farmed by the owners and that Pond Hall Farm consisted of:

> 396 acres of First class Corn and Root Land (40 acres of grass). Valley Farm had 198 acres, 14 of grass, and Ramsey Farm 142 acres, 6 of grass. Each has excellent House and Buildings, (cottages additional if desired), all situate in or near the town of Hadleigh at a short distance from the Station and 8 or 9 miles from Ipswich. A good retail Milk Trade is attached to Pond Hall.

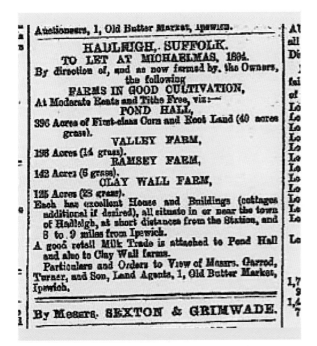

This advertisement for the Pond Hall Estate appeared in the *Ipswich Journal*, 1894.

The land had belonged firstly to Caleb and Robert Kersey, who sold part of their land to the Tollemache family in 1846 for £11,000. Felix appears to have negotiated for the property together with Alfred Harwood of Belstead Hall in 1895, originally as Alfred's banker. Then Felix paid £4,200 to the vendors and £200 to Alfred to become sole owner. At this time the Kersey family still owned the land abutting on the west, and Pond Hall was adjacent to the Hintlesham Hall Estate on the east. The Pond Hall land appears to have first become available for sale in 1892 although only offered for public sale in 1893 and 1894, but Alfred Harwood is named on the deed as having been involved in the purchase from 1892.

Gary Farm, Hadleigh

In 1906, a young man called William Prowse saw an advertisement for smallholdings on an estate just outside Hadleigh, Suffolk. William had been born in Liverpool of a seafaring family, but he decided to enter farming and did a course at Harper Adams Agricultural College. After this, he spent a brief time farming

in Canada but found the climate harsh and returned to England to look for land. The notes he took during his interview with Felix Cobbold survive and show that he would be leasing the land from Felix Cobbold but would be joining a co-operative run by a Tenants' Society registered under the Industrial and Provident Societies Act, 1893. The rent would be fixed at £1 pa, which would include the land tax but not local rates. Loans would be available at four per cent for economic improvements or buildings. The Tenants' Society would act for members and would become 'a Trading Society to do the business of purchasing and selling'. Tenants were also to be offered perpetual tenancies, and continued education – in the form of lectures, etc. – organised by the Tenants' Society.

Scribbled on the back of a postcard from Winnipeg, Canada, are these notes that William Prowse wrote in 1906 during an interview with Felix Cobbold while applying for a smallholding at Hadleigh. (Joan Prowse)

This building – later named Gary Farm – in Pond Hall Lane, Hadleigh, was offered to William Prowse in 1906, along with a cottage for his employees. (Joan Prowse)

William Prowse in 1908 fills milk bottles in his dairy at Gary Farm. (Joan Prowse)

Gary Farm milk being delivered in bottles to a cottage door in 1908. (Joan Prowse)

Domestic milk delivery by churns on a cart by William Keeble of the Orwell Park Dairies to the village of Nacton. The milk was carried in a can from the churn to the customer's doorstep, where it was emptied into a jug. Contrast this with the methods of William Prowse. (David Kindred)

William found the prospect exciting, and accepted a tenancy of just over 26 acres, together with a newly built three-bedroom farmhouse at the side of the Pond Hall Road and a worker's cottage further up the road. He started a dairy herd at his new holding. Two photos from 1908 show William filling milk bottles – pints and half pints – from milk churns in his dairy and then delivering them to a customer. At a time when most milkmen were touring the streets with churns carried on the back of small carts and filling customers' jugs from the churns, William's method showed his advanced skills as a college trainee.[5]

Sproughton and Hadleigh Estates

The original 70 acres of Sproughton land had had considerable improvements carried out by Felix since his purchase in 1900. He installed a water supply to the properties, powered by a wind pump on a borehole, with one of the tenants being given the task of running the pump for several hours each day and oiling the machinery. The water was fed into a reservoir, and several stopcocks installed for controlling the flow. Felix also built houses for occupation by the smallholders, such as the farmhouse at Laurel Farm, Burstall Lane. In addition to the nine holdings there was also an area of five acres let to Sproughton Parish Council for allotments.

At the time of Felix's death in 1909 all this land was in occupation by tenants, and was being overseen by a Mr Diggle, who inspected the estate several times a year and arranged for repairs and improvement requests to be conveyed to Felix for approval. Thus, the Sproughton land played little part in the discussions of the council, other than that of legal acquisition itself.

The Hadleigh Estate was a different matter as it was still not divided or provided with a complete infrastructure. The lands had been acquired later than the Sproughton land and in a piecemeal fashion. The initial purchase of Pond Hall Farm, Valley Farm and Ramsey Farm in one lot in 1895 had been followed later by the purchase of the 'Canterbury Land' which was then merged into Valley Farm. Later he bought a field known as 'Arnold Field' which had once been part of the Kate's Hill estate before being converted into allotments, and then another cottage and garden forming about one acre. The final purchases occurred in November 1908 when he acquired 'Cook Warrens' and then exchanged two fields which were part of Valley Farm for a more convenient small field near the Valley Farm buildings. The result of these acquisitions was a compact estate reaching from Pond Hall Road in the south to the Hadleigh–Ipswich Road on the northern boundary, with another eight fields south of the Pond Hall Road. (See map of the Hadleigh Estate on facing page.)

For a water supply to this estate there was an oil-driven engine installed in 1900 which pumped water to a tank on the west of the property and to a reservoir to the east, and from there water was laid on to Valley and Ramsey Farm premises as well as to several smallholders' houses. This waterworks was in the charge of Mr J G R Smyth, who also acted as farm bailiff and lived at Pond Hall House.

In addition, Felix had used his faithful mentor and servant, George T Harrison, as agent for this estate. George had managed the Pond Hall bank account into which all receipts were paid and from which expenses were paid. At the time of his death Felix was also paying for improvements, which George had hoped to repay as soon as stock and crops were sold from the estate. Further, with the unexpected death of Felix a flock of sheep from Hadleigh had been sent down to Felix's own farm at Felixstowe for winter grazing and a group of four heifers and some pigs sent up to Hadleigh.

The Legacy

When Felix Cobbold died in December 1909 after a

brief illness, he bequeathed to East Suffolk County Council not only his real estate at Hadleigh and also at Sproughton, but also all the growing crops and stock – live and dead – on the farms as well as all the carts and other farming implements at Hadleigh. The land was to be held 'upon trust that they use the said hereditaments and personal estate and the rents and profits arising therefrom in developing small holdings and allotments on so much of the land in Hadleigh as is not already occupied and on any other land that they may acquire by mean of such rents and profits'. If the county council refused to accept the bequest or were disqualified from doing so then the property would revert to his heir, Phillip Cobbold.

The council had a problem: they were loath to lose this gift, but by the Mortmain Act of 1888 the council was not able to acquire land even for a charitable purpose without a special licence. Secondly, by the Small Holdings and Allotment Act of 1908 the council was empowered to acquire land for smallholdings, but allotments were actually to be provided by urban or parish councils. In addition, Arnold Field lay outside the boundary of East Suffolk County Council. Finally, if the various problems of Mortmain and the administration of the allotments could be overcome, the rents derived would have to be kept in a separate fund and administered as a trust.

The council took legal advice in January 1910 from a Lincoln's Inn lawyer, J Rolt, who gave the opinion that the solution was to apply for a licence in Mortmain. On 15 March, the decision had been taken that the council should accept the gift, and the Charity Commissioners were applied to for an order to sanction the retention of the land by the county council, and also to vest the property in the Official Trustee of Charity Lands. The county council became the trustees, and a sub-committee was formed to administer the estates.

The negotiations continued with Philip Cobbold with regard to the bank overdrafts, the payment of tithes, and, not least, the misplaced sheep, pigs and heifers. The clerk – A Townshend Cobbold – wrote a report on 22 April on the outstanding legal points, and described the efforts he had made with the help of George Harrison to provide descriptions of the holdings for the Charity Commissioners.

Two further problems had arisen: when Townshend Cobbold examined the leases he discovered, as noted

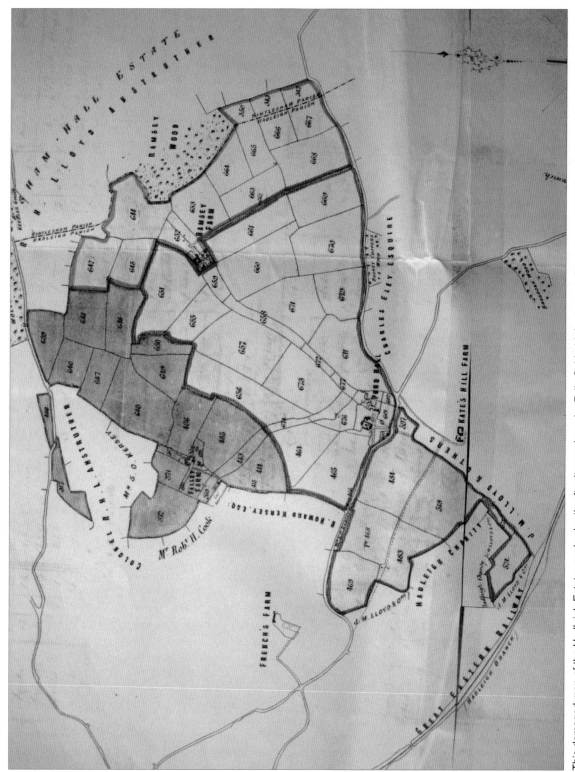

This damaged map of the Hadleigh Estate, made shortly after its purchase by Felix Cobbold, forms part of the deeds of Highfield Cottage, Pond Hall Road, and shows the land before Felix built the houses. On the south side of Pond Hall Road are the fields of Gary Farm, and Highfield Cottage on OS 468. Attached by a narrow strip of land to the estate on OS 524 were the Arnold Field allotments, later added to Gary Farm. (Kenneth Wilding)

above, that Felix had included a clause that a co-operative association should be formed under the provisions of the Industrial and Provident Societies Acts, and also that certain portions of the estate should be demised from the landlord on a lease of 99 years with an option to purchase. If this did not happen within seven years of the start of the lease, then the tenant should have the right to buy within 21 years at 20 times the annual value of the rent reserved, and at 25 times the annual interest on landlord's outlay in erecting houses and buildings. Felix's radicalism was revealed once again.

The Establishment of the Sub-committee

A sub-committee of the council was appointed by the Small Holdings and Allotments Committee on 22 April to visit the properties and to consider a scheme of management under the chairmanship of the third Earl of Stradbroke. The other members were George Fiske, Alfred Harwood, H F Harwood, A H Hucklesby and W W Hunt, together with the clerk, Townshend Cobbold, the county land agent, Lionel Holm Rodwell and Felix's old agent, George Harrison. Two other members sent their apologies: the Rev J F A Hervey and Robert L Everett.

Of this group, Lord Stradbroke was a Tory land-owner from Henham Hall (see Appendix II), and George Fiske farmed the Thornbush Estate abutting Felix's Sproughton lands. Alfred Harwood lived at Belstead Hall and was a magistrate, seedsman and farmer, and had previously part-owned the Pond Hall Estate together with Felix Cobbold. William Hunt lived at Park Farm, Grundisburgh, and Albert Hucklesby was from Lodge Farm, Wyverstone.

The two missing members would have been, in theory, the most sympathetic to Felix's radicalism. Robert Everett had been a friend and fellow exponent of 'advanced radical Liberalism' and had also become a Liberal MP. In Felix's final election Everett had stood in the Woodbridge constituency while Felix stood in Ipswich, and both had been successful. He was a member of a family of yeoman farmers from Rushwell, near Ipswich.

The other missing member, the Reverend Hervey, was an old friend of Felix, and had contributed a long and sympathetic obituary to the *Ipswich Journal*, quoted in the previous paragraph.

The sub-committee had visited the estate at Hadleigh and found that the land was 'being satisfactorily farmed'. The allotments on Arnold Field on the whole were 'fairly well cultivated chiefly for the growing of corn, and were about one acre plots'.

The Hadleigh land which had been described in such glowing terms in the advertisement of 1894 were found to be of mixed quality, some of which was 'unsuitable for the purpose of holdings of a less area than 40 acres, and that to develop the property must be a gradual process. Meanwhile, however, steps should be taken to divide the land into such holdings as the existing houses and buildings would best serve'. The regulations for smallholdings insisted that they should be of less than 50 acres, so permission was to be sought to exceed this limit. Further, it was envisaged that the expenses of adapting the existing houses and buildings and possibly building new ones, would have to be met, 'presumably from the revenue of this estate'. It would thus appear at the outset that the definition of a smallholding held by the committee was far from the old Liberal aim of 'three acres and a cow', or from a piece of land which would give a living to a young man starting in agriculture or a displaced agricultural labourer.

This estate was very much a work in progress, but the trustees had insufficient funds to carry out major transformations at the outset. What could be achieved with good initial funding can still be seen in the Salvation Army smallholdings in Boxted and the Land Settlement Association holdings at Lawford, Essex. Both present a striking contrast with the Hadleigh Estate. At Boxted, General Booth had plucked poor unemployed men from the streets of London, given them initial training in husbandry at the Salvation Army lands at Hadleigh in Essex, and then given them five-acre plots with a modest house with further practical support for the first few years. The holdings and houses still exist, lining Straight Road, Boxted, and are mainly occupied by horticultural nurseries of various kinds. The Salvation Army experiment itself ended in considerable bad feeling as some of the men, unused to hard manual labour and responsibility, were evicted by the Army, which was the kind of publicity that reflected badly on their public image.[6]

The Lawford experiment is still flourishing. Again, the scheme was not catering for agricultural labourers, but unemployed men such as Durham miners. These men, unlike the London poor, were quick-witted and used to hard labour, and thrived in their new life by using members of their families as extra workers. Indeed, when the manager appointed by the association tried to cheat them by selling the crops in London for more than he admitted, a group of them followed him to London and exposed his fraud. These holdings still exist in their original form, lining the road from Ardleigh to Lawford village, and along a specially constructed back road. Both of these settlements echo more closely Jesse Collings' 'three acres and a cow' ideal.

Felix's Hadleigh Estate, by contrast, lacked the kind of funding that Felix had used in setting up the Sproughton Estate. The committee asked that power should be given to the council as trustees (as county rates could not be used) to borrow on the security of the properties, if necessary, to pay the government duties and to employ the necessary agents. They also hoped that a grant or advance under the Development and Road Improvement Funds Act 1909 might be forthcoming for the initial expenses of setting up the property.

Co-operative Farms and Land Purchase

When they came to the problem of the leases, the committee had written to one of the Small Holding Commissioners and to the secretary of the County Councils Association for advice. The advice they received was that the Agricultural Co-operative Society organised the formation of both Land Renting and Agricultural Co-operative Trading Societies, but could not help them with the division and equipment of a farm as their functions were 'confined to propagandist work pure and simple'. The commissioner advised that there were several land renting societies in existence which often rented farms from a council as a whole and divided them into holdings which they then sub-let to their members. The secretary of the County Councils Association surmised that the Central Small Holdings Society might be able to give more assistance with a scheme, and the question would be discussed at the association's annual meeting on 28 May. Memoranda were then being prepared. The sub-committee decided to defer consideration of co-operation until after a promised report from the Board of Agriculture and the County Councils Association memoranda.

What did not emerge from these discussions was that a scheme was already in operation only a few miles away at Assington. One of these farms lasted as a co-operative until 1913, but was then bought out by the foreman, and two other farms remained until 1918, and it is possible that Felix knew about this experiment. There had certainly been discussions in the Ipswich press on this and similar schemes.

The squire of Assington, John Gurdon, started his scheme of co-operative smallholdings in 1830 'to raise the labourer in his class, without taking him out of it, by giving him a stake in the country, and thus rendering him a responsible man, not only to his God, but to his neighbours'.[7] He owned a farm of 100 acres and could find no good tenant, so called together 20 'of the better class of labourers in the parish' and offered them the farm with the loan of the necessary capital '(without interest) if they would undertake to cultivate it conformably to my regulations, each man paying down £2 as a guarantee'. During the next ten years the capital of £400 was paid back and the tenants were in complete possession 'as tenants of a well-cultivated and well-stocked farm'.

In 1852, he divided a second farm, this time of 150 acres for another 30 men. The idiosyncrasies of the scheme were that the men were still employed at their old jobs, and worked on the co-operative farm only if they lost their jobs. Further, no new housing was provided except for the farmhouses, which were divided into two dwellings, one of which was to be occupied by the stockman. The farms were not divided into smallholdings but farmed as a whole, as before, by about five men each. When the Royal Commission on the Employment of Women and Children in Agriculture investigated the scheme's management in 1867 they approved and felt one of the virtues was that it revived the small farm without reviving the class of small farmers, 'a class that neither did themselves nor anyone else much good'.[8]

Both this comment and that of John Gurdon himself reveal a continuing class prejudice, which was far from the aims of Felix Cobbold. The Vicar of Assington, later Bishop of Manchester, complained that the tenants did not occupy the same social position as ordinary farmers or take part in the management of parish affairs, and many were unable to read or write, which Gurdon actually regarded as a positive advantage. His tenants were like a new group of copyholders in the tradition of a mediaeval manor, even committing them to providing the labour of *precaria cariagium* – '1 day's carting with 4 horses and 2 men'.

Felix foresaw that the advantages of a co-operative scheme for his tenants would be that they could buy and share equipment rather than relying on the land-lords, and thus have the advantages of size while remaining the owners of a small acreage.

Allotments

Two parcels of land were designated for allotments: a field at Sproughton already being administered by Sproughton District Council of five acres, and Arnold Field, OS 524, which had been part of the Kate's Hill Estate at Hadleigh. This comprised 20 acres and two roods and consisted of ten allotments at rents totalling £20 8s 6d.

The allotments on Arnold Field were found, on inspection, to be on the whole 'fairly well cultivated chiefly for the growing of corn, and were about one acre plots'. The twenty-first century perception of an allotment is an area of considerably less than an acre, grown intensively with a variety of vegetables which are used to feed the family of the tenant. The term 'allotment' was clearly being defined differently at the beginning of the twentieth century, just as the defini-tion of a 'smallholding' was unclear. Allotments had been covered by the Small Holdings and Allotments Act of 1908 which by Section 27 (3) could include land of above five acres. Indeed, Combs Parish Council applied to the Small Holdings Committee in 1909 to be allowed to let a piece of land of seven acres as an allotment.

The movement to provide allotments had as stormy a history during the nineteenth century as that of the provision of smallholdings. With the Enclosure Acts, labourers frequently lost the small parcels of land that they had traditionally used to provide food for them-selves, adding to their intense poverty. Throughout the century, therefore, allotments were sometimes pro-vided either by philanthropists or parishes to replace the lost land. Before 1894, however, the parish author-ity was the vestry under the chairmanship of the parish priest, and holders of allotments had to be members of the Church of England. One such example in Suffolk, of which Felix may have heard, was the Hitcham Horticultural Society run by the Rev Professor John Steven Henslow in the 1850s. Henslow moved to

Hitcham in 1837 and began to experiment with crop diseases and fertilisers derived from coprolite. Darwin, an old friend, once said of him, 'I fully believe a better man never walked the earth'. Nevertheless, Henslow's allotment scheme rules display a singular lack of pater-nal sympathy for agricultural labourers.

Rule 2 stated that:

> No tenant to work on Sundays. If a tenant be living a grossly immoral life or be convicted in a Court of Justice of any breach of the laws his lease is to be void. He is not to be admitted to a fresh allotment for a twelvemonth at least, and not then unless the Allottees determine (by ballot) that they consider him suffi-ciently ashamed of his bad conduct to justify his return among them.

Henslow's comment on this rule was:

> The allotment system has been established in the hope of improving the condition of the Labourer, socially and morally and not for the purpose of affording him increased opportunity of indulging himself in any way disgraceful to a man and unbecoming a Christian. Unless this rule was properly attended to allotments would be a curse and not a benefit to a Parish and no one would be at the trouble and expense of encourag-ing them. A friend lately wrote to me as follows: 'The circumstances of our Allotment Society at this place have discouraged me. Strangers had crowded in, and we have now a different sort of people among the labouring population, young men, victims of ignor-ance and intemperance, with hideous faces denoting the degradation that results from Beer and Tobacco. The Allotments have been given up.'

Rule 6 was even harsher: 'Any one receiving Parish relief for more than forty days in one year, or for medical attendance in his wife's confinement, unless the Committee decide that very peculiar circum-stances have justified his appeal to the Board of Guard-ians, shall forfeit his lease.' The rule thus attempts to define the sick man as a member of the 'undeserving poor', and would serve to diminish his circumstances still further.

Henslow's comment on this was:

> Poverty is no disgrace. A poor man may be unable to contend against circumstances that have reduced him to a condition in which he may without shame appeal

as a Pauper for relief. But 'pauper-mindedness' is a disgrace to any man, rich or poor, those who under any circumstances have become incapacitated from attending to an allotment, and are obliged to trust entirely or largely to parish relief, ought to resign. They cannot possibly do justice to an allotment, and it is contrary to Rule 1 to underlet it. I have taken pains to ascertain what actual profit, in money value, an allotment of a quarter of an acre might bring to an allottee, who cultivates it successfully. On an average, I believe, each ought to secure a profit of rather more than £5, above the cost of manure. An agricultural labourer may thus add one fourth to the income he can generally make by day wages alone. But the advantages of an allotment . . . are not restricted to the money value of a crop. If therefore a labourer be ever excusable for not laying by, little by little, to meet the charges he so long foresees will be required for medical attendance at his wife's confinement, he cannot often be justified in appealing to the Parish as a Pauper in such cases, after his opportunities have been improved to the extent to which an allotment allows.[9]

These allotments, being of 'a quarter of an acre' would seem to be closer to the modern definition than that of 1908.

Another example of an allotment scheme was the provision in the 1880s by Baron Tollemache at his Helmingham Estate of a number of farm cottages with allotments attached. Once again there were rules attached to the use of this land which are so prescriptive that they limit the value to the tenant, and also serve to keep him in his social place.

> First rule: Not to plough any part of the said Allotment land but to cultivate it with the Spade, leaving one half wheat, and the other half Peas, Beans, Potatoes or other Vegetables, and not to have any Turnips or Beet-root growing for seed without the consent of the Said John, Baron Tollemache or his agent.

> Second rule: to attend some place of worship once on each Sabbath Day.[10]

George Ewart Evans in *Where Beards Wag All* commented that the tenants had to attend church at least once on a Sunday, and that they and their children had to doff their hats or curtsey to Lord and Lady Tollemache or be put off the land.

Both schemes reveal a desire to control the moral behaviour of the tenants and also to dictate the cultivation practices to be used. The Allotments Act of 1887 allowed local authorities to acquire land for allotments, but only after 1894 did the local authority become civil authorities rather than the Church of England parish councils so it was only after 1894 that the religious criteria for being allowed allotments owned by the parish were relaxed. By the 1908 Allotment Act, tenants were also given freedom of cropping in smallholdings and allotments, although land had to be restored to its original state at the end of a tenancy.

The Hadleigh Holdings

The clerk had submitted schedules of the properties to the sub-committee which revealed that while all the 83.014 acres at Sproughton were already let, 635ac 1r and 29p were unlet on the Hadleigh Estate. The Sproughton land was thus bringing in an annual £159 4s 4d in rent, and the Hadleigh Estate only £281 15s 9d but tithes alone accounted for £180 of this. The work of further dividing and letting this land was therefore becoming urgent.

The sub-committee met again on 10 April 1910 at which a commissioner of the Board of Agriculture, Mr Cheney, was present to give advice. He advised against holdings of over 50 acres as these became 'two-horse holdings'. Accordingly the agent, Mr Rodwell, and George Harrison were asked to try to divide up the land into such holdings, making the best use of the existing houses and buildings, but without disturbing the existing tenants. By 24 June, Rodwell submitted a report giving suggestions, and was asked to advertise for applicants forthwith in the *East Anglian Daily Times* at a cost of two guineas. This was followed by a site visit on 6 July to finalise the plans and decide on rents. By now 48 applicants were ready for interview.

The plan was for 16 additional holdings, but of these, four had no houses and two were for cottages with no land. The committee also made an inventory of the equipment which should be retained, such as two pairs of good horses with the necessary harness, one small corn drill, three ploughs, and two self-binders which would be let out to the tenants at a fixed charge per acre. One man and a lad were to be hired by the estate to help tenants with keeping up-to-date with their work.

Finally, Mr Harrison, Mr Smythe – who had been farm bailiff living in Pond Hall House – and Mr Diggle at Sproughton were given notice to leave at Michaelmas, with Mr Rodwell taking over their work.

In July a second meeting was held, followed by one on 23 August. The clerk had been asked to write to the Lord Lieutenant, Captain Peel MP, and Mr Quilter MP, the Charity Commissioners and the Board of Agriculture in an effort to get the scheme adopted, but were advised that it could not be finalised before October but that the county council had the power to agree lettings in the meantime.

Lionel had, by now, a total of 59 applicants, and had interviewed 37 as 16 had insufficient capital, seven had withdrawn, six had failed to send back particulars, 12 lived outside Suffolk and three had subsequently hired other land. The sub-committee then decided to interview 11 applicants on 6 September.

The form of the leases was also agreed, which were to be upon a basis of seven years with rents payable half-yearly; further 'no option for purchase or co-operation was to be inserted' – contrary to Felix's wishes.

The final major decision at this meeting was that Rodwell should be appointed as estate agent to the Trust, in addition to his duties as Small Holdings Officer for the county, at a salary of £100 a year, with the use of part of Pond Hall, garden and buildings, rent, rates and taxes free, but he had to 'provide his own locomotion'.

By 11 October, the scheme had been received back from the Charity Commission, and approval was also given, against previous advice by the Board of Agriculture, for several holdings of more than 50 acres, and for a greater annual value than £50. Reluctantly the board agreed but thought that Holding 7, which was for 105 acres and let to a Mr Cole, should only be let for one year rather than seven. Also on 11 October the final approved candidates were allowed to take up possession.

On 14 October a sale was held at Pond Hall of live and dead farming stock, and Mr Roland Partridge was asked to attend, at a fee of four guineas, to bid on behalf of the council for stock recommended by the agent as being necessary for working the land remaining in hand, and he spent £386 16s.

On 16 October, at the final meeting of the new sub-committee supervised by the Small Holdings and Allotment parent committee, it was reported that the existing tenants had agreed to surrender their present leases subject to being able to retain security of tenure, and the clerk was asked to consider this question. All tenants, old and new, agreed to provisional draft leases prepared by the clerk, and the committee agreed that rents as fixed should include a water supply as at present laid on.

The final minute is headed 'Legacy Duty on Personalty'. It recorded that, 'the sum of £363 18s 4d, the legacy duty on the personalty, was paid out of the Trust Account on the 22nd September 1910 and all title deeds relating to the property have been received by the Clerk of the County Council'.

The stage was set for the new Trust committee to begin their work in earnest.

NOTES

1 *Ipswich Journal*, 17 March 1874.
2 Numbers of women out of work were not quoted, although women were employed in great numbers in the field, especially during the summer, as evidenced by *The Royal Commission on the Employment of Children, Young Persons and Women in Agriculture, 1868–1869*. A number of women had joined the union and thus may have been locked out.
3 Arch, Joseph. *From Ploughtail to Parliament: an autobiography of Joseph Arch*. London: The Cresset Library, 1986. p 222.
4 There is some evidence that this slogan was actually thought up by the Tory party as a joke against the Liberal Land Reform movement, but if so, it was a joke that backfired. George Ewart Evans heard a rumour that Lord Tollemache of Helmingham had been the author. *Where Beards Wag All*. p 118.
5 The property was later named Gary Farm by William Prowse, who enjoyed fishing Loch Gary in Scotland.
6 For further information refer to Booth, General William. *In Darkest England and the Way Out*. London: Diggory Press, 1890.
7 Royal Agricultural Society Journal, 1863, pp 165–6.
8 British Parliamentary Papers, 1867–8, XVII, pp 107–10.
9 Henslow, Rev J S. *Appendix to Hitcham Allotment Report for 1857*.
10 Evans, George Ewart. *Where Beards Wag All*. London: Faber and Faber, 1970, pp 120–1.

Chapter Two

1910–1914 The Establishment of the Felix Thornley Cobbold Agricultural Trust

National Agricultural Scene

The agricultural industry was still in a state of depression which crept over the nation in the 1870s and was partly caused by the import of cheap wheat from North America. By 1900 many plots of poor land had gone out of production and the numbers of employed agricultural labourers had dwindled from 962,000 in 1871 to 621,000 in 1901.[1]

However, certain products, such as dairy, meat, fresh fruit and vegetables, were a thriving market, particularly where good transport – either by road or rail – existed. Farmers were urged to diversify by the Royal Commission of 1895, and along the Suffolk/Essex border apple orchards were established at Stoke by Nayland and Langham, while in Tiptree in Essex and Histon in Cambridgeshire, jam-making enterprises were developed. In 1907, also at Tiptree, a landowner had five acres devoted to growing nasturtiums, mangolds, turnips, cabbages and tomatoes. One farmer in Ardleigh supplied flowers, chickens 'dressed but not pulled' and beef to the London markets.[2]

In 1900 a group of Suffolk farmers visited Denmark, specifically the new bacon factories and co-operative dairies which had helped facilitate a growth – from £2,244,000 to £10,299,000 – in Danish exports of bacon, butter and eggs between 1876 and 1900. The Commission had remarked that 'we have to learn why English markets should not be supplied with English bacon and ham'.[3] The visit to Denmark, however, made little difference to working patterns in the county as the rigid social structure rejected moves towards the Danish model of co-operative marketing. Most farmers and many cottagers kept a few pigs, but large-scale production was not adopted.

The Royal Commission also noted that there was an influx of Scottish farmers into the Eastern Counties looking for cheap land, and commented on their thrift and skills which allowed them to survive and prosper where traditional Suffolk farmers were failing. Many were from Ayrshire, where poor conditions had demanded intense physical labour, rather than a life as minor gentry which many Suffolk farmers had enjoyed. The Commission remarked that the Scottish wives and daughters worked hard on the farms, even mucking out sheds and pig-sties, but for Suffolk farmers' wives this was not typical.

By 1913 nearly 75 per cent of gross agricultural output was accounted for by livestock products, and of these the fastest growing was milk. Pond Hall had been advertised in 1894 as having a good milk business, although we have no evidence as to the condition of this business after the sale of the estate. However, the tenant of Gary Farm quickly established his own milking herd in 1906 and began to prosper by supplying milk to much of Hadleigh.

Nutrition for the poor was becoming a national concern, following the realisation in 1899 that many volunteers to the army were undernourished, and the Pure Food Act of 1906 attacked the common practice of adulterating food.

Government concern over the state of agriculture was manifested in the creation of the Board of Agriculture in 1889, which became the Board of Agriculture and Fisheries in 1903. The ministry appointed honorary agricultural correspondents throughout the country to give advice to farmers and liaise with the government on regional matters. Harry Fiske – who later became a chairman of the Felix Thornley Cobbold Agricultural Trust – set up and ran the Saxmundham Experimental Station, trialling artificial fertilisers from 1899 to 1909 for the pharmaceutical company Fisons.[4]

Meanwhile, the country was becoming increasingly dependent on imported food so that by 1914 the output of home-grown food met only one-third of the country's needs. In spite of concern over the approaching war, the government were confident that the power of the British Navy would protect food imports and so no action was taken to reverse this trend.

The Small Holdings and Allotments Act 1907, revised in 1908, gave county councils the power to buy land for smallholdings and allotments; the East Suffolk Small Holdings and Allotments Committee was formed to purchase and manage land in each area of the county.

Felix Cobbold Trust Committee Governance

On 15 November 1910, almost a year after Felix Cobbold's death, the new committee began work as an independent body by planning to meet quarterly, usually at Ipswich Town Hall. At this point, the new body ceased to report month by month to the Small Holdings and Allotments Committee, and presented an annual report to the county council. All the members of the committee were, however, also members of the Small Holdings and Allotments Committee, as well as being county councillors or aldermen. The councillors were subject to re-election every four years.

The Earl of Stradbroke was elected chairman of the new committee, with George Fiske as vice chairman. The rest of the committee comprised Reverend Hervey, Robert Everett, Alfred Harwood, A H Hucklesby, W W Hunt and H W Mason. Of these, the Earl of Stradbroke was also vice chairman of East Suffolk County Council. George Fiske was an alderman as were Everett and Reverend Hervey. Between them, the committee possessed experience of Suffolk farming from all over the county – from the vast estates of the Earl of Stradbroke to George Fiske's Thornbush farm, adjacent to Felix's Sproughton land, to Hunt's Grundisburgh farm and Everett's Rushmere farm.

The committee confirmed all the previous actions of the sub-committee set up by the Small Holdings Committee, and welcomed to the meeting George Harrison, Felix's old farm manager for the Hadleigh Estate, to provide continuity of management. Townshend Cobbold, clerk of the county council, was confirmed as clerk to this committee from 6 December 1910 and Mr A Gibb appointed as treasurer.

The committee decided to inspect most of the estate land once a year, and for the rest of the year the agent reported on the current situation at each quarterly meeting and made a full annual report. The sub-committee had visited the Hadleigh Estate during the initial months of discussions, and the first annual visit was then made in May 1911.

The financial situation confronting the committee caused some concern. After the debts had been settled and initial payments made, there was 'start-up' money of only a little over £4,000. Rents – the only initial source of income – amounted to £231 15s 9d from the Hadleigh Estate and £159 4s 4d from Sproughton. The Small Holdings Committee was able to obtain money for purchases and expenses from the county council, but this source was not open to the Trust committee, and they were responsible for rates and tithes, and part of the salaries of the land agent, clerk and treasurer. Moreover, early in 1911 Somerset House delivered the long-awaited claim for estate duty and also succession duty. The former was for £1,280 and the committee decided to pay the sum at once. However, they reached an agreement with the government to pay the latter, the succession duty of around £1,023, in eight yearly payments.

The committee also decided to retain eight employees to work on the estate land, which included five farm labourers, a carpenter, a bricklayer and a bricklayer's labourer. In 1911, Lloyd George brought in a National Insurance Act by which every wage earner between the ages of 16 and 70 had to pay 4d a week, while their employers paid 3d a week, and the state contributed 2d a week. This provided an unemployment benefit of 7s a week for 15 weeks in any one year, or 10s a week for 13 weeks and then 5s for the next 13 weeks for sickness benefit. The estate assumed responsibility for payments for their eight men as an additional expense.

In 1912, the Pond Hall Estate account, held by George Harrison, was closed and the accounts were audited and printed. At the end of the year, the accounts showed that the rents from Hadleigh had increased to £780 with £160 from Sproughton. Trees had been sold for £7 and the tenants had paid £3 12s 7d for their corn to be milled. The agent had also sold corn to a value of £144 8s 9d and hired out implements to the smallholders at a cost of £87 16s 4d. However, the following year the agent commented that the tenants had begun to buy their own implements and lend them to each other – spurred on, no doubt by Felix's old plan to see the estate run as a co-operative.

The Agent – L H Rodwell

In 1910, 25-year-old Lionel Holm Rodwell was land agent to the county council and agent for the FTCAT estate and paid an extra £20 per annum for this work. His father was an auctioneer and estate agent in Bury St Edmunds, but Lionel had been living in Ipswich since his appointment. He complained that he often left his home at eight in the morning and could not return until evening. When he asked for travelling expenses, he was permitted third-class travel on the trains and an annual £10 cycle allowance. To further reduce his travelling time, Lionel was also allowed to live rent free in part of Pond Hall and was permitted the use of the stable and gardens.

For a young man, it was a job full of responsibility and during 1911 he struggled with the workload. On 15 August 1911, he asked the Small Holdings Committee to allow him a full-time clerk for his own paperwork, rather than share arrangements with the clerk of the council. The committee agreed that his new clerk should be paid £60 pa, which would rise to £80 pa by annual increments of £5.

The following spring, on 27 February 1912, Lionel came back to announce that he had acquired a motorcycle to replace his old bicycle, and asked for a mileage allowance. Once again the Small Holdings Committee agreed to provide 3d a mile each way for his motorcycle journeys when used on council business; this was in effect from 29 February 1912. In the summer of 1912, he installed a bath into Pond Hall at his own expense, but asked the FTCAT Committee to provide hot water. It was considered that this would prove an asset if the Hall was let at a later date, so the committee agreed to the expense.

However, in February 1913, Lionel announced that

The Grade II listed Pond Hall, Pond Hall Road, Hadleigh. Possibly built by the D'Oyly family in the sixteenth century, and later owned by the Tollemache family until sold in 1845. Felix Cobbold bought it with the estate around the turn of the century and it was sold by the Trust to Suffolk County Council in 1969. The house was then repaired and sold again to a private buyer in 1972. (Strutt & Parker)

he was going into business with his father and taking on a residency in Norfolk. The committee asked him to stay until October at an increased salary of £50 pa, excluding the rent-free use of the house, which they planned to let out. Lionel agreed to the arrangement, as long as he could also continue in his position as land agent to the Small Holdings Committee. As the FTCAT Committee members were also members of the larger committee, this too was agreed.

Rents and Lettings

In the minutes of October 1910, a table was included which purported to show 'the list of tenants of the fresh holdings (all of whom entered into possession on the 11th October) with acreage, rent'.

However, a number of these tenants, like Mr Prowse on Holding 15, and probably also Dyer and the Eastman brothers, had occupied these holdings before Felix Cobbold's death, although the agent and committee now interviewed and accepted 11 more tenants, with a further 138 acres to be let in the forthcoming months. It would appear, therefore, that this table is erroneously described and shows not the new tenants but the original tenants and the rents they were paying (including rates) at the time of Felix's death.

The new committee raised the rents of the tenants, which resulted in a number of complaints. Grout, holding No 12, 'had been asked to pay £112, but wanted to pay £50 at once and the rest in January 1911'. Again, the table printed in the same minutes shows him paying £79 0s 0d, not £112, meaning that the table illustrates a pre-Trust level of rents. Wightman, on Holding 6, did not want to pay 10s per acre on five acres as he had had to spend between £7 and £8 on his new house and on improving the cart shed. The tenant of No 7, Cole, also thought that his land had been over-valued, and indeed further professional advice given to the committee agreed with him that £140 should be accepted rather than the current asking price of £144 16s 10d.

For the first few years up to 1914, tenants appeared to be struggling – there were frequent arrears and some tenants were threatened with eviction. New tenants were required to have sufficient capital to run the holdings before they were accepted as tenants and this deterred many would-be smallholders. Nevertheless, Lionel made a recommendation to the Small Holdings Committee in May 1912 that the council should buy an extra 400–500 acres of land to fulfil demand for smallholdings from applicants.

I have recently heard of several men given notice to quit from farms who have found great difficulty in hiring others, but did not apply to the Council as they

No. of Holding.	Name of Tenant.	Approximate Acreage of Holding.*			Annual Rent of Holding.		
		A.	R.	P.	£	s.	d.
1	R. Dyer	13	1	11	12	2	6
2	A. Alecock	14	1	16	12	2	6
4	G. Keeble	15	2	6	7	16	6
5	E. Catchpole	66	3	30	53	10	0
6	G. Wightman	57	1	20	46	0	0
7	W. Cole	105	3	14	85	0	0
8	G. F. Lambert	60	0	23	54	0	0
9	Eastman Bros.	32	3	33	49	10	0
11	H. Simpkin	44	2	15	55	0	0
12	G. Grout	57	3	35	79	0	0
15	W. Prowse	11	3	33	15	0	0
		480	3	36			
10-13-14-16	In Hand (workable)	138	3	24			
		619	3	20	£469	1	6

* The several holdings will be more accurately recorded when the various roads, &c., have been measured up.

Felix Cobbold Trust: Report of sub-committee, 11 October 1910

had seen how long other applicants have had to wait before being supplied. Although over 800 acres have been acquired since the commencement of the Act (1908) the demand has not varied very much during the two and a half years I have been your Land Agent. Mr Cheney (Commissioner with the Board of Agriculture) in the report of the Board of Agriculture just issued states that other Counties have experienced the same difficulties.

Some of the tenants were not full-time farmers, even several who had been approved by Felix. One tenant in this situation in May 1911 was threatened with eviction at Michaelmas as his land was 'in a deplorable state', but by October he had an agreement from his father to be a guarantor for the rent of £14 15s 11d due that month. In fact, he still owed rent from Lady Day. In mitigation, the agent said that he had difficulty working the land as it urgently needed draining.

The problems rumbled on and again the tenant was asked to leave but he pleaded that he would spend more labour and money on the holding and 'give up his insurance business and start a park business in addition to the holding'. He also had money coming from a life insurance policy for £200, and expected more money later in 1912. The committee had enough, however, and his land was given to the Eastman brothers, who will be discussed on page 26.

Field Drainage

The second urgent matter to be considered at the first meeting of the committee was that of drainage. Grout, at Holding 5, needed pipes for draining one of his fields, and Lionel asked George Harrison for advice on the best method for carrying this out. This was to prove one of the major undertakings for the committee throughout the next few years. Apparently none of the Hadleigh land had previously been drained, and the heavy clay soil turned into a quagmire during wet weather. On this occasion, Harrison was asked to report back to the committee with his recommendations.

At the following meeting, Grout was anxious to have seed for pasturing a field, but the committee agreed that it should first be drained and that they would provide pipes, on Harrison's recommendations. Harrison advised that other fields also needed draining. One tenant went into arrears at the end of 1911 because his crop was ruined, so the committee agreed not to press

for rent but to arrange drainage, along with the land of several other tenants.

Pipes were provided by the committee, but it became apparent that a number of tenants, especially Catchpole on Holding 5, did not understand how to install them. In February 1912, the committee agreed to employ an experienced drainer to supervise the work – at last the situation improved.

Houses and Farm Buildings

Several of the holdings did not have accommodation and were worked by men living locally, but more housing was needed on the estate, particularly for those 'two-horse holdings' of more than 50 acres. In May 1911, the committee proposed that a new house should be built about 30 yards from the road, comprising a living room, front room, scullery, pantry and dairy, with three bedrooms above to be built of local bricks and roofed with tiles. The property was to be built of timber on dwarf brick walls and also roofed with tiles.

An architect was employed to draw up plans, and in August he recommended that the cottage 'should be erected 100 yards up the field on higher ground, which would save on foundations but entail making a roadway'. This was agreed by the committee, but almost at once the Medical Officer of Health for Hadleigh complained that he was unhappy about the proposed drainage and asked for a drainage tube to be carried 30 feet from the house to empty into a dead well, as was the case of the other houses on the estate. By Michaelmas 1912, the house was almost complete but the committee decided that they did not have sufficient funds to provide any further houses at that time.

The farm buildings all over the estate were found to be in bad repair, and each meeting produced another batch of requests for further accommodation – a new cart lodge here, and new piggeries there. Many buildings were not troughed, and several of the thatched sheds 'owing to the continued wet weather' were in a bad state and a rolling programme of repairs and maintenance was set up.

Services

The Sproughton land had a water supply installed by Felix with a wind pump drawing water from a well.

From January 1910, Mr Francis, the tenant who had been attending to the needs of the wind pump, asked for payment for this task, and it was agreed that he should be paid £2 pa for his work. He also pointed out that there were insufficient stopcocks on the system and the committee agreed that they should be fitted. Repairs to the windmill and pump in 1911 were also needed. The Hadleigh land, on the other hand, used an oil pump to raise water and a supply was not at present laid on to the new holdings. This became another common cause of complaint by the tenants.

The Eastman brothers, on holding No 9, were keeping pigs but in addition soon set up a poultry business which thrived, so they asked for more land. They also applied for a water supply to their pig sties early in 1914 as well as a stand pipe in a meadow, and this was agreed by the committee. In addition, they asked for a barn to be match-boarded for use as an incubator, and finally asked that a pantry in their house should be fitted with a bath – the second mention of such a luxury on the estate, following the example set by Lionel. The committee agreed, but said that the Eastmans should pay for the bath themselves.

The state of the roads, which was to be a recurring problem, began to show itself even in the first years. Prowse at Gary Farm, Holding 15, complained that the track to his farm was in such a bad state that moving milk off the farm was difficult, so the committee agreed to repair it at a cost of £8.

George Harrison and the End of an Era

Harrison, who had been Felix's trusted farm manager and adviser, was at first employed by the new FTCAT Committee to wind up the accounts and to provide initial advice to Lionel. However, his work was not

Harvesting in the 1900s required a large group of workers in spite of the 'mechanisation' of the period. Here a 1908 Garretts of Leiston threshing drum and traction engine, a single-cylinder model No 27318, is being used in Northlands Farm, Hintlesham. The thresher separated the grain, polished it, and graded it into two to three different sizes. These were fed into separate sacks hanging from pegs at the back of the drum. An 18-stone sack is about to be lifted from the hoist in the left of the picture.
(David Kindred)

merely financial or advisory: in 1910 he supervised the threshing and sale of the corn for the Hadleigh Estate and was paid £100 for his outstanding salary up to 11 October 1910. In 1911, he again supervised the harvest. Felix had envisaged the tenants being able to buy their own equipment as a co-operative association, but the committee owned the threshing machine and in 1910 proposed charging the tenants for the work. However, the harvest in 1910 was delayed and not threshed until after Michaelmas, which caused financial hardship to the tenants. The actual cost was 1s 4d per coomb for threshing, dressing and carting, but the committee finally agreed to charge 1s a coomb after complaints about the cost from the tenants.

Harrison was asked to leave the estate in spring 1912, when he was 57 years old. He was given a final payment of £50 for his services during the second year of the Trust, and he retired to a house in Hadleigh High Street.

Arson on the Estate

One of the new tenants, Walter Smith, had been given a house and ten acres of land, which caused some ill feelings on the estate, as his neighbour held 35 acres but had no buildings except a hovel built to house the pigs. However, at the meeting on 29 October 1912, the agent reported that there was:

> an outbreak of fire in three distinct places at Walter Smith's cottage, Hadleigh during the early morning of the 25th instant. The fire was subdued before any great damage was occasioned to the Trustee's property, but owing to the suspicious nature of the outbreak he (the Agent) at once consulted a Member of the Committee, and as a result laid information against Smith, the tenant, who was subsequently arrested on suspicion of having fired the property.

The agent submitted a plan of the cottage, showing the position of the fire and also a builder's estimate in the sum of £8 15s for repairs to the damage done.

The agent further reported that he had attended the hearing before the Hadleigh Bench on the 28th instant when Smith was remanded until Thursday, 31 October. He asked for instructions on how to proceed further in the matter. Smith was prosecuted on behalf of the trustees and in the following February was convicted of arson and sentenced to 12 months in prison with no

hard labour. Later, Lionel visited him in prison to pay him compensation for the fruit trees that he had planted on the land. It was a curious incident and no explanation is given in the minutes. He had not been in arrears on his rent, and it can only be concluded that he was suffering from depression.

1913 and a Change of Agent

In May 1913, Thomas William Darby from Dorchester, the new land agent, attended his first meeting. He had been given a choice of a larger salary of £100 with no accommodation or £75 pa with rent-free living at Pond Hall and use of its garden. He chose, like Lionel, to live at Pond Hall, with its splendid new bath and large garden.

The tenants were still – with some exceptions, such as the Eastman brothers – finding the situation difficult, and Darby had a hard time collecting the rents. The carpenter and bricklayer were discharged but then rehired three months later and a new Ransomes, Sims and Jefferies 'Bandet' mower was bought for the estate at a cost of £17 10s.

By July, Darby reported that seven tenants were in arrears for a total of £127 7s 8d. In December a special meeting was held to consider the position, and arrears were now reported to be £120. The first of these defaulters had moved off his holding to live in Milden and was given 14 days to pay. One of the other tenants complained that he should have been allowed a reduction because there was a gravel pit on his land and extraction had caused damage to his crop, but his tenancy agreement made no mention of the pit so his complaint was dismissed.

One of the other tenants complained that his land was poor, the crop had been a failure, and he had had nothing to sell. The committee had some sympathy with his situation as this was one of the areas which had needed draining the previous year and the crop planting had been disturbed. A few months later, he was allowed to leave his holding which, upon inspection, was agreed to be in foul condition. In the circumstances, he was allowed to keep his house and buildings at a rent of £6 pa until he had relocated. In January 1914, the situation was no better: another of the defaulting tenants had been asked to leave, but owed £115 2s 6d and was unable to pay, so the committee agreed that he should pay off the debt in half-yearly payments of not less than £5 plus five per cent interest.

In April, one of the tenants asked for water to be laid on to his land but the committee declined because of the cost. More tenants were in arrears and, as a final blow, of five bullocks bought for feeding purposes by the estate, one was found to have TB and had to be slaughtered.

Two tenants were thriving in this gloomy situation. Prowse at Gary Farm asked for two more rooms to be built on his cottage as accommodation for his men, which would mean a rise in rent. He was now employing a cowman, a milk rounds man, a full-time agricultural labourer and additional casual labourer when required. The Eastman brothers' poultry business was also doing so well that they wanted to expand their holding of 57 acres by another 12 acres, and in July 1914 this was permitted by the committee.

Thus, at the end of this first period, the committee had kept a modest surplus on their accounts only by careful supervision of expenditure and much 'make do and mend' rather than replacement of defective farm buildings or radical improvements. Even during this brief period a number of tenants had left, or been asked to leave, and new tenants seemed hard to find, in spite of Lionel's report of the long waiting lists for smallholdings in the county.

NOTES

1 Wood, Anthony. *Nineteenth Century Britain: 1815–1914*. London: Longmans, 1960. p 273.
2 Howkins, Alun. *Reshaping Rural England*. London: Harper-Adams Academic, 1991. pp 212–3.
3 Royal Commission on Agriculture, 1895. p 53.
4 Russell, Sir John. *Agriculture* Vol LXVI, Dec 1959.

Chapter Three

1914–1920
Suffolk at War

National Agricultural Situation

The First World War affected agriculture in a number of ways – the first being the disappearance of young, healthy men to the fighting. During the first year, the army was composed of volunteers and although a number of young men felt that fighting the Hun was an adventure that should not be missed – and might prove better than digging potatoes in winter – farms were not affected heavily. In the second year, however, conscription meant that more young men and even middle-aged men with experience were called to serve.

The government was initially confident that food supplies would not be affected, as previously noted. While 80 per cent of British wheat was being imported, they believed that the strength of the navy would overcome any problems. They did, however, begin to encourage the home market to produce cereals and this meant bringing land back into production. By late 1916, however, German U-boats began to affect imports and prices started to rise. Other supplies like building materials and timber also became harder to source. In Ipswich, both Ransomes, Sims and Jefferies and Boulton and Paul transferred from producing agricultural machinery and milling to producing FE2 biplanes for the Royal Flying Corps.

In 1917, Lord Ernle, well known for his 1912 book *English Farming Past and Present*, became President of the Board of Agriculture to deal with growing food shortages. His first act was to give additional powers to the War Agriculture Executive Committees to survey land and increase cereal production. By the Corn Production Act of August 1917 a minimum price was guaranteed, as was a minimum wage for agricultural workers and fixed rents. For self-employed smallholders the increased wage affected those who employed labourers, but guaranteed prices increased their profits. Nationally, large numbers of women entered agriculture to compensate for the missing men,

but, there was no apparent influx onto Cobbold land.

The milk industry suffered during the war due to shortage of imported food stuffs; this resulted in lower milk yields. The Hadleigh land was used both for cereals and milk production so this affected some smallholders, notably Prowse at Gary Farm.

1914–1915 and Trust Estates 'Business as Usual'

The start of the war appeared to affect the Felix Cobbold Trust only marginally. The first mention of the war was a minute to the effect that the Eastman brothers, who had wanted an extra 12 acres of land in July 1914, had lost 'some of their staff' to the army by October 1914. Therefore, the brothers could only manage an extra two acres. They were given a maiden ley strip of land by the committee.

The committee were concerned with the bad weather of the winter months. The same rain that was turning the trenches of France into quagmires – together with strong gales – affected the houses and buildings on the estate and the land agent was concerned that many of the roofs needed urgent repair. The houses had also suffered because it had been five years since they had been painted and remedial action was needed.

By April 1915, this work was almost complete and a tender was out for the two additional rooms requested by Prowse and other estate work continued routinely. At this time, one of the labourers employed by the Trust had 'joined Kitchener's Army and was not being replaced'. By October 1915, the tender for the house had been approved and work had begun but continued only slowly with 'the builder being so busy and short of labour'.

The Trust Committee inexplicably discharged two of their remaining estate workers, but kept on a third who was then paid an extra 2s 5d to keep the oil engine running to pump water, commenting that he would then be available for other work if the smallholders needed him. The Eastman brothers appeared to have overcome their labour problem, and they again decided to take on an additional 11 acres for their poultry production. In addition, they asked for a new 100-foot-long shed to be used as an incubator and stable. The committee took time to consider this request as it required a considerable outlay of money.

One minute of note in April 1915 was that Herbert St George Cobbold, Felix's nephew, had become the new East Suffolk County Treasurer and thus also treasurer of the Trust.

In July, the land agent decided to move out of Pond Hall and relocate to Ipswich, and in October the hall was let to a Mrs Emma Deek.

1916 and the War Comes to Suffolk

The bad weather recurred during the winter of 1915–1916, and subsequently, the yard of Cole, the holder of Plot 7, flooded. He was provided with gutters and catchpits to solve the problem. Prowse's new rooms were completed but immediately the roof was damaged by storms so the builder's payment was delayed until repairs were completed. In the spring, heavy snow damaged roofs on the estates, requiring further repairs.

Several tenants wanted better and bigger pig sties as their existing sheds were inadequate, but this was refused by the committee, although one man was given a better stable. The committee also haggled over providing the Eastman's new incubator building. They initially offered to put up a 50-foot shed, but eventually agreed to the 100-foot shed on the condition that the brothers paid an extra five per cent on their rent and agreed to stay on the holding for 12 years. The brothers agreed to these terms and estimates were received for £266, £350 and £1,164 in April. The committee agreed to pay £266, but delayed acceptance of this offer until 30 May 1915. By the next meeting, however, they received a letter from the builders to say that the costs had risen by £18 because 'since that date the price of timber, bricks and tiles have advanced'. Reluctantly the committee paid the new amount.

Land Agents: Darby and Pattle

A further blow to the committee was reported in April 1916 when Thomas Darby, the land agent, was threatened with conscription. Losing a few labourers had been a minor problem, but this presented a serious obstacle to the work of the estate. Generously, the committee proposed that the difference between his army salary and his present land agent salary should be borne by the Trust while he was away. Meanwhile, they proposed asking George Harrison to come back to work for the duration of the war to take Thomas's place.

By the 10 June meeting, Thomas had left for the army but George Harrison had been unwilling to return. An acting agent, Cecil F Pattle, was found; he was an agent for West Suffolk and lived in Bury St Edmunds. However, when Cecil attempted to take over the estate business he found that Thomas's accounts were incomplete and chaotic, with money apparently collected and not paid over, which raises suspicions about the apparent rent arrears in the previous few years. Cecil also discovered that with the exception of the tenants who had been in occupation with Felix Cobbold, none of the tenants had proper agreements stating acreage and rent, which was a situation that needed urgent attention.

The committee met again on 27 June to consider the emergency. Unfortunately, by this meeting the chairman, Lord Stradbroke, had also been called for 'military service' and had sent in his resignation. The committee agreed not to accept his resignation and instead, appointed a temporary second vice chairman – H F Harwood.

Thomas Darby had been asked to leave his army training depot and come to a meeting, but he wrote to say that he could not be there until after 4.30 pm but had managed to visit Townshend Cobbold. The clerk then read a statement showing that Thomas had indeed received the rent money but not paid it over. He also admitted that he had not paid the rates, or the Workmen's Compensation Scheme money. In addition, Cecil said, some lettings had not been recorded, and in some cases wrong amounts had been recorded. The committee were appalled, and Thomas was summarily dismissed in his absence, and again asked to come to speak to them. Meanwhile, Cecil was appointed as permanent agent in his place and began a struggle to make sense of the finances. He also began to draw up new plans of the holdings, showing acreage and annual rent, as preparation for individual agreements.

On 22 August, the committee were told that Thomas had managed to attend another meeting with the clerk and had refunded £94 8s 3d and a second sum of £35 10s 6d which he admitted owing, but said that he would not be able to attend further meetings because of a 'stoppage of all leave' directive issued by the army. The committee noted that he had already been dismissed and that as he was now 'serving in His Majesty's Army no further steps should be taken'.

At the same meeting, a letter was received from West Suffolk County Council, objecting to the appointment of their land agent by East Suffolk, but they grudgingly offered to allow him to remain as a temporary agent until the end of the war. The committee agreed that:

> he be allowed 3rd class railway Season Ticket between Bury and Ipswich, and no charge made for locomotion when visiting the Small Holdings, and no subsistence allowance when he is attending the office only. His salary was to be £112 10s for the Small Holdings Committee, and £37 10s for the Trust work.

He was also to be paid an extra £25 for taking over the work in such difficult circumstances. By April 1917, however, West Suffolk relented, and Cecil Pattle was appointed as a permanent land agent for both East and West Suffolk.

Hadleigh Aviation Ground 1916–1918

A second major concern for the committee in 1916 arose at the April meeting. The War Office had decided to commandeer OS Field 668, which belonged to three tenants, 'for Aviation purposes'. They agreed to pay a rent of 'two years for one', and gave the tenants first refusal on the hay crop should there be any, which satisfied the tenants. The committee replied on 25 February that the War Office must pay to reinstate any fences they removed, and the estate wanted compensation for any timber from felled trees. The War Office replied that this might be a problem.

By 10 June 1916, the War Office had paid compensation to the three affected tenants, and no further problems arose until November, when Cecil Pattle, the new agent, reported that the War Office now wanted to upgrade the field from third class to first class, which would mean expanding the site from 18 acres to 80 acres, with three houses being demolished, and the felling of three acres of fruit trees belonging to Dyer on Holding 1, one of the original tenants.

The agent immediately protested about the trees, but Dyer reported that the War Office was preparing to cut them. The following morning there was an exchange of telegrams between Pattle and the War Office, and at twelve o'clock the War Office said they had just had instructions not to cut the trees. However, the message came too late: the fruit trees and also a number of other valuable trees, belonging both to the Pond Hall Estate and to the neighbouring farms, had been cut down. Cecil inspected the scene of carnage and found that over 150 trees had been felled, and not cut carefully but hacked one and a half to two feet from the ground, with all the foliage and timber still lying on the ground. The agent was incensed, and demanded compensation on behalf of the committee and tenants.

By January 1917, the land had been fully cleared with fences removed and ditches filled in. The timber was sold by the estate for £49 16s, but there was no word from the War Office about compensation, and so in November the committee appointed a Mr Hugh Turner of Ipswich to act for the Trust, and the committee spent additional time trying to decide how to adjust the rents of the affected tenants.

A few months later it was reported that the War Office was now erecting 'extensive and somewhat permanent buildings' on the aviation field, which would prevent easy reoccupation by the tenants, but the War Office had finally agreed to pay compensation to the affected men: Dyer received £132 15s, Catchpole received £15 16s 6d, G Keeble received £50 11s and M Powling received £27 7s. They also paid £64 18s to the committee for the damage caused by felling the estate trees.

The committee decided that given the new circumstances it would be wise not only to raise the fire policies in view of 'the high price of building materials now', but also to take out insurance against damage by hostile aircraft, as the aviation field would presumably be a target for German planes.

The expansion on the field continued and became even more permanent. It was reported in October that 'the Military are desirous of making an arrangement for a supply of water (5,000 gallons a day) from Pond Hall to the Aviation Ground, the water to be pumped to a tank on the ground 30 ft above ground level'. A special sub-committee was formed to negotiate this problem with the officer in charge, when it was suggested that a water meter should be installed by the military and a charge made per 1,000 gallons. Trustees provisionally suggested a charge of 1s 6d per 1,000 gallons, and the committee were not to be held responsible for any failure of the pumping plant. This arrangement was modified slightly by January 1918 so that water would be provided for six months at 12s 6d per week, or 1s 6d per 1,000 gallons, with the figure based on an average of ten hours extra pumping per week.

The compensation claim dragged on into 1918. Not only had the agreed compensation not actually been paid, but the War Office land agent was asked to consider the fact that the land was not likely to be restored in the near future. He agreed to pay additional compensation equivalent to two years' rent for each year. The committee urged their solicitor to try to expedite the payments.

Committee Changes

The committee that was originally formed in 1910 had consisted of eight men, with Lord Stradbroke in the chair and George Fiske as the vice chair. From 1910–1917, the committee frequently had barely a quorum and Lord Stradbroke was often away on official duties, but George Fiske was usually present and usually formed part of any inspection sub-committee.

As noted above, Lord Stradbroke sent in his resignation in 1916 when he was called to the army, but the committee refused it and instead appointed a second vice chairman to aid George Fiske. In fact, Lord Stradbroke never reappeared on the committee and George Fiske remained the chairman. He had chaired the majority of meetings since 1910, carrying much of the load for the establishment of the Trust estate. In April 1917, it was reported that George Fiske was dead and his nephew Harry Fiske took his place as vice chairman. Since 1910, Harry had been a county councillor, as well as a member of the Small Holdings and Allotments Committee, so he brought great experience of the current farming scene to the post.

By April 1918, the committee consisted of Harry as the chairman, with C C Eley, H Hunt, A Harwood, H F Harwood, C C Smith and H W Mason. Lord Stradbroke was still nominally a member. H W Mason became the vice chairman early in 1919.

GEORGE FISKE, J.P.

George Fiske, acting chairman of the Trust from 1914 to 1916, and chairman from 1916 to 1917. An original committee member since 1910, George farmed land adjacent to the Trust's Sproughton Estate. (Nicholas Fiske)

Sproughton Water Supplies

Up to 1916, the Sproughton Estate had rarely been mentioned at meetings. In the annual accounts, income from Sproughton was noted but there were few problems. In April 1916, however, the wind pump became blocked. The agent reported that two elm trees were obstructing it, so the trees were felled. However, in January 1917, the pump failed again and tenants were advised 'to make whatever arrangements they can for water'. The usual firm of repairers, Messrs Smith and Co, could do nothing 'due to pressure of Government work' so an alternative company was found to do the work, and by April the pump was restored. By April of the following year, 1918, the vital pump was found to be clogged with rust; the same scenario occurred again in 1919. A clear pattern of a system under pressure was emerging.

Tenant Changes 1917–1918

In 1917, there were a number of tenant changes, partly due to the loss of land caused by the aviation field. Two men decided to quit, one of them being in arrears with his rent, so the improved financial climate with guaranteed prices was apparently not sufficient to help. Other tenants were also in arrears, but the total outstanding was only £26, which was an unusually small amount after the sums reported by both Rodwell and Darby (although Darby's figures were obviously suspect).

The new agent looked at Arnold Field, Hadleigh, which had been designated as an allotment field by Felix Cobbold. Pattle recommended that one of the tenants should keep his one acre allotment, but the rest of the field should become three smallholdings of around six acres each. One of these smallholdings was to be given to Prowse of Gary Farm, which abutted the field. The committee agreed and by January 1918 the new division was of 1 acre, 5 acres, 8.262 acres and 4.781 acres.

In January 1918, there was news that two of the other tenants, G Lambert and R H Cook had been served notices by the West Suffolk War Agricultural Committee in their drive to increase food production. The Hadleigh Estate as a whole was producing less due to the loss of land to the aerodrome, but Lambert was given instructions to mole drain field OS 372 (16.437 acres). Pattle commented that the field in question had always been very wet and seldom produced more than eight combs per acre, so agreed that the work should be done. Cook, in the next field, was similarly given notice to clear and scour his ditches to improve drainage.

Another change this month was that Mrs Deek, who had begun to rent Pond Hall on the departure of Thomas Darby, now wanted to sublet it to a Mr Cooley of Colchester, who had been discharged from the army through wounds. Another cottage, belonging to Powling, was let to a Lieutenant S A Gibbons, RAF, at £10 pa – possibly one of the officers stationed at the aerodrome.

The defaulting tenants had left their land by April 1918 but there were new applicants wishing to take over the holdings, including two who had been dispossessed by the War Department. Luckily, the committee was offered a further four fields, comprising 30 acres, adjacent to the land of Dyer, by another of the tenants, M Powling. The asking price was £600 but the committee offered £375 and were refused. After further discussion, Powling agreed in July that he would accept £450 on condition that he could also take over the vacated holding, and this was finally agreed. The sale included field OS 48, OS 45, and OS 34, and one of the fields had a well. The purchase was given to Dyer to compensate for his lost holding and acres of fruit trees.

The adjustments went on throughout the year to compensate for the war land in a kind of 'musical chairs'. G Keeble had lost access to part of his land as the road was closed by the War Department, so the isolated acres were given to Catchpole. Catchpole gave the house vacated by one of the defaulting tenants to his horseman, R Green, but Green had been looking after the water pump in his old cottage. In his place, the carpenter of the estate was offered Green's old cottage and the job of becoming the pump man.

One other important comment at this time was that 'considerable assistance has been given to the tenants of Pond Hall and West Suffolk Agricultural Executive Committee in the shape of horses and prisoner labour with beneficial results'.

1919 and the Aftermath of Hostilities

Although the war finished in 1918 the after effects continued for several years. For example, in April 1919, prisoners were still being used as labour on the estate, and the War Executive Committee was serving notices on tenants to change their practices – A P Howard's land was flooded and he was told to clean his ditches; A Tilbury's land was also flooded, and he had planted oats on land that should have been fallowed. One of the national problems in the last year of the war and beyond was that farmers, in a drive to raise food output, were sometimes ignoring the need to allow land to rest or were urged to re-sow fields. As a result, fertility dropped and this is perhaps an example of the trend.

Shortages in supplies were still in evidence: the mole draining needed on a number of fields was delayed into 1919 because of 'coal shortages'.

Services on the Estates and Building Maintenance

Roads, from this point, began to cause regular problems, perhaps due to the increase in motorised vehicles.

The road to Gary Farm had had to be repaired in 1910 but this was the only mention of roads from 1910–1919. Now, in April 1919, there were serious problems. The long road up to Valley Farm was in bad repair, so Pattle had prisoners repair it using materials from the gravel pit on the estate. The even longer Ramsey Farm road collapsed, partly due to the amount of water in the ditches. Prisoners were used to mend the surface and carry out the larger task of strengthening the sides of the road with timber baulks.

Many of the buildings at this point also were found to be in poor repair as little routine maintenance had been done during the war due to lack of labour and materials. They also needed repainting.

In 1919 there was another change – increasing evidence of centralised services for the county. For the first years of the Trust, work had been done by a carpenter and several labourers employed by the Trust itself, with outside contractors for larger works. In 1919 the council set up a Small Holdings Works Department at Copdock, and the estate carpenter, Mr Last, was transferred to working at Copdock while also running the oil engine at Pond Hall two days a week.

Thus, when Mr Prowse at Gary Farm asked for a new cow shed – with dimensions measuring 24 feet by 8 feet by 15 feet – and a yard, because he had built up his stock to 19 head of cattle, it was decided that the work should be carried out by the new Small Holdings Works Department.

Land Adjustments

In April 1919, Pattle had managed to collect all the rents and the committee's finances seemed healthier. In 1918, the trustees had invested £500 in Exchequer Bonds, and £475 in the War Loan (Bank of England), and had been able to buy extra acres from Powling. In January 1919, they were offered land near Hadleigh Railway Station which adjoined Arnold Field – 41 acres in all. They considered the price 'excessive' at £25 per acre. A few months later, 54 acres of Station Farm was offered to them and they decided to inspect the property; however, in July they decided not to buy. Meanwhile tenants were still moving around the land – Dyer had been given Malyon's land and Green's cottage.

At Sproughton there was the first noted change in the holdings since 1910 – C Chisnall's holding was to be re-let to a Mr E W Boreham who was an 'approved ex-Service applicant' in December 1920. Once again a small note in these minutes reflects a national movement. In 1918, the Selbourne Committee had recommended the encouragement of settlements of smallholders, particularly returning ex-servicemen, and in 1919, the Land Settlement (Facilities) Act enabled councils to purchase land compulsorily to provide additional smallholdings. As a result of this, in December 1919 county councils received a circular instructing them to consider what land might be acquired to settle ex-servicemen, promising to cover losses between income and expenditure up to 1925.[1] In fact, it was discovered a few weeks later that Boreham was not eligible, under the Act, for the required financial loan as the holding was held by the Trust rather than by the Small Holdings and Allotment Committee. As a compromise the trustees decided to make their own loan of £100 so that Boreham could take the holding.

Hadleigh Aerodrome 1918–20

By late 1918, the title of the facility had now changed from its first title of 'Aviation Field', and the estate had learned to live with the inconvenience of the lost land. In December 1919, however, the War Department wrote to say that the airfield was now 'superfluous to the requirements of the RAF' but gave no date for their final departure. In the meantime, the committee received a letter from the superintendant of the Road Mechanised Transport, GER, who proposed operating a fleet of about 60 to 70 ex-War Department lorries to convey perishable goods and shop goods to and from the area. They had already acquired Elmswell Aerodrome at a rent of £150 pa, but around Hadleigh they had found that the only suitable depot – which needed to contain garages, stores, a dormitory, and a workshop – was the Aviation Ground.

The War Department Disposal Board said that they could arrange a lease if the Felix Thornley Cobbold Trust withdrew their demand that all buildings should be cleared at the end of the war and the land returned to them for farming. After much discussion the committee reluctantly agreed to this proposal and awaited further correspondence. In February, they instructed their solicitor, still Mr Hugh Turner of Ipswich, to negotiate with the War Department land agent for transfer of the Aviation Ground to the Government Disposal Board, but a few weeks later the plan was dropped, and by March 1920 the War Department had given up their occupation of the land and their buildings.

Finally the committee could contemplate returning to a peacetime regime of smallholdings management. Cecil Pattle remained the county land agent and the Trust contributed £12 10s a quarter to his salary, with £10 travel allowance. Townshend Cobbold remained the clerk for the Trust and was paid a salary of £5 0s 0d a quarter.

NOTES

1   Howkins, Alun. *The Death of Rural England.* London: Routledge, 2003. p 88.

Chapter Four

1920–1929
Post War Reorganisation

National Agricultural Scene

In 1920 the industry was in optimistic mood with high guaranteed prices and a minimum wage for labourers. Many farmers at the end of the war bought land they had formerly rented, and many ex-servicemen were being encouraged by the government to invest their demobilisation money in a smallholding. However, the mood of optimism was short lived with a fall in cereal prices as imports recommenced. A series of government and union meetings that lasted into early 1921 were held nationwide. The meetings explored the possibility of a reduction in wages and as a result, the Agriculture Act was repealed on 7 June 1921, with effect from August. Thus, all price guarantees ended and the Wages Board, established in 1917, was scrapped. This meant an end to the minimum wage and agricultural wages fell by 40 per cent up to the beginning of 1923.

Cereal prices stabilised in 1924, and in the same year the government began offering subsidies for the growing of sugar beet. The subsidies did much to help Suffolk farmers and at least one tenant at Hadleigh started producing the crop.

However, Britain was now entering the years of the Great Depression. Although in America the Wall Street crash occurred in 1929, in the United Kingdom the problems had started earlier with industry struggling from the aftermath of the war. Export markets had been lost not only through wartime destruction of shipping but also by lost business caused by the disruption to trade. This particularly affected export of textiles, steel and coal – products of northern Britain – but even East Anglia was affected by the general economic decline. Churchill, as Chancellor of the Exchequer, reintroduced the Gold Standard in 1925 which made exports more expensive, contributing to a further decline. To offset these losses, wages were cut yet again, leading to the General Strike of May 1926. Unemployment in Britain rose from one million to two and a half million by the end of the decade.

In 1926, prices of crops began to fall once again, and parts of Suffolk and Norfolk around Thetford were reduced to the same kind of desolation noticed by Rider Haggard in 1902. In 1927, S A Bensusan noted that in that area 'the only crop to be seen was weeds, and a multitude of these were seeding generously; houses there were none for miles . . . nor was there any traffic'.[1]

The answer to this desolation came around the turn of the century; it was renewed diversification. The dairy industry profited from cheap grain for cattle feed, and an increased interest in improving the nutrition of the population led to a demand for milk in cities. The Hadleigh tenants, with their easy access to the railway, took advantage of this. Producers of fruit and vegetables did well; the jam makers at Tiptree in Essex and Histon in Cambridgeshire were thriving. Dyer, on the Hadleigh Estate, had replanted after his orchards were destroyed by the War Department. Similarly, the Eastmans did well with their poultry and egg production, not only during the war but also during the lean years of the 1920s. The battery hen farming systems that appeared in Britain during 1925 helped to boost profits.

One trend which is clear from the 1920–1930 Trust minutes is that there was a rapid increase in housing growth, a rise in housing standards, an increase in motorised transport and the need for wider metalled roads in the countryside.

Trustees 1920–1930

In 1918, records indicate that the committee consisted of Harry Fiske (chairman), H W Mason (vice chairman), C C Eley, H Hunt, A Harwood, A H Hucklesby and C C Smith. Attendance was poor at this period; for example, in June 1921, H W Mason was in the chair with only A Harwood and C C Smith attending and in October 1921, only Harry Fiske, A Harwood and H W Mason were present. There was, nevertheless, fairly good continuity in that by 1930 Harry Fiske was still in the chair, while A Harwood, H F Harwood, H W Mason, C C Smith, Fred Smith and W Wilson were still attending members.

The Trust Estates Agriculture

Tenants growing cereals needed to have their corn ground by the mill, but the price charged by the Trust was 1s 3d a coomb, with Simpkin paid 3d per coomb for his labour in carrying out the work. With the fall in prices this charge became a burden on the smallholders and though they complained that the charge was 'excessive', no reduction was made.

More fields required draining throughout the period. In 1923, A P Howard asked for 170 pipes for draining OS 679, and then he asked for more for OS 671 the following year. All the Hadleigh land was affected by heavy flooding in 1924, which was then followed by a drought. In 1925, Catchpole and Reginald Dyer asked if the Trust would supply the pipes so that they could mole drain the whole of Ramsey Farm and Dyer's land with pipes laid nine yards apart. This was agreed.

By the latter part of the decade, many tenants were clearly beginning to struggle again. Three tenants asked for a rent reduction, and of these, two were granted and one refused. Another tenant left owing rent without due notice, after having wavered over his tenancy for some years.

Hadleigh Aerodrome Site 1920

For the Trust, with their expert knowledge of farming, the disposal of the vacated aerodrome produced problems that were outside their previous experience. The early proposal that it should become a distribution depot for food was dropped in February 1920, a few weeks after it was proposed. Unfortunately, this left the committee with a large number of buildings, disrupted farm roads and drainage, as well as large areas of concrete to consider. The idea that this could be quickly returned to farming seemed far from the truth.

The Trust decided to buy the buildings from the War Department for £750 and Pattle proposed

moving the County Small Holdings Works Department from Copdock to this site. The buildings were vacated by the War Department on 13 March but some were found to be badly damaged. A tenant, Mr George Keeble, was asked to take temporary charge of the buildings, and the Works Manager blocked the access entrance from the road. In April, the Disposal Board agreed to accept £250 for the buildings inclusive of fittings and waiver of any claims for reinstatement of the land, and this was agreed.

The inventory of these buildings gives an interesting insight as to the size and use of the aerodrome:

Aeroplane hangar		£500
Workshop		£15
Water tower and pump		£50
Coal shed		£20
Stores		£15
Canteen		£50
Cook house		£50
Sergeants' mess and 3 latrines		£55
MRAF's hut		£5
Officers' hut		£75
Officers' sleeping quarters		£100
Electric light engine house		£15
Officers' latrine		£5
Men's bath house and latrines		£20
Transport shed		£50
Men's living hut	1	£50
	2	£50
	3	£50
Wireless hut		£5
Paraffin hut		£15
Guard hut		£5
Medical hut		£50
Technical stores		£25
Brick wall for shooting – no value given		
Concrete bomb store – no value given		
Total:		£1,215

The committee decided to retain four bays of the larger hangar, all electricity and phone fittings, the brick-built store and its fittings, the concrete store, the water tower and tackle, the engine and pump, and the shooting wall. The remaining buildings were to be offered to the Small Holdings Committee for £1,200 if they wanted them.

By September, many of the buildings had been taken down and removed by the Small Holdings Works Department, but the Disposal Board now wrote to say that they wanted to remove the plant and machinery from the machinery section and this was done by the end of the year leaving a concrete waste-land. The committee tried to sell off the concrete as hard core to the Main Roads Department at 5s a ton, but the department rejected the offer.

A further problem at the end of the year was that the 'watchman', George Keeble, who had been paid £5 pa for his work, died. Despite being asked to leave, his widow did not want to move from her cottage. Mrs Keeble finally left her cottage in 1929, eight years after she had been asked to move, but she had been working the land of the holding, and after her departure asked for compensation for the fruit trees she had planted, and labour in erecting sheds. There was never any question of her being able to take over the tenancy in her own right.

Water Services

Early in 1920, the Sproughton wind pump was damaged by gales and needed to be repaired. However, the shortage of materials still persisted and the makers reported that there would be no spare parts for eight weeks, and that the total cost would be £75. The committee considered using the oil engine from the airfield, but installing this engine would require a new engine house and the removal of the top of the windmill – a costly procedure. At an estimated £90 this was too expensive to be considered further. The tenants were advised by trustees to make 'whatever provision they could' for their water supply.

By September, the parts had still not appeared, although the Eastern Counties Farmers Co-operative had promised the gearing by 8 August. The tenants asked for compensation for having been without water for seven months, but the committee replied that the idea was 'not to be entertained'. This was a harsh decision that is now hard to justify; financially the Trust was on sounder footing, and the whole point of the committee was that it was designed to help agricultural labourers.

The situation dragged on into December, by which time the gears had been fixed but the pump was still losing water and the repairers had to be called back to the site. In February 1922, a new brass pump was installed at a further cost of £22. The problems, however, continued on a regular basis with another bad leak from the holding reservoir in 1924. In this situation, there appeared to be too few stopcocks so the

agent could not find the source and three additional stopcocks had to be installed.

The supply became an even more valuable resource in 1925. Samford Rural District Council (RDC) had built 50 houses nearby and needed a water supply for their tenants. A few months later they tried to buy land for additional houses, but the tenants involved – Southgate and the ex-serviceman, Boreham – were not willing to give up their property. The Trust argued that this was protected charity land, so the RDC was forced to look elsewhere. They were, however, permitted to draw water at a rent of 10s pa, and in 1927, the RDC took over maintenance of the pumping entirely by restoring the wind pump. By the following year, they had an additional 25 council houses, and needed to increase their water volume. The supply seemed ample, and the Trust therefore agreed.

On the Hadleigh site, the Eastman brothers, with their thriving poultry business, asked for water to be laid on to part of their land at Bushy Coopers. Due to the distance from the water main, the committee again said 'the application is not to be entertained' but the same month Prowse at Gary Farm asked for a water supply to Holdings 5 and 26, and this was agreed.

In 1926, a new 8 hp Ruston Hornsby engine was installed to pump the Hadleigh water, at a cost of £77, but in 1928 it broke down.

Housing and Farm Buildings

Throughout the 1920s, tenants applied month after month for additional buildings – a cart lodge here, a house extension there. Boreham, in 1926, asked for a stable and also a bath and connection to the water supply at a total cost of £9 15s 0d – the fourth applicant to ask for a bath. The agent asked him to find a 'cheaper kind of bath' but by 1927 he had two new horse boxes, a chaff house and a bath in the cottage, at a cost of an extra 5s pa in rent.

The Eastmans had also been asking for an extension to their cottage, and a plan was submitted which included a geyser in the bathroom. The committee rejected the idea, and a decision was deferred in 1920, and then again in 1921. This is the third reference to a bathroom on the estate, and clearly at this date the committee still considered it a wasteful extravagance in an agricultural house.

One of the other cottages, belonging to W Cole, was

found in 1923 to be unsafe and past repair, so the Trust decided to demolish it and erect a pair of five-roomed dwelling houses, each with an acre of land, if they could get a housing subsidy from the council to help with the cost. Hadleigh UDC applied for a subsidy from the Ministry of Health, and a grant was obtained. By September 1924, the cottages had been built at the lowest possible cost, but by 1927 they were found to be defective and the architect was called back to inspect them. He found that the rear walls were damp as the rough cast was defective, but also one floor was damp 'due to severance of land drain during excavations' requiring extensive repairs.

Roads and Public Utilities

Road transport was clearly increasing in this post-war period, and Samford Rural District Council asked the committee in October 1921 if they could buy a strip of land on Burstall Land, Sproughton, for road widening. They also asked if they could open a stone pit on the land of one of the tenants, E W Boreham. This was agreed and Samford paid the committee a royalty of 2s 6d per load at 24 bushels of stone. Boreham, on the other hand, was paid 9d per load compensation.

Another sign of the times was that in 1927 the Post Office Engineering Department asked for a wayleave at a rent of 1s per pole to erect some telegraph poles on the Hadleigh land, and this was granted by the committee. In 1929, another five poles were erected at an additional 5s wayleave.

Land Agent Changes

In December 1920, Cecil Pattle resigned from his post after carrying the heavy load of working for two county councils since 1915. His place was taken by A B Johnson at a salary of £50 pa plus travelling and subsistence. The importance of the agents to the Trust at this period cannot be overestimated, and each time there was a change of personnel, the management of the estate altered.

Mr Johnson was asked by the auditor to change his accounting method, so a capital valuation of the estates needed to be made in January 1921. By this, the capital value of the Pond Hall Estate was valued at £13,773 4s 7d, and the Sproughton land at £3,354 11s 6d. The agent reported that 'due to the situation of the land, the number of cottages and conveniences that the tenants on the Sproughton land enjoy, it would appear that the present rents are low'. On the Pond Hall Estate, however, he did not consider that the tenants could bear any appreciable increase. By December 1921, the committee had come to a decision that they would not raise existing rents, but that higher ones would be asked when any holding was re-let or renegotiated. In 1927, another agent, A G Wisbey, took over and his report on the Pond Hall Estate gives a 'snapshot' view of the estate after 17 years of operation. (See page 40.)

Land Sales – Eastman Brothers and Dyer

As previously noted, in the original leases Felix had offered to let his tenants buy their smallholdings at a generous price if they prospered. The original committee had found this arrangement unacceptable, the leases of the original tenants had been changed and all new leases precluded any right to buy. In 1921, however, the Eastman brothers asked if they could buy some of their land, and offered extra land in its place. In April 1922, a proposal was made that the holding in the occupation of A H Eastman could be sold for £1,125 and an additional five acres in the occupation of W Ratcliffe would be sold for £100, subject to permission from the Charity Commissioners. The Eastmans would also have to pay water rates, and be permitted to lay additional pipes from the mains – a facility which they had previously been denied. The Trust were to retain rights to the water main pipes in perpetuity and were to have access, while the Eastmans would pay for any damage to the pipes.

Negotiations continued for months. The Charity Commissioners at first asked for a valuation of the land, but this gave a value of £1,385. The commissioners suggested that they should be given a longer lease instead of a purchase right, but the Trust argued that the Eastmans had shown 'zeal in developing their holding and now want security of tenure'. Finally, the commissioners agreed to the sale, but only at the higher price, and the sale went through in January 1923. In addition, Duncan S Eastman was able to lease a cottage and barn on OS 412 for 20 years at a rent of £8 pa, and he agreed to pay £1 pa for a supply of water for 20 years. The trust planned to invest the money in War Loans bonds, but they were told by the

Pond Hall: 757.048 acres, divided into 30 holdings. Water supplied by oil engine and pump.

Land heavy and difficult to work, some parts are wet. Three sets of buildings:

- (a) Pond Hall divided for the purpose into 1 small and 3 large holdings with 70 acres.
- (b) Ramsey Farm – 2 large holdings with 160 acres.
- (c) Valley Farm – one occupation of 118 acres.

1. Eastman bros: cottage.
2. F Green has cottage, sole old buildings and 43.171 ac. Deeper ploughing would be beneficial.
3. W Ratcliffe: Cottage, bad buildings, 30.786 ac. Fair – but deeper ploughing would be beneficial.
4. A Tilbury: Bungalow and 11.687 ac. Orchard needs thinning, arable not cultivated for 2–3 years.
5. Prowse (26): House, buildings and 30.091 ac. (Also farms a quantity of other land outside the estate and satisfactorily runs a milk business. Could an open shed be provided?)
6. Allen (24 and 27): Land only, of 13.270 ac.
7. Simpkin (11): House, buildings and part of Pond Hall, 49.920 ac.
8. Powling: Cottage at top of Valley Farm drive. Buildings part of Pond Hall. 60.951 ac. Could he have a new cottage at Pond Hall instead of three quarters of a mile away?
9. Howard: House, inadequate buildings. 50.516 ac poorly done.
10. Audus: House, buildings part of Valley Farm 54.664 ac. Very fair. Was bad when he came 2 years ago, and he has improved it.
11. Simpkin: 22.243 ac.
12. Dyer: Cottage.
13. Frost: House, part of Valley Farm, 106.370 ac. Satisfactory cultivation.
14. and 15. Catchpole: House, buildings of Ramsey Farm. 180.058 ac. Also wants drains.
16. Dyer: Buildings, old – from aerodrome. 45.533 acres in bad condition.
17. Cooley: House, Pond Hall buildings, 2.064 ac.
18. Mrs Keeble's bungalow.
20. Dyer: Bungalow. Buildings, small and inadequate. Land, bulk badly done.
23. Mulley: Cottage.
26. Prowse: Land very fair.
27. Allen: Land only, very fair.
28. Howard: New cottage.
29. Lambert: New cottage.

Almost all houses need painting and repairs. No cottages in good state.
All rents paid.

Charity Commission that, by the provision of the scheme agreed in October 1910, they must now buy some additional land.

In 1928, another of the 1910 tenants, R Dyer, also asked to buy his land. His tenancy had been marred by the disruption of the aerodrome and uprooting of his fruit trees, and flooded land, but he now wanted to buy his bungalow, the farm buildings and 12.621 acres of land of his original lease. He was presumably again growing fruit on his land, and this was one area of agriculture that thrived in the early 1920s. Now that the precedent had been set by the Eastmans the sale went through fairly quickly at a price of £559 8s 9d. This meant that the Trust had now sold almost 50 acres which needed to be replaced.

Hadleigh Airfield 1927–1930

In September 1927, the committee was approached by the Suffolk (and Eastern Counties) Aeroplane Club for permission to hire 30–40 acres as a flying ground. After years of disruption and the expenses incurred in putting the aerodrome land back to some kind of agricultural use, the committee might well have refused this offer, particularly as it fell outside the uses provided for by Felix's bequest. However, the Hon. Lady Bailey and Mr and Mrs Courtney Prentice of Stowmarket were interviewed, and in November the committee agreed to lease 35 acres for seven years from 11 October 1927 at a rent of 30s per acre, with the present tenant given grazing rights. The Trust also

An open day of the Suffolk Aeroplane Club at Hadleigh Airfield in 1927. Spectators (dead-heads) looking over the hedge could observe not only the planes and aerial displays, but also the cars belonging to officials and visitors. (*Flight* magazine)

kept rights of way over the site, and gave permission for only temporary buildings to be erected. Finally, the SAC had to accept a clause binding them to take precautions for public safety near the aerodrome as well as on the aerodrome itself.

Courtney M Prentice was an ex-Royal Flying Corps bomber pilot, and had become a successful businessman after the war, but still retained his love of flying. He formed the new club in 1927, with the Hon. Lady Bailey of Leeds Castle in Kent as President. Under his leadership, the club had bought a Blackburn Bluebird in February 1927 and three more planes later in the year.

An article in *Flight* magazine for 3 November 1927, which reported an open day held on 30 October, criticised the 'neglect and decay' of the site with the removal of the War Department buildings and commented that 'it is a pity that the ultimate use of these old aerodromes for civil use could not have been foreseen before the destructive policy was evoked'. This criticism was unfair, as the land was owned by a Trust that was bound by Charity Commission rules to try to return the land to an agricultural use.

Nevertheless, the day was clearly a great success with 'crazy' aerial displays from the Club's own Blackburn 'Bluebird', Moths, Westland 'Widgeons' and a Shell 'Arom' plane. Lady Bailey, Captain and Mrs G De Havilland attended, along with Mr and Mrs Mills who were the New Zealand distributors for the De Havilland Company. Over 400 people were given trips out of the 1,000 that had applied for the 5s tickets. In a photo of the field that showed the cars belonging to officials and visitors, 'a large crowd of dead-heads', or spectators, who watched the meeting by peering over the hedge from the road, could also be seen. (See page 41.)

In 1928, the club arranged an Easter air display, which encouraged potential pilots to undertake flying lessons 'which would enable you to fly to Australia in 16 days – for fifty-five pounds!' Although civilian flying was becoming popular, only seven civilian routes were authorised: Hounslow to Hadleigh being one of them. In 1929, the King's Cup air race visited Hadleigh Airfield as a turning point, with club members acting as judges. Also in 1929, an air taxi service began flying passengers between Hadleigh and Cambridge.

In 1930, Ipswich Borough Council opened its new airport and asked the Suffolk Aeroplane Club to run it for them. The club moved, selling their Hadleigh club house and hangar to Ipswich BC for re-erection on the new airfield. This marked the end of the Pond Hall Estate link with flying; the only exception being that until recently two wooden bungalows on Pond

The president of the Suffolk Aeroplane Club, the Hon. Lady Bailey, is seen climbing into her own 'Moth' in which she gave many of the joy-ride trips of the day.
(*Flight* magazine)

Hall Road were named No 1 and No 2 Aerodrome cottages.[2]

Conclusion

The 1920s had started well, with prices for crops being guaranteed; unfortunately, the rest of the decade saw a gradual decline in prices and conditions. The trust disposed of plots of land but did not find suitable replacements, so they ended the decade with increased investments but decreased acreage. In 1929, they invested another £740 in 3.5 per cent conversion stock, but, apart from building two new cottages, had carried out comparatively few repairs or changes to houses and farm buildings during the decade.

NOTES

1   Bensusan, S L. *Latter Day Rural England*. London: Ernest Benn Ltd, 1928. p 65.
2   Information provided by the Hadleigh Society website (www.hadsoc.org.uk/).

Chapter Five

1930–1939
The Great Depression

The Depression Years

The economic crisis affecting Britain in the late 1920s, led to the election of a Labour Government under Ramsay MacDonald in 1929, but as problems continued to grow and unemployment figures soared to 3 million, MacDonald decided to form a National Government in 1931, which was a coalition of Labour, Liberals and Tories. An election was held to ratify the National Government, which saw a Conservative landslide, although MacDonald continued as PM until 1935. Philip Snowden, as Chancellor, cut public sector wages, cut unemployment pay by ten per cent, and raised income tax from 4s 6d in the pound to 5s. These deflationary measures caused a further decline in trade, so in September 1931 Britain abandoned the Gold Standard, and the exchange rate against the dollar fell by 25 per cent with an immediate easing of trade conditions.

In 1932, Neville Chamberlain, the new Chancellor, implemented the Ottawa Agreement, imposing ten per cent trade tariffs on imports from all countries outside the British Empire, and at last British industry began to recover. As demand for goods and services grew, there was a rush to build new houses by private builders as well as councils. Older properties were also being improved at this time. The electrical industry prospered, with mass production of electrical goods such as cookers, washing machines and radios. By the end of the decade, car production in Britain doubled, which led to increased demand for better roads.

Agricultural Scene 1930–1939

Agriculture experienced an increasingly difficult time during the early 1930s in line with the national crisis. Ronald Blythe's character Leonard Thomson in *Akenfield* recalls that unemployed married farm workers received parish relief, but single men received nothing,

so up to 50 men passed his cottage each night tramping from workhouse to workhouse looking for work.[1]

The Land Settlement Association, mentioned in Chapter 1, was founded in 1934 to provide small-holdings for the unemployed. The first two estates were in Bedfordshire, with 284 acres at Potton and 454 acres at Chawston. These estates had 103 holdings and

Many religious groups provided smallholdings or allotments for the unemployed, both at the turn of the century and during the 1930s. This 1930s poster is from The Friends Allotment Committee, which continued its work until 1951.
(The Religious Society of Friends in Britain)

a further 83 that were set aside for the London unemployed. The Lawford Estate was set up soon after the Bedfordshire settlements and many of these holdings still exist. Allotments were similarly encouraged by charitable organisations: in 1930, for example, the Friends (Quakers) Allotment Committee was set up to assist the unemployed, continuing its work until 1951.

Farm prices fell steeply after 1929, affecting farmers in cereal growing areas in particular, and the numbers of farm bankruptcies each year rose to a peak of 560 in 1932.[2] To ease matters the government passed a number of measures to support farming. For example, the Land Drainage Act in 1930 gave subsidies for draining, while the 1931 and 1933 Agricultural Marketing Acts created marketing boards for bacon, pigs, hops, milk and potatoes, which helped to organise farmers into co-operative marketing associations. In 1932, the Import Duties Act introduced a tariff on many imports, including fruit and vegetables, and set quotas for imports of bacon, ham and other meat products. In 1936, the tithe rent charge was finally abolished.

Towards the end of the decade, the government began, at first secretly, to think once again of the possibility of war and remembered the emergency measures that had been introduced in 1915 to counteract the loss of imports due to enemy action. In 1937, a subsidy was introduced to encourage spreading of lime on agricultural land to boost soil fertility, and the Ministry of Agriculture was given powers to regulate the cultivation of the land, or even to take possession of land under the Defence of the Realm regulations. In September 1939, the County War Agricultural Executive Committees (War Ags) were set up to control food production during times of conflict.

There were other trends during the decade. In 1931, the Agricultural Research Council was established, and an increasingly scientific approach to farming methods began to emerge. One Suffolk farmer near Ipswich remembers attending a lecture given by the Ministry of Agriculture in the mid-1930s where the speaker promised that it would be possible for farmers to get two tons of wheat per acre in the near future, and indeed, in the more distant future, may be even four tons per acre.[3] As current yields were usually around one ton per acre, the farmers who were present listened with some scepticism. Breeding research was carried out to reduce wheat straw length so that energy was devoted to producing a larger head and, sure enough, the yields rose as had been predicted. Fertiliser research allowed farmers to enrich the soil so that eventually the fallow period could be dispensed with and a crop taken every year.

Trust Committee and Governance

In 1930, Harry Fiske was still in the chair, together with A Harwood, A H F Harwood, H W Mason, C C Smith, Fred Smith and W Wilson. The records suggest that as a rule attendance during this period was often low. For example, in May 1933 only Harry Fiske and C C Smith attended a meeting, but H W Mason was now vice chairman of the county council, so had other concerns.

In 1934, Major Norman Everett joined the committee. Norman was the son of Robert Everett, one of the founder members and a friend of Felix Cobbold. There was also another Mason – E Mason – who joined. In 1937, yet another family link within the committee was established when John Rous, Viscount Dunwich became a member. John was the son of the third Earl of Stradbroke, who had been the first chairman, and John became the fourth Earl upon the death of his father in 1947. In 1937, the committee also included T A Crombie, H Scrimgeour and G Stedman, but Harry remained the chairman.

Agricultural Scene on the Trust Lands

Land drainage continued on the holdings, particularly in Hadleigh, but from 1930 the Ministry of Agriculture offered a subsidy of 33 per cent of the cost. Thus, when in the autumn of 1930 three holdings were drained – a total of 85 acres – the cost was reduced to £210 after the grant. The state was offering grants not only for draining the fields by mole drainage, but also for draining ditches and clearing water courses. The following year, 45 acres were drained, followed by a further 125 acres and 324 chain of ditches were cleared. However, as so often happens, in 1931 the scheme ended abruptly on 24 September, so the Trust lost money on the incomplete scheme. After a fruitless appeal to West Suffolk, the agent had to arrange for the work to be done by direct labour at a cost of £150.

In 1934 a Horticultural Advisor was appointed to the county and at once made his presence felt. One tenant on Holding 3 was advised 'to remove each alternate tree in his orchard'. The tenant asked for permission to do the work, but also wanted a rent reduction as he would have fewer trees to crop. The committee agreed that he could remove the trees, but would not give a rent reduction. The following year, another tenant wanted 20 fruit trees, and this was agreed on the condition that the varieties were to be selected by the Horticultural Advisor.

In 1935, with the introduction of the Milk Marketing Board two years earlier, Mr Prowse at Gary Farm applied 'for the provision of a new dairy house in order that he might qualify for production of Grade A milk, with the old dairy to be used as a sterilising room'. This was allowed by the committee and the work was carried out by direct labour at a cost of £15.

The subsidy for growing sugar beet provided another useful crop for tenants. At Valley Farm the tenant was experiencing financial troubles in 1935 and agreed to give all the money from his forthcoming crop sale to the Ipswich Beet Sugar Factory to cover his debt – a desperate temporary solution to his struggles.

By 1937, with the drive to increase the fertility of land, a number of tenants were 'proposing to apply chalk to their lands and wondered whether the Committee would grant assistance towards the cost thereof, in addition to the grant of 50 per cent available under the Government's Land Fertility Scheme'. The committee agreed, 'if the County Agricultural Organiser certifies the land as being deficient in lime'. The committee would bear 25 per cent of the cost, including delivery to the holding or nearest station, with the tenant bearing the cost of the carting and spreading. In 1939, another two tenants asked for help in liming their land with 100 tons for 20 acres and 650 tons for 131 acres.

The Eastmans wanted to expand their poultry farm and applied to take over part of Holding 4 as additional accommodation. This was agreed as a temporary measure.

Timber on the estates had been sold piecemeal by the estate since 1910, usually because trees had to be removed for some reason, such as clearance for the aerodrome, but in 1931 the committee decided to plant trees as a commercial crop and 200 willow sets were planted near Pond Hall. By 1938, the trees had grown well, and the council's Horticultural Advisor recommended that the trees should be topped and cuttings from them planted. The following year they were able to sell five small elm trees for £5 to the East Anglian Electricity Supply Company for poles.

Land Purchases

The Trust had been asked by the Charity Commissioners to replace the acreage lost to the Eastman brothers and Reginald Dyer, but it was not until the early 1930s that they began to search in earnest, encouraged perhaps by the drastic fall in the price of land.

In August 1932, a Saxtead agricultural estate offered the Trust four farms, with six cottages and a total of 222 acres, but in November a decision was made not to buy.

In January 1933, more land became available at Great Blakenham and Claydon, which consisted of two farm houses, four cottages and four sets of buildings. This interested the committee provided that the Charity Commission would agree to them bidding not more than £3,000. By February, the committee heard that the vendors wanted to sell 406 acres, but not all were suitable for smallholdings. The land agent was asked to negotiate a purchase of the smaller land acreage. In October, the agent reported that Tollgate Farm, Great Blakenham consisted of 112 acres which could be turned into two smallholdings with one new set of buildings, so an offer of £1,280 was made. A further plot by Hackney's Corner on the Great Blakenham–Washbrook Road was of interest, but the price was judged too high. By November, Tollgate Farm had been purchased for £1,250 and a plan for a new house and farm buildings had been approved.

At the same meeting, farms at Witnesham amounting to a total of 152 acres were discussed and the agent was asked to inspect. This land consisted of Venn Farm and Low Farm, of which 25 acres were old pasture. The offer included two farm houses, a cottage, a detached house and two sets of farm buildings only four miles from Ipswich, and the agent said the land was 'mostly tender heavy with some mixed'. With the agreement of the Charity Commission, the committee decided to sell some stock to the value of £2,525 for the purchase and adaptation of the property, but the following month they decided that with the additional purchase of the Great Blakenham farm they needed to sell £4,686 15s 8d of share stock. Thus, by the spring of 1934, they had not only two holdings at Great Blakenham being set up, but also four new holdings at Witnesham – Venn Farm and buildings consisted of 72.5 acres at a rent of £100 pa, Low Farm and buildings consisted of 62.5 acres at a rent of £85 pa, Orchard House and new buildings consisted of 10.5 acres at £35 rent, and a cottage with new buildings consisted of six acres at a rent of £20.

From this point, the management problems of the committee and the land agent expanded considerably, with four different sites to be inspected, and a number of new tenants who needed careful nursing through their initial letting period. At Blakenham, for example, in 1936 one of the tenants, Mr Hood, wanted his land drained and 3,000 pipes were supplied to him. Similarly, at Witnesham in 1934, the new tenant F A Walton was setting up an eight-acre poultry farm which also needed draining.

Water

The existing two water systems at Hadleigh and Sproughton continued to give regular problems. A new electric pump was installed at Hadleigh in December 1933 – a No 2 Climax pump producing 900 gallons an hour, a 1.5 hp Compton Parkinson motor with five electric lights to the adjacent farm buildings, and a new pump house built by direct labour. The total cost was £92 13s 3d. However, the pump immediately had problems and in 1935 the contractor was asked to change it.

The water pipes to holdings were now ageing, and in 1939 the 300 feet of pipes to Hill House needed urgent renewal. At the same time, a water analysis was carried out on the spring near the Pond Hall reservoir and it was confirmed as fit for drinking.

For the new properties, the two Tollgate Farm properties were given a Garrard engine for pumping and a 1,000-gallon storage tank. At Witnesham, the committee first planned to install a petrol engine, but there was an East Anglian Electric Supply Company line nearby, so an electric pump was installed connected to the new mains supply.

In 1936, the Tollgate Farm drainage became a problem when the cesspit overflowed into a ditch by the highway. The District Council's Sanitary Inspector suggested that a new cesspit be built under the stackyard and that the open ditch be filled in.

Houses and Buildings

In this period, the Trust came under continuous pressure from tenants to improve their living conditions in line with national trends. Up to this point, cooking seems to have been done on an open fire in the living room, and at least one cottage at Valley Farm, also had the copper for heating water in the living room. Presumably, they used the hot water not only for washing clothes, but also for bathing people in a tin bath. In 1938, the committee decided to 'remove coppers from living rooms, provide new cookers and stoves and make good, and build new coppers in outhouses'.

Tenant after tenant from 1929 until the mid-1930s asked for 'a register stove' in the living room and a cooking range in the scullery which was not called the kitchen. In addition, many more requests were received from tenants for bathrooms and a hot water supply. Several floors had to be changed – one wanted his damp brick floor replaced by boards, while Prowse wanted boards over his concrete kitchen floor. In 1930, Prowse also asked for an indoor lavatory with a window, and in 1935 another tenant was given a new washhouse, coalhouse and an earth closet. In 1938, a second tenant had a coal house turned into a bathroom adjoining the kitchen, while a new coal house and earth closet were erected 'with new drains' at a cost of £75, with the tenant paying an additional £2 10s pa in rent.

In August 1937, one of the new Witnesham properties was found to be very damp and the tenant, F A Walton, asked for a new ceiling in the bathroom. The committee agreed to this and also agreed that the external walls should be treated with boiled linseed oil to cure the damp. In November, however, the recommendation was changed so that the walls were to be treated with two coats of Cementone at a cost of £14 instead of linseed oil.

Farm building changes included not only Prowse's new dairy, but also a new barn, a cart lodge and concrete mangers in his cow houses all of which cost £85. In August 1933, the committee had to provide a new store for one tenant, a new cart lodge for another, and a new chaff house and barn for a third.

There was pressure to improve accommodation not only from the tenants but also from the county. In 1930, it was the local Sanitary Authority which drew attention to a lack of suitable cowshed accommodation at Holding 10 in Hadleigh. This meant that an open shed had to be converted to cover three or four cows at a cost of £25. The note is also interesting in that it shows a traditional farming method of keeping a small group of animals to manure the field and perhaps provide 'pin money' for the farmer's wife in making butter or cheese to be sold in the market. This can be contrasted with the large herd at Gary Farm that was providing a commercial milk supply.

One tenant, H Norman (and sons) – who occupied holdings 7, 15, 21, and 23 – said that he would be leaving unless he could have a new house to accommodate his four sons. In May 1938 this was agreed and a tender was received from Messrs Keeble Bros of Raydon for £664 10s 0d.[4] In February of the following year, the house was almost completed but was already occupied by the sons.

One other change was the arrival of electricity along the Pond Hall Road in 1933; in February, the committee was asked by the East Anglian Electricity Supply Company if they would like a supply to the Pond Hall Estate. The chairman's reply was that the cost seemed prohibitive and 'the tenants hadn't asked for electricity'. By the next meeting in May, however, one of the tenants had paid for his own supply. In August, when the Pond Hall pump became overloaded, the agent was asked to repair it and investigate installing a larger engine with an electric pump; the trustees had evidently begun to appreciate the value of the new supply. For the rest of the period there is a note that two other cottages were given an electricity supply and by 1938 most tenants had been connected.

The newly acquired properties needed considerable repairs and rebuilding. Venn Farm buildings were dilapidated, and some had to be demolished and a new cow house and open shed built, while the old open shed was converted into three loose boxes. Low Farm had similar problems and thatched roofs were changed to corrugated iron.

When a sitting tenant was slow to leave a property in Witnesham, the tenant who was taking over the lease, H C Norman, had to resort to getting the law involved in order to get possession of his holding. The committee compensated him for this. Another tenant at Witnesham in 1936 had a house that was found to be so dilapidated that the committee debated whether to demolish it or to repair. In May, the agent reported that the cost of repairing would be £350 as against £450 for a new house. However, the tenant was badly in rent arrears, and little work had been done on the holding since the previous harvest, so the decision was deferred and the tenant warned. By August, the holding was no better so a notice to quit was issued. The tenant struggled to pay the rent and said he wanted to stay, but in November 1937 he was finally evicted from the land and the decision was made in 1938 to repair the house rather than rebuild.

Roads on the Estates

When the purchase of Low Farm and Venn Farm was made, the private road connecting the Ipswich–Witnesham Road to the new properties was found to be in bad condition and repairs were necessary. However in 1937, the agent noted that the problem had recurred through heavy usage of the road and the committee asked the Roads and Bridges Committee to accept it as a public highway as far as Cockfield Hall. Unfortunately, at this time the request was refused. One problem for trustees was that the track served not only the Trust property, but Pips Hill Farm, near the intersection with the main road, and Cockfield Hall beyond the Trust land. There was a conflict of interests as to who would pay for repairs at any one time, and this continued to be a problem.

The Ramsey Farm Road had been repaired by prisoners after the war, but by 1936 it was again in a bad state. In August 1936, the committee decided to resurface 445 yards as an experiment. It was a success and by November the whole 1,200 yards had been resurfaced.

Public Utilities

Throughout this period, local infrastructure was improving steadily. The electricity supply, which has been noted elsewhere, slowly spread throughout the county; in fact by 1933, the EAESC had erected 14 poles in the hedge banks of OS 460, 482 and 485 in Hadleigh at a wayleave rent of 1s 0d per pole.

The telephone network had also spread. In February 1933, the Post Office Engineering Department were given consent to lay underground telephone cables in a hedge bank at a rent of 2s pa, while in 1934, the same rent was charged for erecting one stay pole and one stay in the hedge of OS 84 at Tollgate Farm. That same year, eight new poles and a stay were installed at Sproughton at the cost of 9s pa wayleave rent. In 1936, there is a minute stating that the tenants at Witnesham were applying to the Post Office for telephones and informing the committee that this will require a line of poles to serve Low Farm and Orchard House. The committee agreed.

Public roads were being improved by the Roads and Bridges Committee of the council. In 1935, they asked for a strip of land, part of OS 268 and 269, fronting the Washbrook–Great Blakenham Road at Sproughton so that the road at Wild Man Corner could be improved.

Conclusion

This was an exciting but difficult period for farming, in spite of the subsidies. For the committee there was the pressure to update the houses and buildings, as the standards changed as to what was an acceptable level of accommodation. The acquisition of the two new plots of land added to their difficulties as both needed investment and improvements.

In 1938 the agent reported:

Land	Acreage	Number of Tenants	Rent
Hadleigh Estate	735.300	17	£791 4s 6d
Sproughton	83.929 acres	7	£192 15s 0d
Little Blakenham	112.124 acres	3	£155 0s 0d
Witnesham	151.910 acres	3 (1 vacant)	£252 8s 0d
Total:	1,083.262 acres	30	£1,391 7s 6d

Properties
1 very large house, Pond Hall
3 large farmhouses (2 subdivided)
11 ordinary smallholders houses – all brick, 10 tile and one thatch
11 cottages – 10 brick, one stud and plaster and thatch
4 cottages – timber and tile

Equipment
Heavy expenditure in the last few years as a number of cottages improved, many more buildings, and thatched barns reroofed in iron.
New track of three quarters of a mile to Ramsey Farm. Now all except one cottage at Witnesham in good repair.

Water
Each property has a good water supply mechanically pumped to elevated storage tanks and distributed to all houses. Hadleigh Estate – by the committee; Sproughton, by Samford RDC in consideration of the water for council tenants; Blakenham, by the tenants; Witnesham by the committee.

Electricity
Available to all properties.[5]

Roads
In consequence of the extensive use of motor transport and particularly in connection with sugar beet, the question of road maintenance is becoming a problem, and I am of the opinion that the committee give the matter special consideration.

NOTES

1 Blythe, Ronald. *Akenfield*. Harmondsworth: Penguin Books, 1972. p 48.
2 Howkins, Alun. *The Death of Rural England*. London: Routledge, 2003. pp 64–65.
3 Interview in BBC TV programme *Mud, Sweat and Tractors* on the history of wheat production, 2009.
4 As at February 2012 Messrs Keeble of Raydon are still in business. They have no relationship to the George Keeble who had been a tenant in Hadleigh.
5 From later minutes it appears that mains electricity was not available to all Hadleigh holdings, as some properties were maintaining generators.

Chapter Six

1939–1945 Second World War and an Agricultural Drive

National Agricultural Scene

On 3 September 1939, war was declared against Germany but this time the Ministry of Agriculture understood the problems that would occur in feeding the population, and had been preparing using its campaign to improve soil fertility on farm land, to drain it, and to establish some control over marketing and supply. However, despite their previous experiences of food shortages due to submarine attacks, in 1939 less than 30 per cent of the country's needs were being produced at home with 90 per cent of cereals being imported. Once again, there was the prospect of disrupted supplies from overseas as in the First World War.

On 8 September 1939, a Ministry of Food was formed with William Morrison as the minister. The organisation became the sole buyer and importer of food and was also responsible for regulating prices, thus guaranteeing farmers' prices and markets for their produce.[1] The following year Lord Woolton succeeded William Morrison. Woolton is still remembered to this day for the notorious 'Woolton pie', a recipe actually created by the chef at the Savoy, which was one of a range of recipes designed to help families maintain a nutritious diet by using whatever vegetables came to hand. In the same year, rationing was introduced and the nation was urged to Dig for Victory so that gardens and even parks all over the country were dug up and vegetables planted to try to improve the situation. Previously, vegetables had been the food of the poor, while meat had been the staple food of the diet of the upper classes, but from this point vegetables became an important part of the diet for all classes of society.

War Agricultural Executive Committees (War Ags) were established in each county. These committees organised widespread ploughing-up of pasture land to grow cereals. Pig farms and poultry farms suffered from lack of animal feed or lost their land. To combat this, some residents of urban areas were urged to save vegetable peelings and other food scraps to provide pig swill, which was collected with the weekly rubbish. Milk supplies were maintained since, despite the collapse of the other marketing boards, the Milk Marketing Board survived to organise supplies. Dietary supplements were issued to young children and expectant mothers – cod liver oil, milk powder to provide seven pints of milk a week, condensed orange juice, and malt extract – but strict rationing of food was imposed from 1940 on bacon, ham, butter and sugar.[2] Meat was added to the rations list in March 1940 and tea, margarine and cooking fats followed shortly thereafter in July. Cheese and preserves were added in 1941.[3] Also in 1941, the US Lend-Lease programme was passed, meaning that food, agricultural machinery and other equipment was supplied to the UK by the USA. However, the situation remained difficult not only during the war years but for years after.

During the war there was continued pressure from agriculturalists who were concerned with the environment and the condition of the land. In 1919, Lady Eve Balfour bought New Bells Farm at Haughley Farm, mid-Suffolk, having studied agriculture at the University of Reading in 1915. In 1938, she read Viscount Lymington's book *Famine in England* and became converted to organic principles by the theories of Sir Albert Howard and Sir Robert McCarrison, which concluded that there was a link between the quality of nutrition and the health of the soil. Lady Eve decided to use her farm as a long-term experiment to discover whether organic methods of cultivation produced crops superior to those fed with chemical fertilisers.[4] During the war years, however, her experiments were hampered, although the increased use of agricultural chemicals in wartime made the need for the experiment even more pressing.

There was also anxiety among economists that care for the agricultural industry and provision of subsidies should not be allowed to lapse as soon as war was over, as happened after the First World War.

Women's Land Army

In the final year of the First World War, with so many men conscripted into the army and food supplies dwindling, young women were recruited into the Women's Land Army to help fill the gap. By the end of the war, the WLA had grown to over 23,000 female farm workers.

In 1939, with war imminent, the lessons learned in the First World War were not forgotten and in June 1939 two groups of women started training to replace male land workers who were about to be conscripted. A total of 100,000 women served on the land during the war and the WLA was not disbanded until October 1950.

Although there is no mention of women working on Trust lands in the First World War, a least one woman worked in Hadleigh in the Second War. At Gary Farm both William Prowse's son, Gordon, and his cowman had joined the territorial battalions of the Suffolk Regiment before the war and were called up for active service, so a young Woman's Land Army girl came to the farm to take the place of the cowman. She remained on the farm until 1945, when she left to get married just as Gordon Prowse returned.

The cowman had become a Japanese prisoner of war, along with many of the Suffolk Regiment 4th and 5th Battalions, and was killed. Gordon became an instructor on Bren guns and remained at home to train new recruits. Towards the end of his service, he met his future wife, Joan, and she accompanied him back to the farm.

Airfields

During the Second World War there were 32 airfields in Suffolk. Nineteen were used by the US Air Force from 1942, but Hadleigh Airfield was not reopened in spite of the fact that it had been used by the Suffolk and Eastern Counties Flying Club between the wars. However, in the surrounding area there were airfields at Raydon, Sudbury, Martlesham, Wattisham, Debach and Framlingham. The Americans moved to Woodbridge Airfield in 1944, but the only mention of the United States Air Force presence in Suffolk that appears in the Trust minutes is a note about damage done to a wall at Tollgate Farm.

The Trust Committee and Administration during the War

Throughout the war years, Harry Fiske continued as chairman of the Trust committee. In 1939, other trustees were H W Mason, Major Norman Everett, H Scrimgeour, C C Smith, G Stedman and W Wilson. In 1944, Stuart Paul appeared on the committee, together with Felix C Smith.

In August 1939, the district auditor asked that the Trust accounts should be included as part of the county council accounts with their assets and liabilities included in their balance sheets. The matter was deferred for consideration and emergency meetings held with the clerk. By October, Townshend Cobbold had produced a long report concluding that it would not be proper for the accounts to be merged as the Trust was not part of the county council under the terms of the Act of 1937. Members were not acting as county councillors but as an ad hoc committee appointed under no statutory powers. This was not strictly a committee of the local authority within the meaning of Section 85 of the Act of 1935. The auditor withdrew his request.

Another problem at this time was that the land agent, W Wisbey, retired in October 1939 due to ill health, and a Mr James Sawyer was appointed as temporary acting agent to the Trust 'for the period of hostilities' at a salary of £50. However, by April 1945, Sawyer's salary had increased to £100, but it is not clear whether this is due to inflation or to an increase in Mr Sawyer's work.

In July 1940, there was a note that 'with a view to economy in stationary and postage, the circulation of copies of Minutes to members of the Committee be discontinued until further notice, and that half an hour before a meeting the Minute Book be laid on the table for inspection'. The minutes from this period are typed instead of printed, and it is possible that this was the work of a Miss K Scopes, because in 1942 there was a further note that 'It having been reported that Miss K Scopes during the past 2 years has undertaken work for the Trust involving a considerable amount of overtime. Resolved that an honorarium of £10 12s 0d be paid to her'.

In 1943, 1944 and 1945, Miss Scopes was again rewarded with further sums of £10 10s 0d, so this is a salary that did not increase. In October 1945, it was also necessary to buy two new steel filing cabinets at a cost of £20 – perhaps filled with Miss Scopes' typing.

In 1945, it was noted that Herbert St George Cobbold, Felix's nephew, who had acted as treasurer to the Trust since 1915, had died, and his place was taken by R R Leawood, who had been the auditor. A new auditor was appointed – Mr S J Prosser – at a fee of £2 2s 0d.

Trust Lands in War Time

Even before war began, H Norman and sons, the tenants of Hadleigh Holding No 7, asked for permission to break up approximately 35 acres of rough grass to qualify for a government grant of £2 per acre, which was agreed. On an adjacent holding, Mr Palfreman asked for 46 tons of chalk to dress his land, but the committee deferred a decision. At Witnesham, J J Mann asked for 100 tons of chalk for application to 20 acres of his land. The committee were unhappy but asked for a report from the land agent. The land was found to be acidic, so the Trust agreed.

In April 1942, Palfreman at Holding 9 asked if he could plough four acres of pasture, but again the committee response was not enthusiastic. Consent was given 'if reseeded at the end of his tenancy'. However, despite the obvious reluctance of trustees to sanction ploughing up of pasture, in 1944 the War Ag asked five tenants to plough up 47.630 acres of grassland at Hadleigh.

Grants were still available for draining land, and in 1941 the agent reported that the main water course dividing Pond Hall Estate from its neighbour was in a neglected state and responsible for land flooding. The committee applied for a grant of 50 per cent of the total cost to cleanse the water course. The same month they agreed to the draining of 14 acres at Venn Farm, which would also be eligible for a grant.

In July 1941, the Trust received a request for the use of 1.75 acres of OS 69 – part of Holding 22 at Hadleigh – as a government emergency timber store. This was part of the old aerodrome land and thus had been disturbed in previous years. Consent was given,

and the government paid for increased fire insurance for the adjacent cottage and farm buildings. In January 1942, the Ministry of Works and Buildings also requisitioned part of OS 612 for the store and made a private entrance road to the site. It was enlarged a second time in January 1944. The store lasted until 14 January 1946, when the Ministry of Works derequisitioned the land and compensation was applied for under the Compensation (Defence) Act 1939.

In 1943, the West Suffolk War Agricultural executive committee said that aerodrome land at Hadleigh – now being partly used as a timber store – should have 61 acres mole drained, as well as 100 chains of existing ditches reconditioned and 85 chains of new ditches dug. The committee ruled that the work should be done by the tenants. The agent liaised with the War Ag and estimated that after grants the work would cost £250. The scheme dragged on due to lack of labour. In 1944, the committee proposed that the scheme should be revived on a larger scale in co-operation with Butterfly Hall Farm next door. At this stage, the old water course channel could be straightened and some timber removed, which would make future maintenance easier. However, the Butterfly Hall Farm owner would not agree to join the scheme voluntarily. Finally, in April 1945, the ditching and mole draining schemes were started, and the War Ag itself were prepared to undertake the ditching work, including spreading and levelling the spoil at a cost of 5s per chain, so the net cost after the government grant was estimated at about £10 only. In October, the agent reported that the mole draining of 61 acres had cost £281 5s 2d with a grant of £91 10s, while the ditching cost £215 17s 6d with a grant of £107 18s 9d. A new culvert would be needed to take the water course under the access road, but again, a grant was available.

In 1944, the Hadleigh Estate suffered some damage 'as a result of enemy action'. A claim was submitted to the War Damage Commission under the War Damage Act 1941 for compensation to five tenants for minor damage to house windows and doors. H Norman also had his barn damaged.

The Trust authorised the felling of some trees on their four estates in 1944, 'where felling and removal would not be detrimental to the property', and in April, sold timber from Hadleigh and Witnesham for £117 to the Stowmarket Timber Company.

Some land was requisitioned on Venn Farm, Witnesham, during the war and derequisitioned in January 1945, with the tenants being left to remove AA poles and wiring. At the end of the work, it was noted that an inspection would be made to ascertain whether any claim for the permanent diminution of annual value was necessary. However, there is no further note about this land in the minutes, and there was no note at the beginning of the war as to the use of this land.

One bright note in these minutes was that in 1945 the East Suffolk War Ag Executive Committee had organised a competition for the best cultivated and best kept farm in East Suffolk, and one of the Tollgate Farm tenants, E Hood, had been awarded first prize in the class for farms of 100–300 acres in the Gipping District. The committee sent him their congratulations.

Houses and Farm Buildings

Property suffered during the war years since, as in the First World War, both labour and materials were in short supply. In May 1939, it had been agreed that Venn Farm (Mr H N Mann) should have a bathroom, a new kitchen sink, alterations to the cooking stove, provision of a picture rail in the parlour, provision of a porch over the back door, provision of a brick-built lean-to washhouse, alterations to the drains and an extension of concrete paths. However, in October 1939, the contractor reported that 'as a consequence of the recent increase in the cost of materials that will be needed to carry out the contract, unless extra costs on the prices ruling at the time of the tender were agreed, the contract could not be carried out'. The committee agreed to increases specified by the contractor on a new price list, but would not agree to any increases for materials not on the list.

In 1940, the agent suggested that only priority repairs should be attempted, which included a new sink at Laurel Farm, Sproughton, and a new flush WC and septic tank at Gary Farm. A few months later, the tiled roof of the washhouse at Valley Farm collapsed and had to be repaired. The contractors also caused damage to a gateway and a wall, which needed further repair. Throughout the rest of the war, the agent set up a regime of overhauling and painting a quarter of the properties each year to maintain their condition. Nevertheless, at the end of the war many properties were in a poor state.

There were other minor problems: a boundary wall at Tollgate Farm was damaged by the US Army and a claim for £5 7s 6d was sent to the US Army Claims Commission. Tollgate Farm also suffered at the hands of Gipping Rural District Council who removed an iron gate and posts for salvage in 1943. A claim was submitted to the Compensation (Defence) Act 1939 for the cost of providing a new gate and posts 'in keeping with the property' at a cost of £8 5s 0d.

In July 1945, a minute on repairs notes that 'an asbestos roof is to be put on the Gary Farm cow house'. For the next few years this is a common solution for roofing repairs rather than the corrugated iron being used previously.

The two new cottages near the Valley Farm entrance were again found to be damp as the rough cast was defective. The solution was to give two coats of Cementone waterproofing on the outside, with defective internal plaster cut out and the wall rendered in Keene's Cement and given a coat of distemper.

Roads on the Estate

One of the private roads at Hadleigh had begun to show signs of wear, so in 1943, the Trust asked the Roads and Bridges Committee to repair it but nothing more was done. The following year, Percy Norman repaired the road himself and asked for compensation.

By 1945, most of the farm roads were in bad condition; the road to Valley Farm was badly potholed and rutted and 30 cubic yards of materials were necessary to repair it. The Witnesham Road was also cause for concern and the land agent remarked that 'both these roads carry a considerable amount of traffic'.

Water Systems

The Hadleigh pump still gave periodic trouble, but the worst problems occurred with the newly acquired land at Witnesham. In July 1945, the well at Venn Farm failed and the brickwork was found to be unsafe. Therefore, a new well had to be driven 220 feet into the water-bearing chalk strata and a 500-gallon storage tank installed at a cost of £175. A grant of 50 per cent was applied for from the East Suffolk War Ag Committee. By April 1946, the new well had been excavated, but there were supply stoppages: a new geared power head had to be substituted for the old direct drive.

Conclusion

The Trust lands and the tenants had a relatively easy time during the period of 1939 to 1945, with support for prices and generous grants for improvements. The smallholders were in a reserved occupation so were not obligated to go to war, but some of their employees did enter the army, e.g. the cowman at Gary Farm.

This was a time of pause after the rapid development of living standards in the immediate pre-war period. It was also a time in which the farming industry was held in high regard, as the public realised that it was the hard work of farmers that had enabled the United Kingdom to survive despite attacks on the food convoys abroad.

NOTES

1 Creaton, Heather J. 'Sources for the History of London 1939–1945.' London: British Records Association, 1998.
2 Huxley, R R, Lloyd, B B, Goldacre, M and Neil, H A W. 'Nutritional research in World War 2: the Oxford Nutrition Survey and its research potential 50 years later.' *British Journal of Nutrition*, Vol 84, Issue 02. Cambridge University Press, 2000. pp 247–251.
3 Howkins, Alun. *The Death of Rural England.* London: Routledge, 2003. p 133.
4 Conford, Philip. 'Eve Balfour: the founder of the Soil Association.' The Soil Association's *Living Earth* magazine. 2003, Summer Edition.

Chapter Seven

1945–1950
Aftermath of a War

National Agricultural Scene

The scene remained bleak partly due to the need to give whatever food aid could be spared for a devastated Europe. In addition, many men were being demobbed from the forces, resulting in a flood of people into the labour market. Food rationing remained in place throughout this period and, indeed, became slightly worse. Bread was rationed from July 1946 to July 1948, and potatoes during the winter of 1947–1948. American lend-lease ended in August 1945 leading to a dollar shortage, which, when combined with the continuing shortage of available cargo ships, made imports of food difficult.

Farmers had profited from the years of conflict with farm incomes tripling during the war because of particularly high prices for oats and barley. The Four-Year Plan for agriculture of January 1944 had promised continuing assured markets for home-grown farm produce based on an annual price review each February, and in 1947 a new Agriculture Act was passed to:

> promote a stable and efficient industry capable of producing such part of the nation's food as in the national interest it is desirable to produce in the United Kingdom and to produce it at minimum prices consistent with proper remuneration and living conditions for farmers and workers in agriculture, and an adequate return on the capital invested in the industry.

Prices were maintained by the annual meeting between the National Farmers Union and the Ministry of Agriculture which negotiated minimum prices for the coming year. Where market prices fell below these figures, 'deficiency payments' were made from general taxation to cover the gap.

The second aim of the Agriculture Act was to maintain good standards of agriculture, and in accordance with this, the War Ags were continued under the new name of County Agricultural Executive Committees, although in practice they had little powers.

For farm workers this legislation did little, though they did share in the prosperity of their employers to some extent. Wages had risen since 1939 by 170 per cent to a peak of 94s a week in 1949, but this still left them behind the average wage of 142s 8d a week.[1] During the years from 1946 to 1950, it is estimated that the number of agricultural labourers fell from 865,000 to 678,000 – a decline of 20 per cent.[2] This was a result not only of poor wages compared with factory work, but also the slow decline in the numbers of labourers required on farms due to increased mechanisation. At the same time, farm sizes began to rise, particularly in arable areas.

Labourers frequently lived in tied cottages; the statistic was 34 per cent in 1949. This was a continued source of grievance since, although farmers saw them as a perk, when a labourer lost his job it also meant eviction from his home. Between 1947 and 1970, the National Union of Agricultural Workers fought 12,482 cases of eviction; the actual figure would have been far greater if non-union labourers were included.[3] The Union Secretary, living in Akenfield, reported in the union journal, *The Land Worker*, that up to 50 tied-cottage court cases were reported each month.[4] Trust minutes quote a number of occasions on which they were considering taking action to evict tenants, or their widows. We have already seen the problem that occurred after the death of George Keeble at Hadleigh and the long fight to evict Mrs Keeble from her home. However, in 1948 the government passed the Agricultural Tenancies Act, which gave tenants improved security of tenure and rights of compensation, together with a system of arbitration for tenancy agreements and rent disputes.

For land owners, death duties and income tax were rising and for many, the best option was to become farmers themselves, rather than to rent out their land.

The Soil Association and the Organic Movement

In 1946, Lady Eve Balfour, see Chapter 6, decided to establish the Soil Association to examine organic cultivation of her crops at her farm in Haughley. She worked alongside a group of like-minded thinkers, such as the founders of the Peckham Experiment, who were also concerned with the state of the nation's health.

> The farm was divided into three units, one farmed using the new intensive techniques, one farmed traditionally and one with mixed system. At the end of this period the results were not as clear as had been hoped (hardly surprising since we still have a poor understanding of what we truly mean by health of land and food), however a much clearer understanding had been built up of how the best of old and new traditions in land husbandry could be combined, and so the first organic standards were compiled defining this system.[5]

The farm represented a threat to the fertiliser industry, but nevertheless Lady Eve's work drew respect from agriculturalists and membership of the new association grew steadily.

Trust Committee 1945–50

In 1945, Harry Fiske was still chairman of the committee, but he stood down in July 1946, after serving for 29 years in the chair. He then remained on the committee until his death in January 1947. Thus, since 1910, a Fiske had been either chairman or vice chairman; it was the end of an era.

His place as chairman was filled by Felix C Smith, who served until 1949. In April 1947, Captain Lord Alastair Mungo Graham, youngest son of the fifth Duke of Montrose, became a trustee, and in 1949, he accompanied Felix Smith in the annual inspection of the estate.

In 1949, Sir Peter Greenwell, who farmed a large estate at Butley, also joined the committee. Sir Peter became chairman in August 1949, and Lord Alastair became vice chairman the same year. Other committee members at the end of 1940s included R H Rash, B C Smith, C C Smith, E V Barber and G Stedman.

In 1947, the clerk of the committee also changed. Commander Sir Cecil Oakes retired, and George Cecil Lightfoot was appointed. The Trust paid Lightfoot a salary of £20 pa. In 1948, the auditor, S J Prosser, also resigned and was replaced by H A Aimley.

Trust Land Situation 1945–1950

The Trust minutes rarely give glimpses of the crops being grown by tenants. However, it is known that Orchard Farm at Witnesham was growing fruit and in 1948 needed a new fruit store at a cost of £178 5s 0d. In the same year, Low Farm asked if they could plant 30 fruit trees. The Eastmans wanted extra land for their poultry farm in 1948, and Boreham at Laurel Farm, Sproughton, wanted extra accommodation for pigs and bullocks. In 1950, one of the other Sproughton tenants, F G Pegg, asked if he could erect a 'dutch light' greenhouse on his land, which was agreed as a tenant's fixture. Two of the Witnesham tenants asked for additional dairy accommodation in 1946 but the committee said that this 'be not granted' with no further explanation.

Two tenants, one at Hadleigh and one at Sproughton, were affected by sugar beet eel worm infestations in January 1949. By the Sugar Beet Eel Worm Order 1943, infestations had to be notified and the land graded 'sick', 'heavily infested' or 'infected'. After this, certain crops could not be grown on the land, except with the consent of the County Agricultural Executive Committee, until 1954 for 'sick' or 1952 for 'heavily infested' and 'infected'. These outbreaks were classed as 'sick', so restrictions remained in place, in fact, until 1955.

In 1950, a minute from November records the request from Mr W J Farrow on the Pond Hall Estate as to:

> whether the Committee would carry out certain improvements to the premises to enable them to qualify as TT milk producers? The work would include the provision of tubular steel manger partitions and an additional light to the cowhouse, re-arrangement of the dairy, and the conversion of an existing box into an isolation box.

The cost was estimated at £5 18s for the tubular steel manger, £136 10s for the alterations to the partitions and £14 for the isolation box. The committee had no choice but to agree, but the tenant would then pay an extra £13 pa (£238 pa instead of £225 pa).

Concern about tuberculosis passing into milk was first raised in 1935 and TT herds were encouraged, but by 1936 only 414 herds existed. Progress was slow and hampered by the war, so that by 1947 still only 14 per cent of herds nationally were free of the disease, of which only 8 per cent were in England. In 1950, therefore, the ministry decided to create areas of eradication of tuberculosis, and owners of TT herds were granted 2d extra on a gallon of milk for four years and 1d a gallon thereafter. The scheme worked well, so that by 1959, 95 per cent of animals fell within the scheme.[6] Suffolk was clearly becoming part of such an area in 1950.

Rents and Land Arrangements

During this period, the committee found that their decisions were hampered by newly passed legislation (page 54) that improved the security of farm tenants. Several apparently harsh decisions were made, perhaps reflecting the financial pressures being imposed on landlords.

In spite of the apparent good times for agriculture, several tenants found that they could not continue. One such tenant had farmed a large acreage at Pond Hall Farm, Ramsey Farm and the old aerodrome land and his departure in 1946 after several years of rent arrears left a large piece of land unoccupied. The agent recommended that this land should be divided into smaller plots, so Pond Hall Farm became a distinct holding of 157.5 acres, Ramsey Farm became a 119-acre holding, and part of the aerodrome land separated into a holding of 150 acres, with the remainder being added to Hill Farm. The rearrangement would bring in an extra £150 in rents when tenants were found. The Charity Commission wrote in 1948 to remind the committee that under the existing scheme holdings should not be more than 50 acres or exceeding an annual value of £100 (a rise of 100 per cent since the 1910 agreement). The committee, as before, wrote to the commission to ask for amendments to the scheme. In 1949, they again appealed that the value should be up to £150, and the Charity Commission recommended that the decision should be deferred until Part IV of the Agricultural Act 1947 came into operation.

The following year, the agent commented that he thought all the rents were low and should be revised 'by voluntary agreement'. By April 1947, these agreements had been reached so that the Hadleigh rents rose from £785 13s 6d to £1,060 10s 6d, the Sproughton from £195 6s to £283 19s, Great Blakenham from £163 to £215, and Witnesham from £271 18s to £291 8s. In October 1947, the chairman commented that the 'Increases have been negotiated on a purely voluntary basis, in my view, which affords ample evidence of the good relations existing between tenants and the Committee'. Only one tenant at Witnesham objected and asked that the additional payment for £10 pa should be regarded as 'a contribution towards the cost of maintaining the farm roadway and not as a rent'. The committee agreed that this man should have a separate agreement drawn up incorporating his suggestion.

As to the cottages, in 1948 the Rent Restrictions Act had been passed and the agent reported that planned increases in rent for the cottages were not possible as they were now controlled.

The 1948 Agricultural Holdings Act also affected the estates. In 1949, the tenant at Great Blakenham wanted to erect a concrete and asbestos general purpose farm building of 60 feet by 30 feet. The agent recommended that this should be approved, but the plans had to be approved by the county land agent. In addition, the tenant had to get approval under the Town and County Planning Act 1947, and the building was to be regarded as a tenant's improvement so any compensation would be paid to the tenant as under Section 47 of the Agricultural Holdings Act.

Timber was still in short supply in the UK so the Trust, in common with all other local landlords, derived a steady income from the sale of trees demolished for various reasons. The bat willow plantation, near Pond Hall House, planted by the committee in 1921 with considerable foresight, was now a valuable resource and 29 trees were sold from the group for £205.

Houses and Farm Buildings

At the beginning of this chapter we noted the thorny problem of tied cottages. By the late 1940s, some tenants had been in place for over 30 years and many were becoming frail and unable to work, which meant a move out of a home they had occupied for much of their working life. H H Howard was one of the Hadleigh Estate workers, but in 1947 he retired. The Trust asked him to move from his cottage, which was to be given to Gary Farm. However, Prowse at Gary Farm did not actually need the cottage for the time being, so Howard was allowed to stay until Michaelmas. When he moved in October he asked for compensation for 14 fruit trees he had planted, but this was refused.

In 1949, another of the original tenants, Reginald Dyer, died. He had been one of the two tenants that had been allowed to buy his land, but he had kept a water supply from the estate at a rate of 10s pa. Now his widow, who lived at Oak Villa, Hintlesham, wanted to keep her water supply, and this request was granted at a rate of £2 pa.

Many of the houses were in bad condition. At Tollgate Farm, for example, the tenant was given permission to put up some new buildings at his own expense, but he also complained of a bad smell in the bedroom. When the smell was investigated, a nest of dead rats was discovered under the floor. The floorboards themselves were decayed and infested with dry rot and had to be replaced by the Trust at a cost of £21 0s 1d.

In 1949, Orchard House, at Witnesham, had an old cooking range in the living room which meant that all food must be boiled, and the tenant asked for a register stove in its place. This was agreed by the committee, but the tenant was asked to make the change at his own expense. The agent's report reveals one reason for this harsh decision: the budget for repairs in 1949/50 would have to be raised to £1,000

which reflects the difficulties experienced in getting contracts complete, due mainly to shortage of labour and supplies. It is becoming increasingly difficult to maintain the various properties in a reasonable state of repair without considerably reducing the Committee's annual revenue surplus and it is anticipated that the figure for 1949/50 will be in the region of £230 as compared with an actual surplus of £481 for the previous year. During late years tenants have been required to undertake more of the repairs for which they are responsible under the terms of their agreements, and I feel that an even more realistic interpretation of the tenants' covenants is desirable in the future.

He continued by reminding the committee that they had the statutory right under the Agricultural Holdings Act 1948 to raise rents if they had carried out improvements on the holdings, and were urged to exercise this right 'in all applicable cases and thereby secure some contribution towards loss of investment income that will result from the provision of improved equipment'.

One further part of this report is interesting because it reflects the ministry's desire to facilitate improvements to farm buildings:

> With regard to proposed new buildings (at Laurel Farm, Venn Farm and Orchard House) it is proposed to make use of standardised components sponsored by the Ministry of Agriculture and Fisheries which, though unlikely to effect any economy in initial outlay, will considerably reduce maintenance and facilitate future extension or adaption.

Another interesting entry from this period was the note that in 1949 B E Farrow at Hadleigh Holding 2 wanted to erect a permanent garage. He was to be allowed a 'temporary portable garage' only, and the tenant had to be responsible for getting consent and pay the charges under the Town and Country Planning Act 1948. This would be a tenant's fixture and not an improvement for which compensation would be payable under Section 47 of the Agricultural Holdings Act 1948. This is the first mention of a garage, but is evidence of an increasing use of private cars and not just farm vehicles. It also reveals once again the increasing amount of national legislation which had to be adhered to.

Electricity

In 1946, the Trust approached the East Anglian Supply Company Limited (EASCL) to extend a supply of electricity to some additional properties. The quotes which were received in April were regarded as 'prohibitive' in each case. Ramsey Farm, for example, would cost £450 which would require a Trust payment of £290. The Borough of Ipswich Electricity Supply Department, on the other hand, would extend a supply to three of the Sproughton tenants – Pearl at 5, Harvey at 6, and Pegg at 7 – without a guaranteed minimum account or contribution.

In July, Prowse at Gary Farm had agreed to guarantee a minimum annual account of £27 10s for five years to the EASCL, and this was accepted rather than the £80 originally asked for a capital outlay. However, he was also told that the wiring would be considered as a tenant's improvement to be taken over by valuation at the end of the tenancy.

Throughout these years the Trust was also asked to allow additional electricity poles and stays on each estate as the power grid was extended. Most notably, in 1949 the British Electricity Authority asked if they could erect two towers at a rental of 10s pa on the Hadleigh Estate.

Water Supply

The water on each site was still being provided by pumps from bore wells with storage tanks or reservoirs, which meant continued problems with broken pumps and lost supplies. At Sproughton, the council had taken over the work of maintaining and working the wind pump as they needed water for their council houses nearby, but this arrangement came to an end in 1949 when they connected their properties to a new mains supply.

The Hadleigh pump was replaced by a Climax Quadruple Action pump in 1946, and the Witnesham water supply to Venn Farm needed a filter at a cost of £285 13s 2d. A government grant under the Agricultural Water Supplies Scheme was available for £78 12s only, but the committee appealed for an increase as the work cost more than originally planned. In 1947, the grant was raised to £116 19s 1d.

A grant under the same scheme was also used to bring water to a meadow at Ramsey Farm in 1950. Palfreman had been asked to pay half the cost of bringing in an extra water supply, but refused and offered labour only. The dispute went on for some months, but at last the County Agricultural Executive Committee agreed to provide a grant of £5 1s 0d, the tenant paid £3 17s and the Trust paid £4 17s.

The Witnesham water supply in 1949 was found to have an excessive iron content which was corroding the pipes, so the committee investigated the possibility of connecting to the water main which had now been laid along the main Westerfield–Witnesham Road.

The Great Blakenham water also had some problems. The bore well supply failed due to corroded pump rods, meaning that a new length of rising main had to be renewed in August 1949. However, in September it was found that the well had silted up and had to be cleared to restore the supply.

Roads

The various farm tracks needed periodic resurfacing, particularly after the depredations of the war years, but the Witnesham private road continued to be the worst headache – hence the objection being made by one tenant when he was asked to pay more rent. The Roads and Bridges Committee had refused to adopt the road, so in both 1945 and 1946 around £40 was spent on resurfacing the heavily used track. A further £70 was spent in 1948 and 1949.

Conclusion

For the Trust this was again a period of 'make do and mend' as they were faced with the problems of lack of income to make changes, poor supplies of materials and rising costs. Guaranteed prices for crops did nothing to help the Trust itself, although the days of constant rent arrears by tenants had passed. The only remedy was to take heed of the agent's advice: raise rents where possible and refuse many tenants' requests for improvements.

NOTES

1   Howkins, Alun. *The Death of Rural England*. London: Routledge, 2003. p 147.
2   Ibid p 164.
3   Ibid p 174.
4   Blythe, Ronald. *Akenfield*. Harmondsworth: Penguin Books, 1972. p 98.
5   The Soil Association website (www.soilassociation.org/), 2010.
6   Macrae, W D. 'The Eradication of Bovine Tuberculosis'. Paper presented at the Zoological Society Symposium. London: Zoo Society, 1961. pp 81–90.

Chapter Eight

1950–1960
A New Europe

International Agricultural Development

Europe recovered slowly from the disruption of war during the first half of the decade. In 1950, the European Coal and Steel Community was established, initially between France and West Germany, to heal wounds and ease the threat of further war between the two countries. They were joined by Belgium, Italy, Luxembourg and the Netherlands. This led in 1957 to the Treaty of Rome, which established a European Economic Community between the same six nations. Plans were laid down in Article 39 to introduce a Common Agricultural Policy.

The initial objectives of Article 39 were:

1. to increase productivity, by promoting technical progress and ensuring the optimum use of the factors of production, in particular labour;
2. to ensure a fair standard of living for the agricultural community;
3. to stabilise markets;
4. to secure availability of supplies;
5. to provide consumers with food at reasonable prices.

The CAP was designed to recognise the need to take account of the social structure of agriculture and of the structural and natural disparities between the various agricultural regions and to effect the appropriate adjustments by degrees. In fact, CAP did not fully come into operation until 1962.

The United Kingdom chose not to join the EEC in 1957 but soon found that this put them at a disadvantage. As the original six member countries prospered, British exports began to suffer. This led to Britain proposing the establishment of a European Free Trade Association (EFTA), which was formed in May 1960 between Britain, Sweden, Switzerland, Norway, Denmark, Austria and Portugal. Britain's strong trading links with the Commonwealth countries was certainly one reason for not wishing to be drawn into the EEC group.

National Agricultural Scene

Food supplies eased slightly during this period and most food rationing had ended by 1950, although meat rationing continued until 1954. Rationing of poultry mash also ended in 1954, which meant that poultry farming increased. Hybrid chicken breeds were developed and deep litter houses were used by some producers. Broiler chickens were introduced in 1954 and in 1956 specialist broiler hybrids were introduced by R Chalmers Watson and G Sykes. This paved the way for the mass production of chicken meat, thereby changing it from a luxury food to the cheap source of protein that it is today.

The grants previously noted – for draining, for using artificial fertilisers and for bringing additional land into production – continued during this period in order to encourage higher food production. However, from 1953 farm subsidies began to attract criticism from the public.

Suffolk reinforced its tuberculosis-free status, with another herd at Hadleigh becoming TT in 1951. Also during this period, Friesian cows gained popularity, so that 40 per cent of dairy cows were Friesian by 1955. Gary Farm, for example, had a herd of Friesian crosses, with one Jersey cow.

Mechanised farming became more common. In 1946, there had been twice as many horses as tractors, but between 1950 and 1960 tractors at last became more plentiful than horses on farms.[1] The Trust minutes reveal the continued problem of road surfacing as motorised vehicle use became more popular.

Lady Eve Balfour and the Soil Association

In the late 1950s, Lady Eve Balfour's experiments into

organic cultivation at her mid-Suffolk Haughley farm came to an end through financial problems. However, the Soil Association she had helped to found continued to thrive and membership grew steadily throughout the decade.

Trust Administration

The November 1955 minutes reveal a major disagreement between the Trust and the county council. On 4 October 1955, the council had decided that in future members of the Small Holdings Committee should constitute the committee of the Felix Cobbold Trust, but it would not include non-council members on the Small Holdings Committee. There were 11 people present at the meeting, including a Miss M H G Hambling, but the chairman, Lord Alastair Graham, was not present as he resigned in protest to the council's decision. The committee as a whole supported his action and argued that the Trust should not lose its separate identity as the past system had worked well. It was agreed that the vice chairman, R H Rash, should discuss the constitution of the committee with the chairman of the council, and try to get the decision reversed. Luckily on 10 January 1956, the council rescinded its decision and the committee reverted to eight members again, with Lord Alastair back in the chair and free to join in the annual inspection of the estates on 22 January. The eight included Lord Alastair, R H Rash, D R Dickson, E J W Fiske, B W Smith, Sir Peter Greenwell, J S Schreiber and J O Youngman.

In 1958, Lord Alastair Graham made a triennial report to the county council describing the history of the Trust and the original bequest. In this he reported that estate lands were now: 735.3 acres at Hadleigh, 83.9 acres at Sproughton, 122.8 acres at Great Blakenham, and 151.9 acres at Witnesham – a total of 1,093.9 acres. They had 18 full-time holdings and three other lets. The rental income totalled £2,503.

The final passages of the report are interesting as they reflect Lord Alastair's fierce determination to remain independent after the fracas of 1955. They also show his admiration for Felix Cobbold:

> As already mentioned, the Trust is financially independent, and in contra distinction to the Small Holdings undertaking, and free from loan debt and relieved from the necessity of making repayments on loan principle and interest. The surplus of net income over expenditure continuing to appear in the annual statements and accounts remains available for reinvestment in the estates.
>
> Also investments built up during the last war to absorb accumulated cash balances arising from slow down of repairs and virtual cessation of improvements. The present state of the market, however, dictates that realisation be avoided.
>
> In concluding this Report the Felix Cobbold Trust Committee feel bound to remark that their fundamental principle underlying the present statutory small holding legislation, namely, the provision of holdings to enable agricultural workers to make a career in agriculture as farmers on their own account, is a tribute to the foresight of the late Mr Felix Cobbold when he made the decision to establish small holdings on his own estate some 52 years ago, and to provide for their continuance under the Trusteeship of the County Council.

Farming on the Trust Lands

One tenant at Sproughton took advantage of the end of rationing for chicken feed, and in 1956 introduced a deep litter poultry shed for intensive rearing.

In dairy farming, Pond Hall Farm attained Tuberculin Tested (TT) status with an improved dairy in 1951, but was then charged an extra £13 pa rent. The following year, Low Farm at Witnesham also converted to TT.

Evidence of increased use of chemical fertiliser appears in one set of meeting minutes from 1955. For some time there had been complaints that the water at Hadleigh had an unpleasant taste. The agent arranged to have the water analysed and this showed chlorophenol contamination, which was believed to have occurred after the tenant had sprayed 'Phenoxylene' in 1954. The analyst said it was not injurious to health and predicted that the taste would diminish. However, there were also high levels of coliform bacilli in the water, so the tenant reduced the amount of stagnant water in the vicinity and the pump was fed from flowing spring water. The Trust planned to commission a new analysis in due course.

The land infected by sugar beet eel worm in 1948 was retested in 1955. Lord Alastair and E J W Fiske met with County Agricultural Executive Committee officers, who agreed that the land was probably not entirely free of infection, but instructed that a licence could be issued if the land was divided into four sections and cropped in rotation. They also said that fences should be erected to divide the land, and it was agreed that the committee would pay, but the tenant would install them. In 1956, fresh land – OS 268A (part) (six acres) and OS 352 (13.816 acres) – was 'infected' and orders were served by the County Agricultural Executive Committee. The OS 352 land was then divided in two, and a licence to grow was issued for two acres only on the west of the field.

There was a continuing move to bring unused land back into production. In 1952, for example, two meadows comprising 5.646 acres of Sproughton land were overgrown and of little use. The tenant was willing to bring them back to arable land or to surrender them to the committee for afforestation. After inspection, the committee decided to have them cleared and returned to arable, but the ditches needed cleaning, the hedges needed cutting, and overgrown timber and dead trees needed removing. The shrubs on OS 342 were removed by gyrotiller – mechanised removal rather than the use of horses to drag out the vegetation. By 1956, the work was complete and the new land had been sown with barley. The tenant was paid £65 for his work in clearing trees and the ministry paid a grant to the committee for 50 per cent of the cost.

Water Supplies

The problem of providing all their tenants with water and sewerage during this period became acute as the move was gradually made from well water and septic tanks to mains water and council sewerage schemes. The Hadleigh pollution problem has already been mentioned, but there were also the perennial pump failures. In 1952, it was found that the motor was not capable of driving the pump and repairs would take nine months. Therefore, a new 1.5 hp Metropolitan Vickers repulsion induction motor, complete with switch gear, was installed at a cost of £64 12s and the old motor sold for £10. Further failures occurred, so in 1955 it was agreed that it would be serviced by Warners at two- to three-monthly intervals in order that the sand accumulating in the sump pit could be cleared.

The Tollgate drain problem recurred in 1952, with overflows from the culvert taking water from Tollgate Farm and the Chequers Inn as well as surface water from the highway. Discussions were held with Gipping RDC. In May 1953, a report from the County Sanitation Officer recommended that the defective vent pipe at Tollgate Farm be repaired, and that Gipping RDC should ask the Ministry of Housing and Local Government for permission to proceed with the Claydon and Great Blakenham sewerage scheme, putting forward the alleged nuisance from Tollgate Farm drainage as a reason for prompt action. However, by 1954 permission had still not been received so the Trust was urged to isolate slurry into a cesspit and divert other drainage into the normal drain, at a cost of £186. This was complete by May 1954. In 1954, there was also a leak from the 1,000-gallon storage tank, which was replaced by a second-hand tank from another council site.

In 1950, Laurel Farm at Sproughton had new farm buildings with a piped water supply to the buildings, with a 50 per cent government grant under the Agricultural Water Supply Scheme. In 1954, there was a water mains leak so an additional stopcock had to be inserted. Samford RDC was using this reservoir for their council house supplies, but nevertheless it had to be drained and refilled again after the repairs.

The worst problems, however, were at Witnesham. A new 240-foot bore hole had been sunk in 1946, but the high iron content in the water caused problems at Venn Farm so pipes to the dairy and the house had to be renewed in 1952. By 1954, it was found that all the pipes were heavily corroded and an attempt to filter the iron was a failure. The Trust decided to try connecting the estate to the Deben RDC mains 600 yards from Venn Farm at a cost of £450, although there would be a grant available. In May 1954, the agent reported that 'owing to the aggressive nature of the soil, the use of pipes resistant to corrosion was essential'. 'Alkathene' polythene tubes were to be used at a cost of £664, with a £25 connection charge, although a grant would reduce this to £517.

In August, the supply failed once more so urgent negotiations were started with the RDC for a mains connection, but the Agricultural Executive Committee was only willing to allow the cost of the mains distribution to Venn Farm, with the committee paying for distribution to the other four properties. The Trust appealed that the reason for the new arrangement was due to the iron content from the bore well and the connection was finally made in November 1954 with the full costs paid.

Housing and Farm Buildings

The gradual move towards better living conditions increased in this period as wartime restrictions on materials and labour eased.

In 1950, Pond Hall – the largest house on the Trust lands – was declared a building of special architectural and historic interest on the list compiled by the Ministry of Town and Country Planning under the provisions of the 1947 Act. It had been sublet to H J Cooley, but he died in 1950 and his widow and son wanted to extend their right to remain under the Rent Restriction Act.

Valley Farm needed extensive rebuilding after the installation of a new tenant in 1959. A lathe and plaster south wall had to be rebuilt in brick, and the east wall was found to have rotten timbers at the base. It was repaired with bricks up to the level of the good timber, and the lathe and plaster replaced by render on an expanded metal lathing.

In 1950, tenants still preferred installing register stoves for heating and most of the old ranges had been removed; the committee themselves installed a tiled register stove in a Burstall Lane cottage in 1952 after the death of a tenant. In 1952, Corner Farm at Great Blakenham had their old kitchen range replaced with a Torglow slow combustion stove. However, in 1954 the tenant of Valley Farm asked that his 'old-fashioned' register stove in the sitting room might be replaced by a 'modern tiled surround stove with a continuously burning grate' at a cost of £19 11s.

Bathrooms were still gradually being installed: the Valley Farm tenant had one installed in 1952 and he was charged an extra £2 10s rent. Bathrooms were thus still considered a privilege, not a right. In 1953, Low Farm at Witnesham had hot water laid to the bathroom and the tenant was charged £5 extra on the rent.

Most toilets at this period were earth closets, but Low Farm at Witnesham appears to have had a water closet in 1955. When Hope Farm at Sproughton was refurbished after a fire in 1955, the minute recorded that 'the opportunity should be taken to install suitable sanitation in the bathroom at a cost of £25', with the fire insurance company contributing £13 19s 6d to the cost. In 1959, a water closet was installed in Laurel Farm and the two adjacent holdings at Great Blakenham, which suggests that this was becoming the norm rather than an unusual improvement.

New farm buildings were being steadily added to holdings. One tenant at Witnesham erected five piggeries and a garage without consent, but most committee improvements were small – a paved yard there, a new asbestos roof there to replace corrugated iron.

Mains electricity was still gradually slowly extended to the more distant holdings. In 1957, Mr Smith at Hill Farm put in an urgent request for electricity and several more pig sties. The committee replied that they were sympathetic but could not manage it at present. However, at the February 1958 meeting, it was reported that both he and Mr Palfreman at Ramsey Farm were installing their own generators as tenants' fixtures.

Roads

The Witnesham Farm Road remained a continuing source of complaint and expense. In 1951, Mrs Patten at Cockfield Hall, who had a right of way over the estate land to reach the Hall, complained about the state of the road. It had been patched repeatedly, so now the agent recommended that 2,850 yards should be completely remade. However, up to this time the other users, Pipps Farm and Cockfield Hall, had not been asked to contribute to the patching; faced with this large and expensive project, the committee approached them both. In 1952, most of the work had been done at a cost of £338 18s 2d, with a further layer of top dressing to be done at a cost of £77 19s 0d. The agent reported that all cash reserves were now exhausted, and higher rents were not due until the following year, so only a small number of repairs could be done if shares were not to be sold.

In 1958, the Witnesham Road was again in bad condition. In the agent's report, he noted that the road could be divided up as follows: the section from the highway to Pipp's Farm, 237 yards (A-B); Pipps Farm to the Trust boundary, 457 yards (B-C); Trust boundary to Venn Farm, 433 yards (C-D); and Venn Farm to Low Farm and the end of Trust land, 340 yards (D-E).

Of these, C-D was not bad. A-B, B-C and D-E should be reshaped and asphalted at £499 18s, and

£982 14s 4d. The C-D section only required shingle and tar at a cost of £74 11s 0d. This meant that the resurfacing job would come to a total cost of £1,557 3s 4d. The county surveyor waived his fee, and the agent reported that several grants might be available, as the Divisional Land Commission had considered the site and approved urgent work. However, with a total of £2,503, rental income and little other income from shares, wayleave and sale of timber, this was a vast expense for the committee.

The committee was also approached for a contribution of £145 to the making up of Chalk Hill Lane at Great Blakenham by the Roads and Bridges Committee in 1956. The other interested parties were Cobbold Brewers, Gipping RDC, and the Associated Portland Cement Manufacturing Company. The committee replied that it was of no value to the Tollgate Farm land, and refused to contribute.

They were also approached by Great Blakenham Parish Council in 1951 to provide land for a turning circle for people visiting the cemetery, and perhaps also an extension to the cemetery itself. However, Trust lands could only be sold for agricultural purposes, so the committee refused, and provision of land for a turning circle was left at the discretion of the tenant. At the end of the decade, however, the Trust agreed to allow a third of an acre to be transferred from the Sproughton Allotments to provide a larger car park for The Wild Man pub.

Tenants, Tied Cottages and Old Age

By the late 1950s, more tenants were becoming elderly and the harsh reality of losing their homes loomed closer. One tenant, in 1958, 'owing to age and ill-health was now given notice to quit'. However, A R Palfreman, a Hadleigh tenant, managed to transfer his holding to his son without problems.

A second tenant, Mr Pearl at Burstall, became incapacitated and relied on his neighbour to keep the land tidy in 1957. In 1960, the committee made the humane decision that 'to apply any pressure, even to the extent of taking land from Mr Pearl, would be unwise'.

A third tenant at Witnesham wanted to let his holding to his son in 1959, but this was disallowed as the son was an agricultural worker on land outside the estate, and the cottage would be needed for the estate.

The fourth tenant affected was a long-standing smallholder in Sproughton. As his health and fitness deteriorated, he arranged for his son to take over the holding but remained in the attached cottage. However, his son found that he could not afford to run the holding on a sound financial basis while maintaining his parent's cottage and was 'advised by his accountant' to leave. The cottage was severed from the holding and let to the sitting tenant at a rent of £20.

These last two cases illustrate the dilemma faced by farmers and landowners. Ideally, tillers of the land should live close to their fields and livestock. In instances where accommodation was not tied to the holdings or to the jobs, a real problem was created; as the fourth case shows, it was uneconomic for the smallholders to live elsewhere. The Trust, by agreeing to allow the elderly tenant to remain in his cottage, had left themselves with a holding which could not be let separately but had to be added to an adjoining let.

Conclusion

It had been a difficult decade for the committee, and their decisions throughout had been largely reactive rather than proactive. The lack of finance was becoming an even more pressing problem, particularly as infrastructure from 1910 began to fail. This was combined with a general pressure from the government to raise the quality of both tenants' accommodation and farm buildings.

In February 1960, with the start of a new decade, it was announced that their long-standing land agent was retiring in March. The committee thanked him for his service and wished him a long and happy retirement.

NOTES

1   Howkins, Alun. *The Death of Rural England*. London: Routledge, 2003. p 152.

Chapter Nine

1960–1966
The End of the Beginning

International Economic Changes

The European Economic Community slowly began to improve the position of its constituent six countries in the early 1960s, and the United Kingdom found that the advantages of the European Free Trade Association did not compensate them for lost exports in the way that they had hoped. Therefore, the Prime Minister, Harold Macmillan, tried to renegotiate British entry to the EEC in 1961. However, this was vetoed by General de Gaulle. A second attempt to join in 1967 was similarly rejected by the General, but finally Great Britain, Ireland and Denmark were allowed to join in 1972.

National Agricultural Scene

The Common Agricultural Policy began its operations in 1962, while British farmers looked enviously at the subsidies being given to their European counterparts. The aims, as listed in the last chapter, were broadly in accordance with the plans of the British Government, and they were giving their own subsidies to improve the infrastructure of agriculture.

At the same time, British agriculture was in a period of rapid change with the increased use of agrochemicals – fertilisers, herbicides and pesticides – to increase production. Plant breeding research became more important: new wheat varieties, for example, were developed with shorter straws, which diverted plant energy to seed production. In 1963, a warning note was sounded at these intensive methods with the appearance of *Silent Spring* by Rachel Carson and the organic farming lobby increased its influence.

In livestock farming, the introduction of artificial insemination hastened the ability to vary breed shape and performance, and the ubiquitous Friesian cow came to form 85 per cent of the national herd.

Trust Property and a New Agent

On 16 March 1960, the new land agent – Mr Arthur John Potter, MA, ARICS, QALAS – took up his post. As so often before, the appointment of a new agent affected the Trust deeply.

No meeting of the Trust Committee was held between 3 March and 6 September 1960, but business at the two meetings on these dates looked at the recommendations for repairs from the retiring agent, and considered some urgent matters raised by tenants. Valley Farm, for example wanted water laid onto two additional fields, which would attract a grant of 40 per cent.

On 22 November, the agent had had time to inspect the Trust lands and properties and prepare his report on the conditions he found; the result revealed a disastrous situation. Mr Potter reported that recent government legislation on housing had established 12 points of 'standard condition' which needed to be met.

Dwellings should:

1. be in a good state of repair and substantially free of damp;
2. each room should be properly lighted and ventilated;
3. each house should have an adequate supply of water;
4. have an effective and adequate means of supply of hot water for domestic purposes;
5. have an internal or otherwise readily accessible water closet;
6. have a fixed bath (or shower) in a separate room;
7. be provided with a sink or sinks and suitable arrangements for disposal of waste water;
8. have a proper drainage system;
9. be provided in each room with adequate points for gas or electric lights (where reasonably available);
10. be provided with adequate facilities for heating;
11. have adequate facilities for storing, preparation and cooking food;
12. have proper facilities for storing fuel (where required).

However, in the agent's estimation, of the 29 buildings only five farm houses were up to standard, 12 lacked standard amenities in whole or in part and were not up to standard, seven cottages were lacking standard amenities, and five cottages were 'let away' but were lacking in standard amenities. Thus, only five of the 29 properties were in such a condition that they would need no more money spent on them in the next 15 years.

The farm buildings fared no better. He reported that many were:

1. expensive and difficult to work and were badly laid out;
2. they were expensive to maintain from both age and construction;
3. they were expensive to adapt and modernise;
4. and inadequate to meet the needs of a progressive tenant of today.

Most of the farm buildings were those which existed at the time the Trust came into the council's possession. A number of minor improvements and additions have been made at various times, but the major possess inherent disorder.

The financial analysis of the estate was: Hadleigh property value £13,376, Sproughton £4,860, Great Blakenham £2,918 and Witnesham £7,882. The total equalled £15,666.

Investments had been made to the value of £3,069 but the present value was only £1,700.

The tenancies at that time were:		
Hadleigh	8 full-time tenancies, 2 cottages and part time	Rents £2,089
Sproughton	3 full-time tenancies and 4 cottages	Rents £440
Great Blakenham	3 tenancies	Rents £330
Witnesham	3 full-time tenancies and 1 cottage	Rents £542

The total tenancies was thus 23 full time and 7 cottages. The rents totalled £3,401.

Mr Potter estimated that it would take over £10,000 to bring all the houses up to an adequate standard. Unfortunately, only £1,000 was available each year

for capital works and, as long as the limited inflow of capital continued, repair costs would remain high, and should increase to prevent further deterioration. He pointed out that the Trust had been trying to provide a service for which the local authority Small Holdings Committee were having to be subsidised by way of exchequer contributions to losses. The Small Holdings Committee also had access to county funds, which was a source of income unavailable to the Trust.

The conclusions were inescapable: the Trust could not continue in its present form and Mr Potter recommended that properties should be sold rather than modernised, if possession could be obtained. The Farm Improvement Scheme would enable them to modernise rather than replace properties, but would still require more capital than the Trust possessed.

The Trust Chairman had talks with Mr Potter as well as informal, and then formal, talks with the Charity Commission to examine the prospects. Additionally, a working party consisting of Lord Alastair Graham, D R Dickson, E J W Fiske and J O Youngman was established to create a set of proposals. In the meantime, the day-to-day work of the Trust had to continue.

Tenants and Houses 1961

From 1961 to 1962, the management of tenancies was in some disarray until plans could be finalised for the changes, but the estates were also changing rapidly for unrelated reasons.

For the last few years there had been problems with aged tenants and tied houses. In September 1960, it had been reported that G Pearl in Sproughton was incapacitated. Finally in November 1961, he was persuaded to give up 2.498 acres of his worn-out orchard and it was decided that he would retain only his cottage in Bramford Lane and 1.016 acres. The rest of his land was given to Hope Farm. In May 1962, it was reported that Pearl had died in March; his widow was almost blind and remained in the cottage for a few more months.

E W Boreham, who was one of Pearl's neighbours at Sproughton, had already been 'retired': in other words, the Trust let him remain in his cottage while his son worked the land. In January 1961, however, Boreham also died and his aged widow was allowed to stay on 'as some doubt existed as to her circumstances'.

This left two cottages which could not be sold immediately.

The Eastman brothers, who were themselves nearing retirement after their successful careers in poultry farming, applied for planning permission for industrial development on their land, which was partly surrounded by Trust property.

In January 1961, the Pond Hall Farm tenants, W J Farrow and his son, complained about the state of the two cottages attached to their holding, and the committee replied 'that they were aware of the problem and working on the properties'. Mr Farrow also asked whether he could buy his farm but 'the idea was not to be entertained'. This was a strange decision in the circumstances, but demonstrates the lack of clarity the committee members had about the momentous changes they were being asked to make.

At Laurel Farm, Sproughton, it was found that the previous tenant had sublet buildings on one field as a garage for village residents, which only came to light when the holding was relet to Mr and Mrs Golding. However, the buildings were away from the homestead and so dilapidated that they had no agricultural use. Moreover, they were filling a local need, and so it was agreed that the situation could continue.

Sub-committee Report (1) – May 1961

The first report of the sub-committee recommended drastic action to begin to dispose of properties. Pond Hall and grounds should be sold as soon as possible, and the nearby thatched cottage demolished as soon as the tenant, who was an employee of the Trust, could be found new accommodation. Four cottages in Sproughton should be sold, along with Corner Farm and Tollgate Farm at Great Blakenham. At Witnesham, Venn Cottage and Orchard House would be sold and the useless Orchard House buildings demolished.

At the same time, steps were taken to try to form the remaining holdings into saleable plots. Thus, the Eastman brothers were asked whether they would sell either of the two old cottages on plots which were encircled by Trust land. Similarly, the owner of OS10 in Westerfield, adjoining Venn Farm, was asked whether he would sell the land to the Trust to round off a boundary.

The sub-committee recommended that the Trust should apply for a loan from the county council loan pool to provide ready finance if any or all of the suggested sales fell through. However, this was not possible, so the committee asked the Agricultural Mortgage Corporation (AMC) for help. At this point, Sir Peter declared his directorship of the AMC and had to withdraw from the discussions.

Sub-committee Report (2) – May 1961

Later in the same month, a second report by the sub-committee was presented and gave the welcome news that the Charity Commission would allow any money raised from sales to be used to provide improvements to remaining properties. It was estimated that after grants this would amount to between £30,000 and £45,000.

The committee carried out their own inspections and their reported findings echoed those of Mr Potter, which meant that preparations for sales must be made. At Sproughton, for example, they reported that the farm buildings were poor and that 'additional buildings would be needed for the intensive methods essential on a small acreage'. This reflects the change in agriculture over the preceding 50 years – the first tenants did not use 'intensive methods' but often grew traditional crops on a tiny acreage.

In September 1961, it was reported that the loan from the AMC was agreed subject to the Charity Commission's approval so that there was a financial cushion to ease property sales. By now the tenants were aware of the plans to sell: Venn Cottage at Witnesham was to be sold to the son-in-law of the tenant. The price was low – only £500 – but the property was in poor condition and there was no vacant possession. The owner of Tollgate Farm also made an offer to buy but agreement on the price was not reached until September 1962.

Repairs and Renovations

Before sale, many properties needed urgent work to bring them up to an acceptable standard and work was carried out as a matter of urgency on both houses and farm buildings. Mains electricity had still reached only a quarter of the Hadleigh properties in 1961, but the connections were planned within the next year.

Orchard House at Witnesham was up to standard,

except that it had no water closet and no proper drainage: the bathroom waste discharged into a ditch and caused a nuisance. In September 1961, the committee decided that the fourth bedroom should be turned into a bathroom with water closet and the old bathroom on the ground floor turned into a larder. The old earth closet nearby would be turned into a water closet as well. Hill Farm in Hadleigh also gained a bathroom and had repairs carried out.

As to farm buildings, it was agreed that Ramsey Farm's cowhouse should be turned into a milking parlour and dairy, which would attract a subsidy from the Milk Production Officer, and Valley Farm gained three new pig sties in the stackyard.

In May 1962, it was decided that the old thatched cottage, near Pond Hall, was to be demolished, and replaced in May 1962, but W J Farrow, who the previous year had asked if he could buy his farm, now felt that 'he was disturbed at the future of agriculture' and needed time to consider whether he needed a replacement cottage.

Sub-committee Report (3) – September 1962

The third report signalled the end of the Trust in its present form. The group had reassessed the situation, and now reported that they feared that the cost of the retained estate would be more than at first envisaged, and of such magnitude that economics would defeat the continuing of the Trust in its present form.

> In effect it is impossible to operate on a charitable basis a service which in its statutory guise depends for its existence on both central and local government financial assistance. Therefore, an alteration in the function of the Trust is essential. Any alternative will have to be within the framework of the original scheme and relate to its objective in a broader sense, that is, to assist persons to make a start in agriculture.

The alternatives had not, however, become clear at this stage, so the work already begun to improve and rationalise the holdings continued while further discussions with the Charity Commission were held.

Thus, Highfields Cottage was offered to W J Farrow as an alternative to the demolished thatched cottage and the offer was accepted. Mrs Pearl at Burstall had vacated her cottage so the cottage and garden were put

up for auction and sold for £2,200, while the remnants of Mr Pearl's old orchard were given to Hope Farm. Tollgate Farm was sold for £8,000 to Mr Hood. The Eastmans at Hadleigh had now agreed to let their land to Cookson & Zinn who were manufacturers of steel storage tanks, and L J Sheppard who made concrete blocks. Both works needed a water supply from the estate so metered supplies were arranged from the Trust.

Sub-committee Report (4) – January 1963 – Demonstration Farm Vision

At last the group had begun to formulate a new plan for the future: 'A suitable and practical alternative would be the setting up of a demonstration farm on which the improved techniques and developments in agricultural methods could be practised, a farm open to inspection by farmers and available for training purposes, if possible in collaboration with the Education Committee'.

Here was an ambitious plan which required agreement from all concerned bodies, and thus at the committee meeting of January 1963 a legal assistant from the Charities Commission, Miss A M E Jacobson, and also the land commissioner, J F Smithies, were present.

The Charities Commission summarised the Trust's situation with the following statements.

(a) (The Trust) No longer fulfilled its objects in the present economic conditions and should be revised.

(b) The principle object of the Trust – 'the advancement of agriculture' – should be kept.

(c) The Trust will exist in perpetuity and therefore the objects should be framed as widely as possible to allow flexibility and to obviate the necessity for repeated revision whenever economic circumstances change.

(d) There appears to be a conflict of interests arising between the Trust and the county council due to incompatibility between the carrying out of the objects of the Trust and the existence of the statutory powers of the council. Therefore, the Trust should be revised to become an independent body of trustees from the council.

The Commission were happy with the idea of a demonstration farm as a suitable revision of the activities of the Trust. It was then agreed that 'the new farm should be run on a commercial basis as this was essential if the respect and interest of the farming community were to be established'.

As to the farm itself, the agent recommended that it should be of about 500 acres and on boulder clay, if possible, like the Kent Farm Institute.

Suffolk Agricultural Education

It was agreed that members of the Education Committee should be invited to meet with representatives of the Trust. Thus, on 29 January 1963, the planned meeting took place between Lord Alexander Graham, D R Dickson, Sir Peter Greenwell and J O Youngman from the Trust and Captain the Honourable C B A Bernard and A E Pye from the East Suffolk Education Committee. Also present was P O Trist, the County Agricultural Advising Officer from MAFF.

The Education Committee representatives were clearly pleased with the new proposals. They had been operating a small agricultural education establishment at Witnesham which was inadequate for demand. (See Chapter 16 for more information on Witnesham.) Fortuitously, they had been considering whether to establish a farm which would be devoted to agricultural education, and they had wanted to follow the example of Oxfordshire, where a private Trust operated a farm of some 400 acres on a commercial basis providing the education authorities with facilities for agricultural education on mutually agreed terms.

At the end of the meeting it was agreed that:

1. A demonstration farm should be run by the committee on commercial lines.
2. A new school should be set up as soon as possible with the agreement of the Charities Commission and the Trust lands should be sold.
3. The size of the farm would be 300–500 acres – 'large enough to be typical of present and foreseeable trends and permit demonstrations to be realistic from both practical and economic aspects'.
4. The soil should be boulder clay, like the majority of the county farms.
5. It should be easy to access from the whole county and probably in the Ipswich or Framlingham area.

In October 1963, the committee were told that the Charity Commission had approved the draft scheme, but that MAFF needed to be asked for approval. By the February meeting both had given their approval, and the Charity Commission had been asked to draft a final version. However, it would take about three months before the final version could be received by the committee.

The End of the Estates

Despite the constant round of meetings at this period, the work of the estates had to continue. In January 1963, the long awaited electricity supply to the Hadleigh holdings was complete, and the farms and buildings had to be wired. In October 1963, negotiations for mains water for the estate had begun, and the Trust needed to contribute £1,300 for connection and metering of the supply. At the same time, Valley Farm was to be given new drains and water closets, which would make the property more saleable.

Another large outlay was a realignment of the Ramsey Farm Road in May 1966 to allow heavy lorries to reach the farm; cattle grids were installed at the same time. The new road ran beside Beehive Farm.

The six acres of Ramsey Wood were sold in 1966, and Valley Farmhouse had major structural repairs. Laurel Farm, Sproughton had new farm buildings, and the Corner Farm buildings at Great Blakenham were repaired.

Lord Alastair Graham, E J W (Jack) Fiske and the New Committee

In April 1964, Lord Alastair Graham announced his retirement. He had been a member of the committee since 1946 and chairman since 1952. He had also been chairing the sub-committee considering the future of the Trust, and had thus contributed hugely to the success of the work.

The chair at the next meeting, 28 July 1964, was taken by E J W (Jack) Fiske – the third member of his family to take that position. He was charged with the difficult task of carrying forward the changes.

With the arrival of the draft scheme in May 1965, there was also to be a change in the status of the committee. When the new scheme came into operation, the county council were not to be trustees of the estate, but the new Felix Thornley Cobbold Trust Committee assumed the role of trustees. The county council agreed, if seven nominees of the county council were kept on the committee for their usual three-year term. The clerk, the treasurer and county land agent would be ex-officio trustees, and four of the nominated members should be members of the county council. Also, the Trust would submit annual reports and accounts to the county council.

The money derived from the sale of the Trust lands would become the working capital for the new Trust. However, there could be an interim problem during the period of buying and selling land, and the Charity Commission agreed that capital assets might be released as long as they were replaced eventually.

Continuity was achieved between the old and the new in that the seven members of the existing committee became the new seven nominated members of the Trust.

Charity and Stanaway Farms

In February 1966, the Trust was offered a possible site for their demonstration farm – Charity and Stanaway Farms at Otley. This estate comprised 272.351 acres of medium/heavy land, together with two farmhouses, two pairs of cottages and two sets of farm buildings. The position of the site was ideal as it was only seven miles from Ipswich and one and a half miles from the Witnesham Agricultural Centre.

It presented, however, rather less than the acreage the Trust had been seeking, but the offer was made to them before the land was offered on the open market at a price of £81,600 with possession by 1 June 1966. There were also tenant rights of £6,000, £500 for redemption of tithe, stamp duty of £816 and the cost of raising a mortgage of £800 – a total of £90,000.

The Charity Commission approved the deal, and so in May the agent reported that he had completed the purchase at a cost of £81,600 together with tenant rights. The Department of Education and Science and MAFF had also given their agreement to this arrangement.

The agent reported at the same meeting that he had intimated – unofficially – that the Trust would be prepared to make a site available to the council for a new education centre at Otley, and the council offered to fund a loan of £7,800 for five years at 7.5 per cent to assist initial funding.

This purchase meant that the old holdings needed to be sold as a matter of urgency, and tenants were given the option of purchasing them, although the offers had to reach the market price in order to raise funds.

Stanaway Farm at Otley was purchased by the Trust in 1965 together with Charity Farm as the site of the new demonstration farm. It had formerly been owned by Lord Cranbrook, and then run as a dairy farm by Mr Buchannan of Witnesham. (Otley College)

Conclusion

During the fifty-odd years in which the Trust had been running smallholdings and allotments, they had supported a number of men throughout their working lives, and the end had a feeling of inevitability about it with the deaths of tenants like Pearl. Felix's infrastructure was obsolete, the buildings were not fit for purpose and modern farming could only be continued on the estate land with an influx of capital that was simply not available. It was time for a change.

Chapter Ten

1965–1978
Demonstration Farm Project

National Agricultural Scene

Alun Howkins, in his book *The Death of Rural England*, characterises the period from 1965 as one in which output expanded but at a slower rate, and was often tied to government or EU grants.[1] For example, grants for drainage were available for 65 per cent of the cost by the mid-1970s, so it became an affordable improvement for most farmers. It was also a period in which interest in mechanisation grew steadily, along with the use of pesticides and herbicides which could be spread accurately by the new machines. To benefit from these chemicals there was an increased need for technical advice from agencies, such as the National Agricultural Advisory Service (NAAS) which was founded as a result of the 1947 Agriculture Act.

In the late 1960s and 1970s a number of pieces of fundamental legislation began to impact on the agricultural scene. British industry was still suffering from the legacy of the Second World War despite the improvements of the previous decade, and the response of the government was the 1964 Act under which industry could set up training boards, financing them with industrial levies. Thus, the Agricultural Training Board, East Anglia, was established in 1966 with a view to promoting the training of young people entering the industry. Similarly, the 1967 Agriculture Act established the Meat and Livestock Commission to promote the quantity and quality of red meat production, with consideration for the interests of the consumer.

An even greater change came in January 1973 when the United Kingdom became one of the three new countries joining the original six members of the European Community, and was thus able to become part of the Common Agricultural Policy instead of remaining a bystander. It not only affected markets and commodity prices, but in January 1974, the EEC Directive on Farm Modernisation opened up new sources of funding to British agriculture, which was of interest to the Trust.

A second Act – which had major consequences for the Trust – was passed in 1973: the reformation of counties. East and West Suffolk together with the County Borough of Ipswich were combined to form the new Suffolk County Council so that the Farm Training Centre at Chadacre, the Agricultural Centre at Witnesham and the new Otley demonstration farm came within the same county area.

Trust Reorganisation and the Committee

The Charity Commission was busy during the winter of 1964, so the draft agreement for the new Trust did not arrive until February 1965 and could not be fully discussed until the meeting in May 1965. The committee voted to adopt the new scheme, and the first meeting of the new governing board of the Trust was held on 7 June 1966. The board consisted of E J W (Jack) Fiske in the chair, D R Dickson as vice chairman, H C Meadows, J S Schreiber, B C Smith and J O Youngman. R H Rash sent his apologies. Also attending were the ex-officio members, or their representatives: R W Gash (representing G C Lightfoot who was to be the clerk), A J Potter (the land agent), and H Ainsley (representing F Wroe, the new treasurer with Ainsley as the auditor).

The new Trust deed stated that:

> The object of the Charity shall be by establishing and maintaining a farm or farms as centres for demonstration, training and apprenticing and by other means to advance and improve agriculture, and in particular to educate farmers and young persons in agricultural methods, development and techniques.

As noted above, the national priority at this stage was to improve the skills of the workforce and to provide farmers with good technical knowledge so the

Trust objectives were precisely in line with these needs, and the work would fulfil an urgent need for practical advice in the Suffolk area.

Farm Planning

At the May meeting, the new board confirmed the purchase of the Stanaway and Charity Farm Estate at a cost of £81,600 together with tenant rights, and looked at their options. The Trust envisaged a period of two to three years in which the new estate would be developed, and an outline plan for the first period was agreed in consultation with the Chief Education Officer and MAFF. The responsibility for running the farm would be the Trust's, but every effort would be made to provide educational facilities.

The first phase provided for:

1. A basic crop pattern as at present with winter wheat, winter oats, spring barley and sugar beet.
2. The initial labour force would be a good foreman, together with two labourers. The contract for the foreman should have an incentive element, but he would be told that the post might not continue after the first period.
3. Farm machinery purchases would be approved by the chairman and vice chairman and two of the ex-officio trustees.

The Education Centre

It was anticipated that the land would provide not only the space for a demonstration farm but, after consultation with the Department of Education and Science and the Ministry of Agriculture, it would also become a new centre for agricultural education. The ideal partner for this enterprise was the struggling Agricultural Education Centre based at the school in Witnesham – a short distance from the new farm. As previously noted, the agent had already agreed unofficially that the Agricultural Department might transfer to a new site made available by the Trust. The county council agreed to fund a loan of £7,800 for five years to help with the initial financing.

The centre at this stage had the use of two class-rooms and an adjacent woodworking room, but student numbers had gradually climbed from 50 to 300, although they spent the mornings at Suffolk College and attended Witnesham in the afternoons for practical work. (See Chapter 15.) Thus, in September 1966, the Trust agreed to form a small sub-committee to negotiate the transfer of the Educational Centre to Trust land, although they expressed the wish that 'in line with the wishes of Felix Cobbold, the centre would continue to place and empower the training of farm workers rather than farmer's sons'.

The June 1967 meeting of the trustees was held at Stanaway Farm, which gave an opportunity for inspection of the new purchase. The Trust decided that they could provide part of OS 25 and OS 26 – a total of 4.79 acres – for the next Education Centre, with a 99-year lease. The Trust provided a range of one-storey buildings, including a reception area, several classrooms, a canteen and library area, and administrative offices. There would also be a large barn nearby housing farm machinery on one side, and a milking parlour, milk room, pig sties and a bull pen on the other. While small, this presented better facilities than the centre at Witnesham had, and the students would also have access to the demonstration farm to observe the techniques being used. An area for parking was allowed on Charity Field and cycle storage was provided beside Charity Farmhouse. In the meantime, the Trust decided to issue a *Farm Notes* booklet for use in

This photo from the late 1960s shows the original buildings erected by the Trust to house the East Suffolk Agricultural Institute. (Otley College)

East Suffolk and Ipswich schools, and also arranged for the machinery lecturers at Witnesham to provide a demonstration on ploughing and cultivation at Charity Farm during the autumn.

Residual Estate

For the first couple of years the Trust were concerned not only with setting up the new estate, but also with the disposal of the old smallholdings. The Trust had a duty to sell at market value, which meant they could not sell to tenants who had occupied their holdings for many years if the tenants' offers were not high enough. For example, it seemed possible that Gary Farm, Hadleigh, and Orchard House and Low Farm, Witnesham, might be sold to the tenants but negotiations dragged on for months. Finally, the Gary Farm 'best offer' fell through, and Gordon Prowse, the son of William Prowse who had been the tenant since 1906, was allowed to buy the farm himself in 1967. Orchard Farm was sold to F A Finbow the same year, and Low Farm was sold to J C Norman in 1968. The tenant at Venn Farm, Witnesham, made an offer, but this was thought to be too low. The tenant of Corner Farm, Great Blakenham, left his holding at Michaelmas 1967 and the farm was sold at auction with most of the land going to the Portland Cement Manufacturing Company Ltd and a small section going to E Hood.

At Sproughton, F G Pegg at Hope Farm wanted to retire and part of his land was let to the Goldings at Laurel Farm. By the end of 1967, a total of £47,000 had been raised in the sale of land and the remainder of the Hadleigh Estate was bought by the West Suffolk Small Holdings Committee in 1968 for £110,000 rather than being sold to tenants. Hope Farm and Laurel Farm at Sproughton were retained by the Trust along with the Witnesham holdings. It was an uncomfortable end to the old Trust, but legally the Trust had no option but to sell to the highest bidder or retain county ownership of the lands.

The Demonstration Farm 1965–1969

With the acquisition of the demonstration farm, trustees now found themselves with a substantial amount of money and an unusual opportunity to put all their combined experience in agriculture to the task of producing a farm which would be a symbol of good management.

The basic infrastructure needed much work, and visibility on the roads surrounding the farm had to be improved. Grain storage proved a problem as did beet loading facilities so a Massey Ferguson Store-N-Dry of 216 tons was bought, and preparations for drying grain in the store with a Lister Moisture Extractor Unit and ventilated brick floor were made. A Ransomes Crusader Combine Harvester was acquired and it was anticipated that this could be used by the Education Centre in due course. The trustees were embracing mechanised farming in line with the national trend, but were also serving as a source of information and inspiration to the county.

An old barn at Charity Farm was demolished for road improvements, but a new store of 3,000 square feet was approved at Stanaway Farm. The Trust also bought a Massey Ferguson MF34 15-row combine drill and a John Salmon Hydro-Depth Control Unit. At the same time, both Middle Field and Bottom Field were mole drained. Charity Farmhouse was occupied by one of the new employees, Cyril Jaye, but it needed extensive repairs, and the Charity Farm Cottages were sold, as modernisation would have been prohibitively expensive. Two new cottages were built beside Charity Farmhouse, together with a garage.

A new foreman – Roger Leggett – was appointed, together with two labourers, but one of them decided to emigrate in June 1967 and it was decided that he would be replaced with a trainee or apprentice. Roger had initially trained at the Witnesham Centre before completing additional training elsewhere; he rapidly proved his worth as an excellent choice for such an unusual post.

In March 1968, several trials were set up in partnership with NAAS and the National Institute of Agricultural Botany (NIAB) and more machinery demonstrations were held with East Suffolk Machinery Club. In June, the Education Centre held its prize-giving and open day at Charity Farm. These events proved not only a challenge to Roger Leggett, but also to the trustees who found themselves responsible for managing an influx of people from all over the county. At the demonstration of autumn cultivation over 6,000 people came to see over 50 tractors working on different soil conditions. Cars were parked on road verges, on the paved areas of the farm, and even on the edges of fields, and the trustees were concerned that crops would be damaged. It was later discovered that the soil of Charity Field had suffered compaction, so the initial fears were realised.

The Education Committee had not provided for large car parking areas, and the Trust objected to car parking on the hard areas of the farm. One of the main problems that would beset the trustees throughout the next 20 years was thus exposed: the need to be representative of the farms of the area, but nevertheless to fulfil their charitable objectives at the expense of commercial practice if necessary.

By 1968, the management of the demonstration farm was becoming easier to plan, and Roger Leggett's salary increased, partly due to the fact that the Trust acquired another parcel of land at Corner Farm in November 1968 and yet another 5.697 acres from Snipe Farm, Otley at a cost of £1,435 in June 1969. The farmhouse and gardens at Corner Farm were considered to be superfluous to the demonstration farm needs and so were sold. Thus, the estate consisted of 314.5 acres, although it was planned to lease 20 acres to the Education Authority rather than the initial estimate of 4.79 acres, providing the centre with its own mini-farm. In 1970, a further 5.5 acres were bought from A G Day, making a total of 320 acres.

A financial analysis by the District Agricultural Advisor in 1969 showed that the farm was now achieving the county average in results in spite of the many distractions. The only blemish was a poor pea harvest.

Unfortunately, one of the 'founding fathers' – J S Schreiber – died in 1968, and another, H C Meadows, died a few months later in 1969. This exposed another of the problems of the Trust, and possibly of all Trusts run by a committee: continuity of thought and purpose was important, but many of the trustees were men in the second half of their lives who had already led successful careers before becoming county councillors. In addition, county council elections every four years meant that changes in the composition of the Trust Board were perhaps too frequent, as it took every new appointee some months to become familiar with the situation and to become effective trustees. The third problem for the council-appointed trustees is that they had their duties as councillors, and often held a variety of other posts and responsibilities, making attendance at Trust meetings difficult.

The ex-officio members also changed in quick succession. In 1971, G C Lightfoot retired and was replaced by Sir Peter Hutchinson, Bt., S Elsmore replaced F Wroe, while Mr Potter, the agent, was replaced by M J Lusby Taylor. Ex-officio members, in fact, attended meetings rarely as they had their county responsibilities; more often than not, they sent representatives to the meetings who were not familiar with the whole picture. The change in land agent so soon into the new venture was unsettling, as it was Mr Potter that had supervised the momentous change from smallholdings to demonstration farm.

The trustees now included E J W Fiske in the chair, Capt R J Sheepshanks, B C Smith, D R Dickson and J O Youngman.

East Suffolk Agricultural Institute

In 1970, the new buildings were ready for occupation, and on 4 July the grand opening of the new institute was held with Lord Netherthorpe, the chairman of Fisons, cutting the tape. The Honourable C A Bernard, chairman of the county council, attended along with a large group of distinguished visitors. Throughout the day, guests were able to visit the demonstration farm, guided by Roger Leggett, as well as inspect the new institute buildings and farm land. Graham Boatfield became the first principal of the East Suffolk Agricultural Institute, and Brian Bell, the secretary of the East Suffolk Farm Machinery Club, became head of farm machinery. Brian had already worked closely with the Trust to provide machinery demonstrations.

The institute had a small governing body which was originally a small sub-committee of the Suffolk County Council. At the time of the move, the chairman was Eric Chapman, who served from 1970 to 1974. He was a Suffolk farmer, who had been prominent in the affairs of the Suffolk Young Farmers and the National Farmers Union. He was succeeded by Robert Black, who had already served as a governor since 1964, and remained as chairman until 2004.[2]

The trustees were delighted at the fulfilment of their plans, but the demonstration farm had changed in character. There was daily activity on the institute site, and frequent visits to the demonstration farm fields by students. The trustees had decided not to acquire livestock at this stage, but the institute kept a small dairy herd and some pigs, and an apiary appeared at the bottom of the Bee Field, just south of the new buildings.

Demonstration Farm 1970

Roger Leggett was now responsible for conducting students' visits to the farm and answering questions. When yet another 5.5 acres of farmland were acquired in 1970, he was given yet another rise in salary – to £1,050 plus £275 expenses – and renamed farm bailiff rather than farm foreman to reflect his changing role. He was also responsible for giving lectures and conducting walks for the young farmers, as well as supervising the various trials. In 1972, the salaries of the farm manager and the two staff were controlled by the Agricultural Wages Board.

Infrastructure changes continued – the new grain store with conveyors was in place by the spring of 1971, and an implement store and workshops were constructed, aided by a £7,000 Farm Improvement Grant. A Catchpole 33 tanker sugar beet harvester was bought, Stanaway Farm rewired, and a concrete roadway at Charity Farm was laid on college land by Roget Leggett and his staff. Only a year later it was decided that the grain store should be enlarged. Several more tractors were also purchased.

In 1971, John Doe staged a crawler tractor demonstration on the farm to compare its performance with a normal four-wheel tractor. In 1972, the National Ploughing Championships were held on the demonstration farm; the previous event had been a disaster due to bad weather and the organisers had suffered a crippling financial loss, so at first it appeared that the 1972 event might not be staged at all. However, Brian Bell, with the East Suffolk Farm Machinery Club, offered to organise the event using the institute premises and the demonstration farm venue was offered by the trustees. The National Ploughing Championship was a great success, and the plaque recording the event can still be seen mounted on the wall of the college Millennium building. In the same year, the farm was able to host trials of winter wheat and spring barley varieties on four acres, together with a trial of herbicides on winter wheat on a small plot in co-operation with the Agricultural Development Advisory Service (ADAS), so that the farm incurred no costs.

In 1972, the trustees decided to hire extra tractors from the Ford Motor Company. This minute was repeated on several occasions, and demonstrates an increasing trend to hire or lease rather than buy farm machinery which was becoming larger, more complex, and consequently more expensive for outright purchase.

British Sugar staged a demonstration of sugar beet harvesting in 1973 on 40 acres, which cost the Trust nothing but haulage. Also, in the summer of 1973, the Countryside Commission asked the Trust to hold two open days, and they agreed to pay 75 per cent of any loss incurred.

With three members of staff, the overheads for the farm were higher than for commercial farms of similar size, so it was decided to take on contract farming of 8.99 acres of land belonging to Farlingaye School, Woodbridge. This worked well and was continued until 1976.

In November 1973, the demonstration farm was awarded the Cranbrook Cup for the best farm in Class 2 (200–600 acres). Roger was given a gratuity of £25 and the other two men were given £15 each.

Trust and College Co-operation

In 1972, the institute wanted to send some agricultural students on a study tour and asked for funding, and £300 was provided by the Trust. The grant increased to £1,000 in 1974 and the practice continued each year from this point.

Graham Boatfield suggested buying 60 calves for fattening which would initially be housed at the institute alongside their existing 60 calves, but in December he wanted them to move to the demonstration farm. There is evidence to suggest that the Trust had been considering the question of acquiring livestock and since this fitted in well with their objectives, they agreed to build a beef unit at Stanaway Farm. Students would still have involvement with the work at Stanaway, but the farm bailiff would be supervising the project at this stage. The beef unit was built at a cost of £7,300 aided by a Farm Capital Grant of £3,000. This signalled the beginning of the co-operative project.

In 1973, the institute were also interested in a pig rearing and fattening unit, but the trustees were not happy with this suggestion so a decision was deferred. HM Inspectors visited the institute in 1974 and again asked the Trust to reconsider as a pig unit was felt to be educationally desirable. In a statement the trustees said that there were doubts as to the economies of pig rearing and fattening, a disease risk, and lack of

Bob Hainsworth and Graham Boatfield with a batch of calves in the new livestock unit at Otley around 1973. (Otley College)

evidence that a farm pig unit would be any more valuable than a small pig unit in the institute itself.[3]

Suffolk County Council Formation and New Trustees

In 1973, government legislation redrew county boundaries, and the Suffolk County Council was formed, which meant a possible change in ex-officio members of the board, and delay in projects until the elections of county councillors and appointments of staff. Once elected, the new councillors needed to look again at the council's responsibilities and redefine its policies. There was initial confusion over possible grant support to the institute, which meant that decisions were deferred until grants could be confirmed.

To make matters worse for the Trust, on 31 March 1974, Roger Leggett decided to move on in order to further his career, and B E B Reynolds was appointed in his place as working farm manager, and a small van was bought for him by the Trust and a pension was arranged. One of the labourers also left and was replaced by Barry Quinton. Barry was initially paid 165s per week, but this was raised to 192s per week, and then 222s per week (£11 2s)

In June 1974, several new trustees came to their first meeting. Yet another death had occurred – that of J O Youngman in December 1973. He had been a keen supporter of the Trust and had usually attended meetings despite being in poor health. The new board thus consisted of chairman Jack Fiske living at Thornbush Farm, Sproughton; R R Harvey from Braisworth Farm, Tannington; D R Dickson from Barrow Lodge, Barrow near Bury St Edmunds; H A Mitson from Alanor Lodge, Buxhall, Stowmarket; Capt Robin Sheepshanks from Rookery House, Eye; C C Smith from White House Farm, Levington; and C G James from Ipswich. C W Smith, the new chief executive of Suffolk County Council, also attended with E Knott as treasurer, and M J Lusby Taylor as agent. Jack Fiske, it was announced, had also become a governor of the institute.

The institute also changed its name in summer 1974. The Education Department had decided to move the horticultural education department from Witnesham to the Otley site, so the institute became Suffolk Agricultural and Horticultural Institute with an increased staff and a range of new courses.

Residual Estate 1974

By 1970, the residual land consisted of two farms and three cottages at Sproughton, and Venn Farm, Witnesham. In June 1972, the estate was listed as Laurel Farm, Hope Farm, Oakdene Cottage and Bramford Lane Cottage, and the Sproughton allotments. Venn Farm, at Witnesham, had 72.349 acres, the demonstration farm at this date was 312.751 acres, and the Institute held 5.267 acres; together with the Sproughton acreage this amounted to a total of 472.975 acres. It posed a complex management situation for the trustees.

Venn Farm had farm buildings which were deemed to be unsuitable for modern methods and the agent recommended that they be demolished and replaced. However, the tenant said that he did not want new buildings, so his rent was kept at the old level.

In Burstall Lane, Oakdene Cottage became vacant after the death of the elderly widow, Mrs E Boreham. The house was modernised with a 50 per cent Housing Act grant and then relet to Suffolk County Council for staff housing. Hope Farm and Laurel Farm were redecorated and the Goldings at Laurel Farm were provided with new farm buildings.

A few months later, negotiations about building a major road to Cambridge from Ipswich took place. Of

Laurel Farm, Burstall Lane, Sproughton. This was one of the first properties built by Felix Cobbold for his smallholders, although it has been altered and enlarged over the century. Mr and Mrs Golding, photographed in 2010, have been in residence since September 1960, and have thus spent most of their working lives on this farm. (R Thomas)

of wheat on Charity Field.[4] The prize of £1,000 was shared between Roger Leggett, and the new farm manager, Brian Reynolds, who had trained at Writtle, and gained an NDA and a college diploma (2.1) in agriculture. The two labourers, Cyril Jaye and Barry Quinton were given prizes by the Trust in recognition of their good work.

Machinery purchases, such as bale handling equipment, a new Farmhand Flat 8 accumulator fork and hitch and a new 26-foot-long trailer, increased each season. Bins were provided for storing separate crops at Stanaway Farm. A new Claas Combine Harvester – 'preferably with an air-conditioned cab' – was also being bought. The addition of the comment about air conditioning once again demonstrates the extraordinary changes in tractor evolution since the beginning of the century. The first tractors, with their uncomfortable metal seats, exposed their drivers to the elements like the farmer with a horse-drawn plough, but this minute highlights the change to a sophisticated machine with weather-protection and air conditioning.

the proposed routes, one would have impacted Hope Farm and another would have impacted Laurel Farm. Local protest against the road was led by Nicholas Fiske, Jack's son, and eventually the plans were dropped in favour of the route from Copdock to Huntingdon now in place as the A14. The Goldings asked if they could buy 11.26 acres of their farm and surrender the remaining 33 acres to the Trust, and this land was offered to Hope Farm.

The other elderly widow, Mrs Pegg, was still living in her unmodernised cottage in Burstall Lane but Samford District Council wanted to demolish it and re-house her. When the Trust finally agreed to the demolition, Mrs Pegg was moved to a council house. The site was cleared and the land once again went to Hope Farm.

Demonstration Farm 1974

The farm was running well at the time when Roger Leggett decided to leave. At the harvest of 1974 the farm won the National Man's Hunstman Competition organised by the National Seed Development Organisation (NSDO) with a record yield of 86.1 cwt per acre

Chadacre Farm Training Centre

Following the merger of East and West Suffolk the new county was responsible not only for the institute at Otley, but for grant aid to the Chadacre Agricultural Institute, which had been started by Lord Iveagh in 1920. By the mid-1970s, however, Chadacre needed a higher grant in order to continue. A sub-committee was formed by the County Education Committee which consisted of D R Dickson (not only a governor of Chadacre but also an FTCAT trustee), Lt Col J M H R Tomkin (a Chadacre governor, an East Suffolk Institute governor, and vice chairman of the Further Education and Youth sub-committee) together with J Turner (East Suffolk Institute governor, Chadacre governor, and also a member of the Further Education and Youth sub-committee).

The group carried out a review of agricultural

education in the county, inviting comments from many other organisations, such as the East Anglian ATB and the National Farmers Union (NFU). There was strong support for Chadacre with its large estate of 537 acres plus a further 284 at Stanningfield and 51 residential students. By July 1976, a decision was made to give additional grants to keep Chadacre open, but it was suggested that some money might be made available from the FTCAT. Chadacre needed a new dairy unit, as their present buildings were too small and out of date, and they proposed increasing the herd to 100 or 120 cows from 70 cows, with a new unit containing covered cubicles with a herringbone parlour.

In the middle of these negotiations, the Trust suffered another blow with the death of Jack Fiske. He had been a trustee for 23 years and chairman since 1964 and had provided continuity through the difficult years of the transition while all around him shifted and mutated. His death was also keenly felt at the institute,

and a memorial garden and plantation was planted across the road from the institute entrance in his memory. As a double blow, the vice chairman, R R Harvey, also died a few weeks later, so the Trust representatives that finally visited Chadacre included C C Smith, as the new chairman, and D R Dickson as vice chairman once again.

The group met John Paton Philip, principal of Chadacre, for a tour of the site, but were concerned that the new project had not been costed correctly. The Trust agent estimated that the new cows would need 58.5 or 97.5 extra acres of pasture, which would mean halving the sheep numbers to compensate. The fixed costs were therefore at variance with the estimated costs produced by Chadacre and the Trust referred the problem back to the Education Committee for further thought. It was finally agreed that the Trust would support the Chadacre Centre with a grant of £50,000 so that a dairy unit could be constructed.

Demonstration Farm 1975–6

In 1975, the results were good and the new agent, Michael Taylor reported a surplus of £32,139. The livestock had been bought cheaply and their purchase attracted a subsidy. There was an increased yield of wheat with an average of 42 cwt per acre. The pea crop was good, and sugar beet had averaged 12 ton per acre at 16.5 per cent sugar. In addition, the book value of the various properties had increased. However, the farm report of September 1976 was disappointing, partly because of a drought in the summer of 1976.

The farm manager was interested in the theories of Professor R Laloux on the danger of blanket treatment of disease and discussed possible future treatment of wheat. He also recommended the tramline system. An Amazone twin disk fertiliser spreader was recommended as it could reach to 42 feet – the width of tramlines to be used on the farm. He advised buying two new tractors – an International 674 and a Ford 4600 with DAB loader. On the advice of ADAS/NIAB, he was sub-soiling much of the farm and the farm was also metricated.

At this meeting, once again there was a change in the composition of the Trust committee: C C Smith decided to retire, leaving Capt R H Sheepshanks to take the chair for the September meeting. For the following meeting, however, Lt Col J M H R Tomkin was

E J W (Jack) Fiske, chairman of the Trust from 1964 to 1974. He is commemorated by the Fiske Memorial Plantation on the college land. (Nicholas Fiske)

elected as the new chairman, and he declined to have a vice chairman as he thought it unnecessary.

In October 1976, the weather changed from drought to deluge, with 19 days out of 31 having rain during the month. Beet was only lifted on two days and it was necessary to hire a contractor with a crawler to plough as a 2WD vehicle would have caused too much damage. By the end of 1976, however, it was reported that the farm again compared well with the regional average and Brian Reynolds was congratulated. He was also sent on an advanced course in farm business run by the Worshipful Company of Farmers, with the Trust paying the fees, but in January 1977 he announced that he would be leaving his post in March. At the same meeting it was announced that Cyril Jaye had been chosen by Ransomes to drive one of their demo machines at the National Sugar Beet Demo in November 1976.

Since the beginning of the demonstration farm project, the trustees had been searching for an area of light land, but none was available close enough to be practical, meaning that although the topic was often referred to, the problem was never resolved. In January 1977, the Trust, however, found and were able to buy 29 acres of land at Pear Tree Farm at a cost of £23,250.

The new land was immediately drained and some hedges removed before it was brought into cultivation. Some of the original land still required draining so South Field, and parts of West and West Middle Field were drained at the same time. Luckily, the Power in Action demonstration in 1977 had drained nine acres of New House Field at no cost to the Trust, but for the rest of the work a Farm Capital Grant was available. Unfortunately, inclement weather postponed the final completion of some of the mole draining, and some work was held over until 1978.

In June 1978 a new land agent, Hamish Anderson, reported to the Trust that the demonstration farm was also eligible for grants available from the EEC Directive in Farm Modernisation. The directive provided higher grants than the Farm Capital Scheme and also covered more items, such as livestock and machinery purchases. At the time, the Trust was investing in a cattle handling area at Stanaway Farm, with a cattle race and cattle crush ready for the arrival of the beef from the Institute joint scheme.

Conclusion

The characteristics of this period for the Trust continued to reflect national trends, namely the reliance on grants from whoever would provide them and the growing interest in mechanisation and techniques for making the best use of equipment. Machines were becoming larger and more expensive every year, and the entrance to the farm had to be widened in order to be accessible by larger vehicles. However, the heavy machinery also permitted work on a large scale, including draining and re-sculpting the landscape, as well as the chance to experiment with controlling farm weeds and diseases with chemicals. Centuries-old methods of farm management were being abandoned in the race for bigger yields and ruthless efficiency.

NOTES

1 Howkins, Alun. *The Death of Rural England*. London: Routledge, 2003. p 152.
2 Information supplied by Graham Boatfield.
3 The decision to exclude pigs from the farm was strange if the farm were to represent Suffolk farming. There were a number of successful pig farms in the county, including two at 'Akenfield' (Charsfield) not far from the farm in Otley. In Ronald Blythe's book, *Akenfield*, his character 'Terry Lloyd' was studying pig farming at Witnesham Training Centre and keeping Essex pigs on his own smallholding (p 247), while 'Col Trevor West' had a successful herd of 200 pigs, producing about 2,500 weaners a year (p 201).
4 For more information on the development of the National Seed Development Organisation (NSDO) see *The Plant Breeding Institute: 75 Years, 1912–1987*. PBI, 1987.

Chapter Eleven

1978–1985
Education, Trials and Profit

National Agricultural Scene

Support from the Common Agriculture Policy for agriculture was helping British farmers, as can be seen from the constant references to grants and subsidies in the Trust minutes. However, by 1985 there were signs that support was perhaps working too well, and there was growing criticism.

In 1984, milk quotas were introduced, limiting the amount of subsidised milk that dairy farmers were allowed to produce. Arable farmers did not face reforms until May 1992; this will be discussed in Chapter 12.

In 1967, the Meat and Livestock Commission was created to promote the production and sale of red meat. It lasted until March 2008, when it became a subdivision of the Agricultural and Horticultural Development Board.

The farming revolution had had other effects: farmers of small acreages could not afford the new giant machines, and even if they could, the machines were unprofitable to use on small farms. Farm labourers were once again under threat of redundancy as one tractor driven by one man was capable of doing the work of several men using old machinery and methods.

Another effect of the previous drive towards great production was the environmental impact of these agricultural methods. The numbers of birds and small mammals began to decrease alarmingly in arable areas due to the widespread loss of habitat, causing public concern for biodiversity. Between 1946 and 1974, 45 per cent of hedges had been grubbed out in Norfolk and 40 per cent in Cambridgeshire. Overall, over 120,000 miles of hedgerows were removed between 1946 and 1974 in England and Wales.[1]

The period also saw a rise in concern for animal welfare and animal rights. The RSPB membership, for example, grew eightfold between 1971 and 1994, while the RSPCA saw a similar growth. Concern about the use of DDT and the effect it was having on the bird population led the RSPCA to openly oppose its use, leading to a ban on utilising the substance in British agriculture in 1984. American opposition to DDT had led to a US ban in 1972. A number of legislative acts protecting birds were passed in 1954, 1964 and 1967, but these were superseded by the more wide ranging Countryside and Wildlife Act of 1981. During the late 1970s and 1980s, therefore, the role of farmers began to change from being merely producers of high quality and cheap food, to accepting a dual responsibility for becoming protectors and stewards of the countryside.

Public concern for the countryside was linked with a renewed surge of interest in visiting the countryside, not only for rambling and bird watching, but also for leisure pursuits like fishing and playing golf. Rights of way were guarded jealously, and there was anger at landowners' 'Trespassers Will Be Prosecuted' notices, which eventually lead to extended 'Rights to Roam' legislation in 2000.

Pollution caused by agricultural processes became a matter for particular concern during this period. The Royal Commission on Environmental Pollution 7th Report: Agriculture and Pollution (1976) (Cmnd 7644) and the 11th Report: Managing Waste: the Duty of Care (1985) (Cmnd 9675) discussed possible pollution from farm slurry, straw burning, silage liquids, chemical wastes, containers for sheep dips and pesticides among other things. Thus, straw burning became a problem for the demonstration farm in 1983.

Suffolk had been a major producer of sugar beet since the 1930s, with British Sugar Corporation plants at Ipswich and Bury St Edmunds, and we have noted its importance as a crop not only to the smallholders, but also to the Trust's demonstration farm. In 1977, a rights issue meant that government holding of shares in the company was reduced from 36 per cent to 24 per cent. With further troubles in the sugar industry, plants in Ely, Felsted, Nottingham and Selby were closed in 1981. In 1982, the company experienced a takeover by S & W Berisford, and its name was shortened to British Sugar PLC. During the takeover struggle, the NFU made an abortive bid to take over the government shares, and the Trust supported this effort. The company was later resold to Associated British Foods in 1991, still using the title British Sugar.

Trust Committee 1978–81 and Land

Lt Col J M H R Tomkin was in the chair, with D R Dickson as vice chair. Other members included C G James, who was also the trustees' representative on the governing body of the college. A G Barker joined the trustees in October 1977. The remaining trustees were H A Mitson, C C Smith and Capt R Sheepshanks.

However, during this period there appear to have been few meetings, with a gap from October 1977 to June 1978. Brian E B Reynolds left his post as farm manager in 1977 and was replaced by Robert A Fletcher in October 1977, which meant that he was supervised only by the new land agent, Hamish Anderson, during this period.

The Demonstration Farm and Conservation

The Trust's role in agriculture soon began to change. In June 1978, Hamish Anderson advised the trustees that the Countryside Commission would give grants for planting trees on suitable sites. Up to this point, the Trust had been following national trends, enlarging fields and taking out hedgerows to simplify work with large machinery, but from this point onwards, the Trust began to balance conservation and the environment with commercial farming practice. The Trust land had lost trees to disease and to the process of grubbing out during field rationalisation. However, the initial response of trustees was to find ways of taking advantage of this grant by trying to identify unproductive areas of the estate which could be planted to take advantage of the subsidy. In November 1978, with Lt Col Tomkin in the chair, the trustees agreed that eight acres of trees would be planted at a gross cost of £12,000 to create a 'new agricultural landscape'; this work attracted a 50 per cent grant from the Countryside Commission.

At Hope Farm 1.3 ha of hillside were planted with trees in 1978 and by entering the Dedication Scheme of the Forestry Commission the Trust were given a grant of £200 for this work. The farm was also given a 60 foot by 30 foot open shed with the help of a 30 per cent grant from the MAFF Farm Capital Scheme. For the farmer, the result was that his rent rose from £1,000 pa to £1,350 pa.

At the June 1978 meeting, the trustees began to consider the results of hedge removal on the network of footpaths over the fields. The public had a right to access, but new cropping areas needed protection, so a review process to move paths to the edges of new fields began.

Agricultural Demonstrations

In 1978, an ADAS herbicide trial on 32 acres of trust land investigated 30 different treatments for black grass and wild oats. One highly successful ADAS trial on pea crops used pheromone traps rather than pesticides, which not only had the result of reducing the need for spraying chemicals but was also in line with the emerging concern for encouraging environmental solutions to problems. The trials were visited by students and staff from the institute, an ADAS/NIAB trial evening had 140 visitors, and on another day, 30 Suffolk County Council farm tenants visited the site as well as 24 students from Plumpton Agricultural College.

Farm Reports 1977

The farm began to suffer in 1977 and the 1978 report showed a total loss of £397.07. Twenty tons of grain with 16–20 per cent moisture had overheated in storage and been lost. However, the first batch of beef had made a profit of £248.48. In addition, the farm had successfully produced barley, peas and sugar beet.

With a view to claim money through the Farming and Horticulture Development Scheme, Hamish Anderson, the land agent, produced a potential shopping list for the farm which included a new concrete pad for sugar beet at Pear Tree Farm, more land drainage, a toilet and mess room for farm staff, three-phase electricity at Stanaway Farm, bulk feed silos and automatic feeders, and a new beef fattening house. All of this was expected to attract a grant of

25 per cent from the scheme. The trustees asked Hamish to produce full costings and a prioritised list for their next meeting, but meanwhile they had agreed to buy a Jumbo Buster Chisel Plough and grain weigher spout for the combine harvester.

When Hamish reported back in July 1979, as there was again no spring meeting, he announced a profit for the 305 farmed acres, which matched the local average for a heavy land arable and stock farm. The beef unit had, in fact, done badly but Hamish recommended that the project should continue in the likelihood that matters would improve. There had been a transport strike earlier in the year and cattle performance suffered as their usual feed was not delivered and had to be replaced by lower quality emergency rations.

For equipment, he recommended purchasing a Proctor and Watveare 1.5-tonne rear-mounted fork lift, which could handle palletised loads. He estimated that the handling of bags in the old way would be refused by drivers in the foreseeable future, and later on even the farm staff would refuse, so mechanised handling would become mandatory.

Machinery was now so expensive that Hamish asked the Trust to consider whether it should be acquired by outright purchase, leased, hired, or bought through loans. MAFF figures showed that leasing machinery produced an overall cost saving, so a Manitou 25P Fork Lift Truck was leased. The total cost amounted to £15,855 over three years, with an initial payment of £5,699. After three years, the Trust would have the option of paying £160 pa to extend the lease. VAT would be payable but recoverable by the Trust. Interest would be paid at a rate of 8.16 per cent.

At the same meeting, the trustees were given a report from Graham Boatfield, principal of the college, on the cattle situation. He thought that the present two-unit system was wasteful and asked if all the cattle could be reared at Stanaway, with the college students being given access to calves in adequate numbers for their education. The college would underwrite any losses due to this educational use, and the county council would indemnify the Trust against any deaths or other losses due to student intervention. The Trust agreed to the changes and decided to join the Meat and Livestock Commission Recording Scheme on behalf of the beef unit at a cost of £30 pa.

In July 1979, the effects of the 1974 Health and Safety at Work Act began to impact on farm work so the new farm manager, Robert Fletcher, produced a policy statement in line with requirements. A few months later the local HM Agricultural Inspector visited the farm for an inspection, and both the demonstration farm and the renamed East Suffolk College of Agriculture and Horticulture premises were given a clean bill of health, with minor recommendations for changes. The recommendations were:

1. that the grain drying air tunnels should be provided with latches on both sides of the doors,
2. that there should be changes to the fencing of the bull beef unit,
3. that there should be changes to the pesticide and chemical store, and liaison with the Fire Prevention Officer was necessary,
4. and that a broken parking brake on a Ransomes tractor should be fixed, and all the other tractors should be fitted with them at a cost of £900.

Chadacre Agricultural Institute

During this period, the Chadacre Institute was continuing to experience financial difficulties, and in November 1978 a possible merger between Chadacre and the Trust was discussed as a way of solving the problem. The views of the Charity Commission were sought, but the Commission rejected the proposal in July 1979. Chadacre had by this time lost half its acreage 'but was achieving satisfactory results from the remaining 400 acres'. By December 1979, Chadacre were seeking another £12,000 from the Trust for conversion of a Dutch barn into a grain store. A loan was agreed by the Trust at a 1.75 per cent interest rate – less than the current building society rate.

In 1982, Chadacre asked for a suspension of capital repayment on the £12,000 loan as they were again suffering financial problems. This would have meant a loss of £8,000 to the Trust, so they refused the request. In 1983, Captain Sheepshanks, now chairman of Suffolk County Council, co-ordinated a meeting between the Chadacre trustees, Lt Col Tomkin – the FTCAT chairman – and the land agent. At this meeting it was suggested that an independent body should be set up to co-ordinate agricultural training in the county; later, however, the FTCAT trustees decided against this idea and also decided not to lend Chadacre more money.

The institute was at this time offering residential,

two-year, full-time courses only; these ran from October to March so that students could work on farms during the busy summer months. However, the West Suffolk Agricultural Education Advisor, Michael Hosken, arranged to lease land from the institute in 1966 to provide day release courses for West Suffolk, specialising particularly in farm office work, accounts and record keeping. With the merger of the counties, the Chadacre Farm Training Centre became the responsibility of Suffolk County Council and continued to run in parallel with the Otley College site.

Demonstration Farm as an Educational Resource

Under the management of Robert Fletcher, the farm began to grow several new crops – Finale protein peas, durum wheat, and 12 acres of forage rape for seed. He also increased the number of demonstrations and visits. In June 1979, more than 100 local farmers attended a demonstration and a second day in July attracted another 100. Over 1,200 school children visited in the first half of the year alone and 390 college students used the farm facilities, with 240 doing practical work. Still, Robert complained that 'there is a constant struggle to find enough equipment and facilities for the purposes of student practice and student assessment including livestock, pigs and cattle, and, to a lesser extent, sheep'.

The farm results, however, showed that the farm was doing well. In the 1980 harvest report, Hamish said that the durum wheat had achieved 45.4 cwt/ac. ADAS had conducted spring barley trials and these produced 50.3 cwt/ac. Robert had then drilled 22 acres of oilseed rape, 28 acres of winter barley, 149 acres of winter wheat and 38.5 acres of sugar beet. The final report on 1980/81 showed that the farm had produced one lot of sugar beet at 7.10 tons per ha and another at 37 tons per ha.

At this point, relations between the farm and Otley College began to suffer largely because Robert was responsible for reporting to the Trust as well as the college principal. There was friction over wages: the college staff were paid a different rate from the farm staff. The college was still running its own beef unit and Robert complained that there was duplication of work. He was also unhappy because the annual Power in Action demonstrations disrupted farm work and this

was affecting profits. The 1980 event provided demonstrations of direct drilling, mechanical handling, subsoiling, minimal cultivation, ploughing, manure spreading and mole ploughing. The days were very popular with local farmers, but the Suffolk Farm Machinery Club was now told that demonstrations could only be hosted every other year and must fit in with farm cropping plans. The next Power in Action day would, therefore, be held at a convenient time in 1983.

A series of recommendations from Hamish were considered by the Trust but did little to calm the situation as the first was that 'the farm manager is to be directly responsible to the principal of the college but still retain full responsibility as farm manager'. Another recommendation was that the County Education Officer might become a trustee, and that there should be a joint annual meeting between representatives of the Trust and the governing body of the college. The recommendations also included the advice that the Trust should accept a slight (controllable) reduction in net farming profits accountable within the objectives of the Trust. Trustee discussions in 1980 noted that the first recommendation was a stumbling block, but welcomed the suggestion of a co-opted trustee from the board of governors, along with the County Education Officer. The Trust also thought that joint monthly meetings might be held, rather than annual meetings, on a set day, including special advisors where applicable. Also, they thought that there should be daily contact between the farm manager and the college heads of agriculture, machinery and horticulture.

It was also agreed that the beef unit at the college should close and that students should be able to use the Stanaway Beef Unit, with the county indemnifying any loss. Half the calves had to be castrated so that they could be handled by students and this resulted in a loss to the Trust.

In June 1980, the college had another proposal: John Pearson, head of horticulture, wanted to begin commercial vegetable growing and asked for help. The Trust did not want to grow vegetables themselves, but agreed to make four acres of New House Field available, together with some labour and equipment, including spraying equipment, at minimal cost to the college. Staff issues were again a problem, as the college could not recruit a foreman responsible for such a wide range of activities as landscape, turf, nursery stock, glass crops, fruit and amenity and field scale vegetables. It was therefore agreed that the college foreman would market the products via a local wholesaler and undertake some tasks, while the farm manager would grow the vegetable crops and hire casual labour where necessary, but would be given technical help from John Pearson. In addition, the farm manager would have day-to-day responsibility for the crops, which were to be on a five-acre, rather than a four-acre, site.

This aerial photo of the college site around 1982 shows the importance of horticulture at this stage of the institute's development. Almost a third of the site is now covered with commercial greenhouses and polytunnels, outdoor gardens and vegetable plots.

Hamish Anderson and John Pearson agreed upon:

1. a one-acre tree bank run by the college,
2. one acre of daffodil bulbs cared for by both the college and the farm,
3. three acres of vegetables, including rhubarb plants in the autumn of 1981; summer cabbage, including blocked and drawn plants; cauliflowers, including blocked and drawn plants; leeks, sprouts and onions – direct drilled; potatoes – three rows grown annually alongside bulb crop for horticultural and machinery training.

Hamish argued that these crops would be more valuable than the traditional cereal crops and would provide valuable experience for students. Also, there would be no charge for college labour and the college would pay £150 for integrated rotation work.

For staff, the demonstration farm was employing Robert Fletcher and two craftsmen tractor drivers –

Cyril Jaye and Barry Quinton. The college were employing Henry Kemp, who was said to be 'not good with pigs' but managed the other livestock. The college pig unit had problems and the Trust insisted that they did not want to be involved, in spite of pleas from the college. They had only 20 sows, which were unprofitable and they wanted to increase to 50 sows, provided they could employ a specialist pigman.

It was finally decided that the college needed two pigmen to handle 50 sows. Henry Kemp could care for the Trust calf and beef unit and the college sheep as well as assisting with the arable work. Barry and Cyril were given revised pay scales and a new bungalow, together with the purchase of 15 acres of land, was found to house one of the pig men at Otley Bottom.

It was an ambitious programme and for the first year it seemed to work well. Joint meetings were held between Robert Fletcher, Ted Barnes (the assistant agent) and Graham Boatfield, John Pearson, Bob Hainsworth, Ken Miller and Ron Brown from the college. This did much to improve communication. The vegetable plot broke even in the first year and was allowed to continue for a second year for its educational value. There was, however, some friction between staff and Ted Barnes almost had to stop the work at one point.

The calf and cattle unit suffered from disease and lost £800 for the 1980/81 season due to ringworm and salmonella. The ringworm was eliminated but the salmonella problem proved more intractable. Hamish commented that salmonella was present in the national herd and was tolerated, and would probably continue to be tolerated unless there was an outbreak of disease in the human population that could be attributable to cattle. However, students were not able to handle diseased cattle, so a search was started for a local source of disease-free animals.

In February of the second year, however, the whole horticultural scheme began to unravel. Some of the farm leeks had been criticised by the market inspector where they were being sold and they were downgraded to 'poor quality'; the farm manager responded to this by complaining that the farm staff 'did not like doing horticultural work'. The joint vegetable venture was then abandoned.

Unfortunately, worse things were to come. In April 1982, Robert Black, chairman of the Otley Governors, was invited to a Trust meeting to discuss the problems.

First Robert Fletcher was asked to outline the problems and he then was required to leave the meeting while discussion continued. Trustees agreed that the role of the farm manager needed better definition, particularly with respect to the pig unit. One suggestion was that the Trust farm should revert to the 1975 plan, with the college running its own farm.

The trustees pointed out to Robert Black that the cost of running a demonstration farm for the benefit of the college was too high. Trustees would allow the arable part of the farm and the livestock unit (with the exception of diseased animals) to be used by the college if convenient, but college livestock must be separate and self-supporting. Robert Black then presented a report from Bob Hainsworth, head of agriculture at the college, on the requirements of the college from the demonstration farm, which in parts made grim reading.

In the report, Bob asked that the demonstration farm should present an above-average appearance of tidiness and cleanliness – not just to the standards of a normal working farm, but those of a demonstration farm. Trials and demonstrations should only be held when 'husbandry standards were at a high level'. For tidiness, he did not want students to see 'discarded baler twine, empty bags, leaking taps, blocked drains, lack of bedding materials for animals, accumulated dung, obviously sick and deformed animals, and dirty water bowls'.

Many of his demands were clearly beneficial not only to the students but also to other farm visitors. These demands included integrated conservation areas, identification of fields by name and size, production of a farm guide, and that records and accounts being kept in a similar manner to those of a progressive commercial farm with copies made available for students. There should be a 'blueprint' agreement on procedures – crop choice, involvement of students in planting crops, a regular supply of animals of all kinds including baby piglets and young calves. Grass plots should be available for grass husbandry, and hay for the college stock. Trust machinery should be available for college use. There was an annual need for land for students to plough. Conservation should be of high standard and technical information about it made available. All machinery must conform to Health and Safety Regulations, and everyone should have a good understanding of those regulations. Technical help

might be needed by students from the farm staff, and any costs for this would be reimbursed by the college. The college also asked for a large quantity of unsprayed hay for horticultural use – about 300 bales pa.

Finally, it was suggested that it would be helpful for Robert Fletcher and the other staff to attend an 'effective supervision' course.

The Trust agreed that with the demise of vegetable growing things might improve and so they decided to continue with the frequent meetings to iron out co-operation problems. A second joint meeting was held in February 1982 to monitor the situation. A list of machinery borrowed and shared was now being kept by Robert Fletcher and Dick Waterson of the college. For the livestock, six steers had been bought by the Trust and kept in the hay barn for student use, and they were doing well. Salmonella testing had been done in Norwich but the service was slow and this was hampering student access to cattle.

On the plus side, a demonstration of hedgelaying had been held by students and had proved popular with visitors. It also demonstrated the growing interest in environmental conservation and best practice at the college.

In the mid-1980s, after decades of removing hedges, farmers were encouraged to replant and protect wildlife. As part of the drive for conservation in the countryside, college students were taught the ancient art of hedgelaying. (Otley College)

Ted Barnes, assistant agent, reported that the new computerised accounting from the Suffolk County Council Treasurers Department should help in producing useful information for the students. However, the farm had to produce two sets of accounts: one normal set and a second ADAS Farming Account which would enable comparison with other farms. The demonstration farm was not a normal farm, particularly with regard to staff costs. However, the dual system was producing anomalies so that there were apparent losses where they did not really exist.

Trust Committee in the 1980s

In 1981, D R Dickson resigned after 25 years on the Trust, and his place was taken by Bruce Hinton, a land agent and farmer from Framlingham, who was thus well informed about mid-county farming. Dickson had been one of the key trustees providing continuity over the previous quarter of a century, attending most meetings and serving as a governor of Chadacre. He also served as vice chairman for several periods.

At a meeting in October 1983, those attending were: Lt Col Tomkin in the chair, A G Barker, B N Hinton, C G James and J H Taylor, with apologies from H A Mitson, Capt R H Sheepshanks, and C W Smith and Hamish Anderson, the land agent.

E C Barnes, the assistant land agent, also attended the meeting together with M J Cassedy on behalf of the county treasurer, Miss J Cursley on behalf of the clerk to the Trust, I N Whitaker, the assistant county clerk, and Robert Fletcher, the farm manager.

Residual Estate

In 1982, Sproughton RDC asked if they could buy the allotments. The assistant agent recommended that this be refused, as the land might be redeveloped for housing, which would not accord with the wishes of the Trust.

Farm Report 1983

Robert reported that he was again growing durum wheat, as ADAS wanted it trialled, there was a national demand and it spread across the harvest period. New drying facilities which would be in place by harvest 1984 would enable increased acreage and it should realise a good sale price, whereas other wheat prices were poor.

Of the present grain store at Stanaway, one of the new bins was now full. Weighing the grain was a problem as the combine spout weigher did not deal with other grain, and the committee debated installing

a weighbridge, which would be essential to contract drying or cleaning. Otley College were interested in acquiring the old grain store at Charity.

The farm manager also reported on the trials and demonstrations held on the farm. Information from them filtered back into the farming community through ADAS and commercial firms, but conducting trials was time consuming and disrupted the normal farm schedule. Power in Action was particularly difficult to manage as it was usually held at the busiest time of the year, but it was now to be held every other year to minimise disruption. Cyril Jaye was retiring from his post of craftsman tractor driver to the Trust, but Robert argued that the farm still required two craftsmen plus a trainee to cover all the work.

At the end of the meeting, however, Bruce Hinton reported that he had done a calculation of expenses and estimated that while the farm was still making a small profit now, by 1984 the farm would make a loss. The trustees asked the assistant agent to make his own financial prediction for the next meeting.

Straw Burning on the Farm

As noted on page 79, one Royal Commission report had already discussed the problem of straw burning after harvest: one estimate from 1976 suggested that over 2 million tonnes of straw had been burnt in that year. In a report to the meeting of October 1983, the agent asked the Trust to consider the matter. As yields of cereals increased, the volume of straw had increased also: 120 acres of straw had been baled for use by the Trust and the college, but 150 acres had been burnt off and on two occasions nearby houses had been affected by the pollution. It was anticipated that the practice might shortly be restricted by law, so other disposal methods must be explored and possible trials held.

ADAS wanted a trial of 3.42 hectares of North Charity Field incorporating straw at 20 cm, 15 cm, 10 cm and 5 cm with monitoring of slug and disease build up. Older ploughs did not cope well with this regime but new ploughs had deeper throats, so an extra 125 hp 4WD tractor was needed with a six-furrow plough to replace the old three-furrow plough, and a straw chopper mounted on the combine with a flexicoil roll. Straw incorporation was a slower process than burning and it impinged on the muck spreading time, but this would be compensated for by doubling the plough size. A combine-mounted straw chopper was available at a cost of £900 and the Trust agreed that one should be purchased and used on 50 acres for an experiment in straw incorporation.

For other trials, Norsk Hydro was trialling a nitrogen fertiliser, Power in Action used 111 acres and ICI had been conducting a direct drilling trial. However, bad weather had made the land unusable and the ICI trial had to be cancelled. Ted Barnes also reported that when Robert Fletcher took up his post as farm manager, three trials a year had been held, but there were now nine, with two more under consideration, causing a strain on the farm staff.

Cyril Jaye was replaced by Stephen Podd in January 1984, and later that year Stephen was awarded a Craft Certificate by Suffolk Agricultural Wages Board, and his wages upgraded. The Trust recognised that the trials and demonstrations were taking up the work of one man, but felt in November 1984 that the general aim should be to demonstrate methods of farming to Suffolk farmers rather than to assist large companies. Apart from Norsk Hydro, the farm was now giving 12 acres of land to the British Sugar Beet Corporation for a demonstration of cultivation and growing, for which they were paid compensation of £240 per acre (a total of £2,880 for the 12 acres).

In other ways the year was a bad one and profits were low. Wheat gave a bad yield, particularly 'Hustler', although the durum wheat paid well. A third of the straw had been chopped and ploughed into the soil, but Robert reported that they had had a problem with the straw handling and corn carting, and asked for more tractor horsepower. The Trust agreed that, in future, the farm should use more student labour in straw handling rather than buy another tractor.

The agent reported that machine repairs and maintenance were high, considering the acreage of the farm, and labour costs contributed to a poor overall performance.

He also raised the question of the provision of an area of light land again. There was the possibility of 72–83 acres of medium/heavy land becoming

The 1983 harvest results were:		
148 acres	Feed wheat	2.7 tonnes per acre
33 acres	Soft milling wheat	3.951 tonnes per acre
20.6 acres	Kunzler milling wheat	3.1 tonnes per acre
30.7 acres	Durum wheat	1.79 tonnes per acre
34.4 acres	Winter barley	2.73 tonnes per acre
3 acres	Triticale	2.8 tonnes per acre
57.6 acres	Oilseed rape	1.38 tonnes per acre

available, but there was still no immediate prospect of finding light land. The Trust decided to ask the County Education Officer to make his intentions clear. At this point the college asked for more land for cultivation, so Far South Field was given to them.

The Trust decided that they would no longer pay a subscription to NIAB or continue updating *Farmers' Handbook*. They would, however, join the Farming and Wildlife Trust at a cost of £100.

Farm Management Consultants

In January 1985 there was an emergency meeting of trustees to consider the future of the demonstration farm.

Trustees had decided after the October meeting that the slide in profits could not be allowed to continue and standards on the farm were unsatisfactory. Tenders were therefore sought from a number of farm management consultant companies.

At the January meeting the Trust decided that Strutt & Parker should be appointed to manage the farm. It was then arranged that the chairman, Bruce Hinton and Hamish Anderson, the agent, should have a meeting with D Allerton of Strutt & Parker to outline the objectives of the Trust and to consider future cultivation plans. This reorganisation would include examining the role of the farm manager and the number of staff to be employed.

NOTES

1 Howkins, Alun. *The Death of Rural England*. London: Routledge, 2003. p 196.

Chapter Twelve

1985–1992
Agribusiness and CAP Reform

This decade was perhaps the most difficult so far for the Trust's demonstration farm. Nationally, the recession of the early 1980s led to high unemployment and rising prices. In October 1987, Black Monday saw the fall of stock market values throughout the world, including a fall of 26.4 per cent in Great Britain. On 16 September 1992 – Black Wednesday – Britain was forced to withdraw from the European Exchange Rate Mechanism (ERM) following speculation against the pound. Agriculture was protected to some extent by the Common Agricultural Policy which was still offering generous subsidies and price guarantees in its continued drive to achieve food self-sufficiency throughout the EU. By the late 1980s, however, this was becoming increasingly wasteful and creating huge food mountains, but reform did not come until the beginning of the 1990s. It was estimated that by 1988 there were a million tonnes of butter, 5 million tonnes of wheat, 4 million tonnes of barley and 800,000 tonnes of beef in store.

In 1992, the McSharry reforms – named after the EU Commissioner for Agriculture, Ray McSharry – were created to limit rising production, while at the same time adjusting to the trend toward a free agricultural market. The reforms reduced price guarantee payments by 29 per cent for cereals and 15 per cent for beef. They also created set aside payments to withdraw 15 per cent of land from production, payments to limit stocking levels and introduced measures to encourage reforestation of farmlands denuded in the race to increase food production. Since the McSharry reforms, cereal prices have been closer to the equilibrium level, there is greater transparency in costs of agricultural support and the 'de-coupling' of income support from production support. However, the administrative complexity involved invited fraud, and placed an additional administrative burden on farmers. The reforms also did not cover some products, such as sugar production, which affected East Anglia.[1]

It was also estimated that by 1992, 80 per cent of farm support was going to only 20 per cent of farmers; total numbers of farmers between 1960 and 1990 in the original six member states had fallen from 10 million to less than 5 million. Thus, one additional ingredient of the McSharry package was to give financial aid for those forced to take early retirement from agriculture.

Prices were also affected by the General Agreement on Tariffs and Trade (GATT) 1994 in Uruguay. For the first time protection afforded to agriculture was included in the debates and with the creation of the World Trade Organisation there was a movement towards improved access for agricultural products and reduced domestic support for agriculture with price-distorting subsidies and quotas. This gave greater access to British markets for products from New Zealand, for example.

Genetically modified foods began to appear in 1990 with a variety of tomato in the United States. In the UK, their introduction has been fiercely opposed by the Soil Association, organic growers and Friends of the Earth, although past governments have welcomed investigations into the value of the techniques for British agriculture. However, attempts to conduct trials have often led to the destruction of the crops by activists, fearful of cross-contamination of other plants and wildlife in the area.

British Sugar PLC continued to have problems. In 1991, the factories at Peterborough and Brigg were shut down as a programme of closures and consolidation continued. The trials on the Trust farm continued at the beginning of the period, and the Trust still included sugar beet in their cropping plan when possible.

This was a period in which the effects of intensive farming methods appeared to be affecting the health of the nation adversely. Contamination by crop sprays and run-off from pesticides entering the water supply led to increasing public concern over the direction that agriculture was taking in the drive to raise yields and produce cheap food. The reports on pollution mentioned in Chapter 11 fed through to legislation in this period; public disquiet led not only to the continued growth of the organic movement, but also public lack of confidence in both government management of the food supply and bewilderment over frequent food scares.

In the last chapter we have already noted concern on the demonstration farm at salmonella in the beef unit animals, its presence in the national herd and the agent's view that nothing would be done until there was a public outbreak of salmonella due to beef. This was a foreshadowing of an even worse problem.

Bovine Spongiform Encephalopathy (BSE)

During the early 1970s, commercial cattle feed was frequently supplemented with additives such as antibiotics and hormones to boost performance. It could also be contaminated with pesticides and herbicides. Worldwide, soya bean meal was used as a major source of protein, but, as it grows poorly in Europe, meat and bone meal produced from ground-up and cooked residues from the slaughtering process were used. This meat also included the carcases of sick and injured cattle, sheep and chickens. In the early 1980s, a change in British law allowed a lower temperature for the sterilisation of products from the rendering process. It was suspected that this led to infection remaining in the food, although a later British inquiry denied that this legislative change could have been solely responsible for the emergence of BSE. More recent findings suggested that the cause was a genetic mutation within the prion protein gene. Whatever the reason, in 1984 the first cases of 'mad cow' syndrome appeared, with the oft-repeated television pictures of a cow staggering to maintain its balance on farmyard cobbles. By 1986, MAFF accepted that this was a new animal disease and took measures to eradicate it from the national herd. The long incubation period of four to five years hampered identification, but it was estimated that 179,000 cattle were infected and 4.4 million were slaughtered to prevent disease from spreading.

Even more disastrous to the beef industry was the realisation that there was a link with new variant Creutzfeldt-Jakob disease (vCJD), which was apparently caused by eating the nervous tissue of infected beef. The effects of this infection are still unknown due to the long incubation period in humans, but it is estimated that over 460,000 BSE-infected animals entered the human food chain before controls were introduced in 1989.

At the height of the epidemic, over 1,000 cattle a week were identified as being infected. Government measures to ensure British beef was safe included: an upper age limit of 30 months for all cattle fit for human consumption, and the removal of central nervous tissue and all bones from healthy cattle to prevent any possibility of infected material entering the human food chain. The elimination of cattle and sheep residues from animal feeds had also been imposed.

The effects on the beef industry were a disaster which had widespread consequences. A ban on exports of British beef lasted from March 1996 to May 2006, but there was also concern about the safety of bovine insulin used for diabetics as well as by-products used in cosmetics, surgical sutures and gelatine production. In Britain, many people temporarily stopped eating red meat, and some became vegetarian.[2]

Salmonella in Eggs

A second food scare to emerge in the 1980s was caused by the statement of the Minister of Health, Edwina Currie, in a 1988 television interview that 'most of the egg production in this country, sadly, is now affected with salmonella'. Egg sales fell drastically and pregnant women and the vulnerable were told to avoid using recipes, such as mayonnaise, that called for uncooked eggs. Government measures to repair the damage included the slaughter of 2 million birds and tighter regulations for hygiene in egg production. Despite this, in 1996 the Public Health Laboratory Service found that whereas one in every 650 eggs had been contaminated in 1991, in 1996 the infection rate was still one in 700.

Trust Committee, Staff and Management Changes 1985

Following the appointment of Strutt & Parker (S&P) as management consultants, David Allerton presented his initial assessment of the position at the meeting in March 1985. He noted the falling profits and lack of control on the farm, and recommended that:

1. The present farm manager should be made redundant and replaced by a foreman recruited from Writtle Agricultural College or Chadacre;
2. The trials programme should be simplified and organised to meet the agricultural needs of the community, not run to meet commercial interests;
3. And relations with Otley College were at a low ebb so a meeting with college officers should be organised in the near future to discuss the way forward. The college should also be asked to do their own carting, baling and manure collection and a proper charge made for some of the work done by farm staff.

The Trust was pleased with this summary and took the advice of S&P to inform the manager that he would become redundant at Michaelmas 1985. Unfortunately, council elections were due in May, so by the June meeting there was a change of trustees and further decisions had to be postponed.

On 17 June, the new committee met and elected Captain Robin J Sheepshanks as chairman, but he was absent for the meeting, so Bruce Hinton took the chair. Other attendees were P B Atkinson, F Barker, P E Koppel, B E Rosher, C W Smith, J H Taylor and Lt Col J M H R Tomkin, who had been invited to attend as an additional trustee. H A Mitson was still a trustee, but sent his apologies. In addition, W H Marshall, the new land agent, attended as did I R Rands, on behalf of the clerk to the Trust, and I N Whitaker, deputy county solicitor. F Barker was also a governor of Otley College.

The major business of any first meeting after an election was usually to acquaint new trustees with the Trust aims and describe the present situation rather than make major changes. On this occasion, however, the management of the farm was changing hands, and decisions had to be made. Lt Col Tomkin had retired from the council, but trustees asked him to return to negotiate the redundancy of the farm manager. Later in the day a meeting with Otley College had been arranged to explore new methods of help and co-operation, and to facilitate this David Allerton had already had a preliminary meeting with Graham Boatfield to set the scene. The committee reconvened the following month with Robin Sheepshanks in the chair to consider the meeting with Otley College, and

Tomkin was formally thanked for his work as chairman from 1977–1985.

As to the college, Graham Boatfield outlined the imminent changes in the college work, not least of which was the coming retirement of the principal himself. Student numbers were creeping towards 700, and the range of courses was widening, so that the trend was away from being merely a college of agriculture and horticulture, which also meant divergence from the aims and objectives of the Trust. The college was developing the site with buildings which had not been formally agreed with their landlords, including a new practical work area and a pig unit; the whole costing more than £100,000. The county architect recommended a new formal agreement between the college and Trust to take cognisance of these changes.

It had also become clear that the college and also the local farming community misunderstood the Trust changes, so in November the Trust agreed to issue press releases, to write to the local NFU branch, and for the chairman to attend the college open day in 1986 to give a talk about the new Trust management.

Demonstration Farm 1985

A report for the new trustees in 1985 gave a summary of the estate as follows:

> The residual estate at Sproughton consisted of 70.003 acres, with a book value of £15,913. Venn Farm at Witnesham consisted of 72.349 acres, with a value of £3,787.50. The tenant is 70 years old, but has a son who could have a claim on the tenancy.

> The demonstration farm consisted of 376.656 acres with a value of £168,525 bought in five lots since 1966. It has nine acres of trees, including the Fiske plantation, and 330 acres being farmed.

> The original college lease was 5.267 acres for 99 years and the original rent had been £540 pa. They had been given an extra 0.260 acres for cottages to be built and in 1978 the rent was increased to £885 pa. They now had 32 acres and a rent of £1,440 pa.

A new foreman, Paul Lawrence, had been appointed and he was found temporary accommodation on the Helmingham Estate until Stanaway Farmhouse should become available. He had a difficult start as the autumn weather was bad and the oilseed rape failed completely and had to be redrilled with winter wheat.

S&P decided to simplify the cropping plans for the first few seasons, and concentrate on a programme of spraying for weed eradication and general husbandry matters. The farmhouses were painted and maintenance work carried out to improve the appearance of the farm. Demonstrations and trials already agreed were to continue but no new trials started. All in all for the next few seasons, the emphasis would be on restoring the standards of the farm before embarking on fresh initiatives.

Otley College and Trust Co-operation

A second meeting was held in September 1985 between college representatives, N J Purse, the senior assistant education officer, Robert Black, chairman of the college governors, and Graham Boatfield, and Trust representatives, including the chairman and F Barker, the land agent, and David Allerton from S&P.

Once again the college presented a paper on what they wanted from a demonstration farm as an example to the students. They wanted 'a well-run farm in technical and management sense and in appearance and presentation', which should be:

> typical of the better farms of the area – up-to-date but not too ahead of current practice. There should be a reasonable range of crops and enterprises, a farm which is attractive in appearance and purposeful, tidy and with some regard to the requirements of visitors and those concerned with the conservation of the countryside. Equipment should form a sensible balance between what is normal and up-to-date, without being excessively large or too advanced.

The college also wanted the farm records and accounts to be available as teaching material and information boards displayed throughout the farm. Staff should be competent and well trained (and attending refresher courses regularly). They should have 'the right attitude to the occasional interruption and special demands of visitors'. There should also be a joint blueprint for dealing with conservation and wildlife covering all the land in joint occupation.

As on the previous occasion, this paper contained overt criticism of the standards of the farm, which were not lost on the Trust representatives, but the chairman replied that S&P had been appointed to produce a profitable and well-run farm which would be a good example to students and to the farming community at large.

On a matter of divergence, the college pointed out that 'the College covers without preference or priorities agriculture, horticulture, machinery, conservation, floristry etc. over a wide range of country-based interests'. David Allerton was sympathetic and agreed that he would try to make areas available for horticulture, but 'hoped floristry might be avoided'.

The college reiterated that they wanted to acquire the grain store and would also like to take over Charity Farmhouse when it became available. The agent suggested that the college might be able to take over the grain store when the new one was built at Stanaway.

Trading Report

S&P made a further series of reports at this period on the general trading situation. The beef unit, for example, had been having problems with ringworm, so students under 18 were excluded from working with the animals. The bull beef unit had low output and high costs, and was not making money. The calf rearing unit also had a gross margin that was 25 per cent below the budget figure, and was making a loss of £43 when it should have been making a profit of £1,022.

For the cropping, yields were of poor quality and quantity. The durum wheat had been of such abysmal quality that it could not be sold for seed or milling but only as feed, and the total harvest income was £14,000 lower than had been hoped. The new cropping plan was therefore to drop durum wheat, and sow only winter wheat of the Galahad variety, to be used for milling, winter barley and oilseed rape.

The trials report noted that three commercial trials had been withdrawn, but British Sugar was continuing and still paying £240 per acre. Norsk Hydro Fertilisers had agreed to compensate for any loss caused by their trials. For the Ministry of Agriculture trials, much of the work was done by ADAS staff and therefore cost the Trust nothing; as these trials had importance for local farmers, it was decided that they would continue. The whole farm regime was thus simplified and pared down to basics before the new work could begin.

Landscape and Conservation

One of the demands of the college was that a higher priority should be given for conservation over the whole estate, and indeed this was a matter that had been ignored for the previous few years even though the college was introducing courses on conservation.

In April 1986, the landscape section of the County Planning Department prepared a landscape and conservation plan for the estate. Further tree planting was recommended, but as the estate was an 'upland exposed Suffolk farm' those trees already planted had taken some time to establish. Future planting would have to be on useable land, rather than on waste land. Hedges should be replanted over the farm with thorn bushes. The college offered to plant a hectare of land between the Fiske Memorial Garden and 'Silver Dene' as it would offer valuable horticultural training for the students. The plan also required that some water areas should be dug in the future. In 1987, the Landscape and Conservation policy was reviewed again, and the Trust considered introducing shooting rights when the plans were more advanced.

Work went ahead in planting hedges around East Middle Field, using farm labour and materials provided by Suffolk County Council. Grants were also now available for conservation work under the Farm and Countryside Initiative (FCI), and the college had found sponsorship by NatWest, so they undertook to plant a hectare of Charity Field with broadleaved woodland, including oak, ash, hornbeam, alder, hazel, willow and poplar. A pond would be excavated, and the whole would be managed to demonstrate the potential of woodland management for timber, game and amenity. This was the first FCI project in Suffolk. In 1989, the Trust also planted a roadside belt of trees along the B1078 by Nelson Field, and another triangle of trees on the south side of the field, which attracted a grant of £500 of matched funding. As a result of this work, the Eastern Regional Arboricultural Association asked to hold their annual meeting for 1989 at Otley College and to walk the farm to see the plantings; this was a welcome boost to the reputation of the farm.

Environmental Pollution

In 1985, the report on pollution in agriculture had been published, as noted in Chapter 11, and by 1987 the Health and Safety Executive issued a new set of standards for chemical storage. In May 1987, the Trust were planning to erect a new building at Stanaway and decided to wait until the standards were published before completing it. In the meantime, however, they decided to buy a lorry container as a temporary chemical store. By May 1988, the container was in place at a cost of £2,200 at Stanaway, and had proved to be so successful that the Trust asked ADAS to include details of it in their publications, and also asked for a feature in the *East Anglian Daily Times*. Later in that year, not only was it mentioned in the *EADT*, but was used for an article in *Crops* journal as an example of good practice.

Beef Unit 1986–1991

Following the poor report by S&P, the Trust decided to buy calves at 12 weeks old and calf rearing equipment was sold. Pauls Agriculture agreed to co-operate with the unit in providing feed. As a result of this re-organisation, the farm employee, Stephen Podd, was made redundant. Farm overheads were thus lowered as staffing was reduced to the farm foreman, Paul Lawrence, and Barry Quinton, who had now been working for the farm for 20 years. The Trust provided the two men with Citizens Band (CB) radios so that they could communicate with each other across the farm.

The following year, the bull beef unit continued to lose money despite the efforts of S&P, and the agent suggested buying a mill and mix unit to cut feed costs. The college were anxious that the unit should continue if possible so that students could watch the processes, but Health and Safety rules did not permit the animals to be handled by inexperienced stockmen, which included the students.

By 1988, the mill and mix unit was being used, and margins on the beef began to rise to put the unit in profit. In 1990, the sale of beef was being affected by the BSE epidemic and the unit lost £2,700. However, the trustees decided to keep the unit running. One reason was that if the unit was closed the farm would need to reduce its staffing to become a one-man farm and the trustees wanted to avoid this. The animals were now being fed partly on a feed mix supplied by Pauls, but it was estimated that beef fed in this way had gross margins of -£66.51, whereas home-grown feed gave a gross margin of +£8.35. Pauls, however, were meeting any loss for animals fed on their feed mix.

In 1991, the decision was made to run down the unit as the continuing market problem made the possibility of producing contract beef animals for supermarkets remote. A suggestion that the unit might change to pig production was not pursued further.

Cropping at the Farm and New Technology

As standards improved, the harvest in 1986 was good and the Trust offered the staff bonuses to be paid at Christmas. In addition, Cambridge University decided to adopt the demonstration farm for inclusion in its annual surveys of farming in the Eastern Counties, which helped to restore the farm's status.

In 1987, however, there was appalling spring weather, and the ADAS trials had to be abandoned as drilling on land treated with minimum cultivation was contaminated by the previous year's crop. S&P asked if they could hire an agronomist from Deben Crop Management for expert advice on future cropping, and in May 1988 it was reported that the crops looked good despite a bad winter and spring. The crops grown included winter wheat, winter oilseed rape, linseed, winter beans and spring beans – 130.07 hectares in all. Later that year, the trust decided to return to growing sugar beet and British Sugar Corporation was asked if they could have an allocation. However, they were only offered a 250 tonne quota for the 1990/91 cropping season. The Trust asked if any trials might be carried out and their agronomist, Philip Reeve, was asked to discuss the possibility.

New experimental machinery had been obtained from America which separated grain into good milling and feed wheat. There had been teething problems with the machine, but it made a difference of £6.50 per tonne before deductions for the cost of hiring the machine. Another new technique being used was a combine drill incorporating a power harrow and drill, which had been borrowed from Framlingham Farmers. This was used on two fields.

The farm staff were also contract farming, which raised about £6,100, but in November 1988 the farm was still running at a loss of £37,395 due to the disastrous harvest of 1987 and the losses on the beef unit. Trustees realised that half the loss was due to the fact that it was a demonstration farm, rather than a purely commercial farm. The farm report stated that they had winter wheat on 91.55 ha, winter oilseed rape on 13.52 ha, linseed on 8.36 ha, winter beans on 9.82 ha and spring beans on 6.82 ha – a total of 130.07 hectares of crops. Unfortunately, wheat prices had crashed: high quality milling wheat, for example, had fallen from £140–150 to £121 per tonne.

The following year Paul Lawrence, now called 'farm manager' again, decided to leave to further his career. Paul Creasey was appointed to replace him, and in due course, Mrs Creasey was also paid in recognition of her help in running the farm office.

Chadacre Agricultural Institute

Towards the end of the decade Chadacre was again reported to be struggling financially and there was a prospect of having to curtail its educational programme. The Trust had offered them £50,000 in 1979, and in 1980 had offered a second loan of £12,000. Part of these loans had been repaid, but the Trust continued to monitor the situation closely. The Education Committee were still confident that the institute was viable and continued to offer them help.

In 1989, however, Chadacre decided to close and the estate was sold. This meant that the county-run Farm Training Centre also had to close as their site disappeared; equipment, students and even buildings were transferred to Otley where possible. After the sale of the Chadacre Estate, the FTCAT loan money was repaid and Lord Iveagh set up the Chadacre Agricultural Trust as a charity with the object of providing grants for agricultural education and research in East Anglia.

Otley College 1986

Otley, on the other hand, was thriving. Alexander Ferguson had taken over as principal in 1986, and had plans for expanding the college. Relations with the Trust were good with weekly meetings, a farm diary kept to organise work, and farm information being circulated to students as teaching material not only for the agricultural students but also for business studies. In 1988, the college had estate management training courses approved and the farm records became a valuable resource.

The Trust had been making annual grants to the

college to support student overseas visits and in 1987 the annual grant rose to £2,500. An additional grant was given to purchase arboricultural equipment, including climbing harnesses, ropes, spurs and helmets, to enable them to maintain the new broadleaf woodland. Students were walking the fields regularly, and the college asked for more land for car parking as well as use of the grain store. Alexander Ferguson was concerned, however, with the limited number of trials and demonstrations now being carried out on the farm, but S&P wanted to complete their farm improvements before taking on new work.

The lease was reviewed: it still had 80 years to run and there had been no proper review for the last few years to take into account the extra land – now totalling 38.95 acres – and buildings. The trustees agreed that they should pay £6,250 for the first year, and £12,500 thereafter and there would be another review in ten years time. It was also foreseen that the college would shortly be able to take over the old grain store, and would be given Charity Farmhouse when it became vacant. The college were also asking for more land for car parking as many of the students were driving to the site. As the Trust were also giving grants to the college the actual rent was partially offset, but trustees recognised that this was part of their plan to support agricultural education.

In 1989, Capt Sheepshanks had been asked to be a governor of Otley College to further good relations and to keep the Trust informed about the building plans. Due to pressure of work, however, his place was taken by F Barker. The college, however, continued to feel that relations could be further improved, and asked, for example, if Paul Creasey could come to discuss the spraying and manuring policy with students.

In 1990, it was agreed that the farm manager should lunch at the college twice a week and attend formal meetings. In addition, students would be allowed access to agreed areas of the farm each year for experience in ploughing, cultivation, drilling, manuring and spraying.

Elections and Committee Changes 1989

Once again county council elections meant a change in personnel for the trustees. In August 1989, Capt Sheepshanks was re-elected chairman and H A Mitson became the vice chairman. Other attending trustees were P G Batho, M D Cornish, Dr A P Draycott and B N Hinton. The agent, W H Marshall attended, and apologies were received from P B Atkinson, C W Smith and J H Taylor. As three additional trustees might also be appointed it was proposed that F Barker, a former vice chairman, should be asked to serve again if he was willing. It was also announced that E C Barnes was retiring as assistant agent after many years of service, and he was thanked by the chairman.

Lt Col Tomkin had become an additional trustee in 1985 to negotiate the redundancy of the farm manager, but had left the committee in November 1988 as his work was done.

Morley Research Centre

In November 1989, one important agenda item was an approach from Morley Research Centre to hold Mid-Anglian Trials Group (MATG) trials at the demonstration farm. The director, S P McClean, had visited the farm and was enthusiastic about the possibilities for co-operation. ADAS was by now having its funding curtailed by the government so the Trust welcomed this approach as a way of hosting valuable local trials. Morley would pay compensation if the trial site fell below the expected yield so it would not affect the profits of the farm. The 1990 harvest would be the third year of Morley trials at Crow's Hall Farm, Debenham, and the farmer decided that he wanted to pull out of the scheme, and thus the move to a farm dedicated to demonstrating the best in Suffolk farming was of mutual benefit to Morley and the Trust. Members would be visiting the plots monthly from April to July so the trial site needed to be close to a road. The Trust agreed to invite Morley to the farm but the decision came too late for the 1991 season and so the move was postponed. The Trust did, however, offer a grant of £10,000 to Morley to facilitate the move whenever it could take place.

Rhizomania

In 1987 a source of rhizomania was found at a farm near Bury St Edmunds, which was identified by ELISA analysis as Beet Necrotic Yellow Vein Virus. For Suffolk with its large acreage of sugar beet this was a potential disaster, which led to immediate precautionary measures throughout the area to prevent the spread of infection. British Sugar was consulted on precautions which should be taken.

Power in Action 1989 could have brought infection onto the farm so in order to avoid this all machinery had to be washed in baths of disinfectant before entering the farm. The measures worked and no infection occurred on the demonstration farm.

Residual Estate 1989

The tenant of Venn Farm at Witnesham died in November 1989, but the Agricultural Land Tribunal sent an application for a new tenancy for his widow, Mrs V M Cooke, and her son, R Cooke. The Trust would have preferred to gain possession of the farm and issued a notice to quit. The situation was complicated by the fact that Mrs Cooke was herself 75 years old and would not be able to farm the property by herself, but her son, Richard, had been born at the farm and had been farming it for some years in addition to owning 74 acres of land at Church Farm, Whitton. Negotiations went on for many months but in April 1991, the Cookes agreed to vacate the farmhouse, but wanted to keep the farm until after the harvest. By 1992, both the land and the farmhouse had been sold, raising a sum of £202,000.

Hope Farm at Sproughton also had an ageing tenant, Mr Barber. In 1989, he asked for permission to store caravans on an unused orchard area as an alternative source of income and the Trust agreed. The tenant was asked in 1991 if he would surrender some land so that it might be offered to the college for practical training, but the tenant refused this suggestion. In 1993, the rent for the farm was increased, but he went to appeal against the rent rise for the caravan storage land and was adamant that he still did not wish to retire from the farm.

Red House Farm, Ashbocking

In 1991 two parcels of land became available adjoining the B1078 at Ashbocking and Barham Green. The trustees had been looking for land ever since their move to Otley, and had pursued several other possible land purchase opportunities with no success. These fields, however, consisted of 281 acres of medium to heavy land with good access and the purchase would provide work for a second member of staff on the farm despite the closure of the beef unit. Further investigations by the agent were promising: the land was good, but the drainage needed improvement. Eventually, the decision was made to refuse the land at Barham Green, but to purchase 182 acres of Red House Farm at Ashbocking at a cost of £255,100. This amount was raised from the sale of Venn Farm and treasury stock for the value of £53,536.

The farm buildings were occupied by Woodbridge Engineering Company Ltd, and there was planning permission for a new farm cottage. All hedges had been removed, and the fields remodelled, so tree planting and conservation work would be needed. The owner had recently dug a pond in the corner of OS230, and this needed landscaping and conservation work.

By November 1991 the land had been purchased and work began on drilling winter wheat and break crops of linseed, oilseed rape, sugar beet and winter beans. Work began on draining the land after the 1992 harvest. This was costed at £18,000, so the Trust decided to proceed incrementally, and part of the land could become set-aside in the meantime.

John R Forrest and the Trust Committee

In 1991, J H Taylor resigned from the committee and John R Forrest was suggested as a replacement. As a farmer at Stowmarket and a past chairman of the Mid-Anglian Trials Group, the trustees felt that he would be an admirable asset to the committee; he was approached and agreed to serve; in November 1991 he attended his first meeting. The following year he took the place of F Barker on the Otley College board of governors.

Demonstration Farm 1992

In 1992, it was agreed that 7.22 acres of West Middle Field should be leased to the college, along with Charity Farmhouse, which had just become available. The college were also asking for the old grain store at Charity, but could not pay a high rent. A decision to transfer it was deferred.

The farm was now thriving, but unfortunately again the farm manager decided to leave. His place was taken by Tim Whitehead – the sixth manager to be appointed.

Cropping figures from 1991 showed the improvements in standards under the care of Paul Creasey and S&P.

Crops	1987		1991	
Winter Wheat	42.97 ha	5.70 tonnes/ha	78.71 ha	8.37 tonnes/ha
Linseed	6.30ha	0.98 tonnes/ha	24.11 ha	1.99 tonnes/ha
Oilseed rape	32.19ha	3.37 tonnes/ha	17.12 ha	3.31 tonnes/ha
Field beans	15.56ha	2.97 tonnes/ha	—	—
Sugar beet	—	—	6.5 ha	43.86 tonnes/ha
Winter barley	18.18 ha	4.82 tonnes/ha	—	—
Return on capital to tenants	12%		18%	

Paul had also improved relations with the college students during his brief time at the farm, and would be hard to replace. The trustees decided to send Tim, his replacement, on an ATB Supervisory Course at the Management Training Centre at Stoneleigh in 1993. From this course, Tim would gain a NEBS qualification in Supervisory Management, a nationally recognised qualification. It was also thought that this might prove to be an incentive to keep him in the post for a longer period.

One of the results of the increased yields was yet another urgent need for additional grain storage. The agent was asked to look at the existing buildings to see if any could be adapted, but none were suitable. The two existing silos were of 200 tonnes capacity, but while one had a Shivers Circulator in-bin drying system, the other had a low volume aeration floor only. This meant that grain was dried in the first silo, and then transferred to the second. In addition, the elevator system was decaying and sometimes broke down, causing a loss of the facility. The new Food Safety Act of 1990 meant a higher standard for storage, and the old store at Charity did not meet the new requirements. Thus, the farm needed new storage, or grain would have to be sold direct from the combine so that in wet weather the farm would be at the mercy of dealers who would charge for the drying. The agent recommended a new portal farm building measuring 80 feet by 65 feet by 18 feet, with low cost drying ducts and a central fan tunnel, which would store 1,000 tonnes at a cost of £7,500. If the Charity store was not brought up to standard another store measuring 60 feet by 40 feet would be needed to accommodate 450 tonnes of wheat at a cost of £4,500.

In April 1993, the trustees gave permission for the new store, but thought that work might be done in stages as the costs were high. In addition, the concrete outside the Charity store was in a bad condition and might cause accidents so should be replaced, along with faulty guttering.

At the same meeting it was agreed to give the college £25,000 towards a new extension and hoped that a conference room in the new buildings might be made available to the Trust for meetings. The new building would also contain a larger library on the first floor, reflecting the fact that the college was about to embark on degree courses in conjunction with the University of East Anglia.

NOTES

1 University of Essex, Department of Economics, Module EC329, Lecture on 'The Management of Agriculture in Europe' by Alastair McAuley.
2 Howkins, Alun. *The Death of Rural England*. London: Routledge, 2003. pp 228–233.

Chapter Thirteen

1993–1999
Conservation in the Countryside

National Agricultural Scene

Following the United Kingdom's withdrawal from the European Exchange Rate Mechanism (ERM) in 1992, the country experienced years of recession, so much so that Norman Tebbit MP referred to ERM as 'Eternal Recession Mechanism'. Unemployment figures rose steeply, house prices fell and industry faltered. Britain was not the only country affected – Italy, in particular, suffered at the same time.

On 1 November 1993, the Maastricht Treaty came into force, having been signed the previous year. However, uncertainty over ratification by France and Denmark led to market swings, but the British government refused to allow a referendum on the treaty's merits for Britain. Opposition to the social clauses, insisted on by the Conservatives, was criticised by Labour and Liberal Democrat MPs, and John Major's government almost suffered defeat. The treaty set out the route for monetary convergence, leading to the establishment of the Eurozone, but Britain refused to abandon sterling, and thus continued to hover on the sidelines of the European Union rather than become central players in negotiations. On 1 May 1999, the Amsterdam Treaty was signed, modifying the clauses of the first treaty, and paving the way for a further enlargement of the constituent countries.

The McSharry reforms to European Common Agricultural Policy began to have an impact in 1993, with changes in farm subsidies and the land set-aside scheme affecting farms in 1994. Initially, a minimum of 15 per cent of land which had been cropped in the 1993 harvest had to be taken out of production, but this figure gradually fell to ten per cent by 2000. The first regulations also stipulated that a different area must be used for the quota each year, but this regulation was later revised so that flora and fauna could develop undisturbed on the same areas of uncropped land. In addition, it was later agreed that some environmental land, such as woodland, could be used. It was also agreed that industrial crops, such as oilseed rape land, might be grown, although there were penalties for this practice.

Demonstration Farm and Otley College 1993

Average farm sizes were still increasing during this period, and trustees found that they had to acquire more land to make it representative of the farms of the county. Farm staff had dwindled from four men, plus temporary help during busy periods, to two men, and the second man was only needed to cope with the demands of the trials and demonstrations. Otley College was thus finding it increasingly difficult to recruit agricultural students and were forced to diversify into alternative subjects – such as game keeping, arboriculture, business management, sports turf and equine studies – subjects which fell outside the aims and objectives of the Felix Cobbold Agricultural Trust.

For the Trust, 1993 marked the year in which it began to lead the county into managing farmland not only for profit and the production of food, but for stewardship of the countryside and environmental protection.

Reorganisation of sugar beet processing continued in this period, with the closure of the Kings Lynn factory in 1994. The Trust, however, grew the crop throughout the period, which could be processed at the nearby Ipswich factory.

Trustees and Staff Changes

At the April 1993 meeting it was announced that Tim Whitehead, farm manager, would be leaving in July, so a fifth manager needed to be recruited. David Allerton from Strutt & Parker was also leaving, and the Trust estate would be supervised by Hector Wykes-Sneyd in future.

As this was an election year, the Trust also lost its chairman, Capt Robin Sheepshanks, who had been a trustee for 25 years. At the July meeting, K J Doran was elected chairman with H A Mitson remaining as vice chairman. Other trustees were J R Forrest, Mrs J I Girling, M J Gleed and B N Hinton. P F Bye and C W M Penn sent their apologies, along with P B Atkinson, the treasurer, who sent P G Edwards in his place. The agent, William Marshall attended, together with Christopher Storey as assistant agent. Hector Wykes-Sneyd and D J Cousins from Strutt & Parker were also present though this grouping was short-lived because, in 1994, Hector retired and the Strutt & Parker representatives became C A Monk and his assistant, William Gennell. In 1994, there were also changes to the trustees with Sir Peter Batho and R F Durrant attending meetings.

The changes to the trustees and farm staff meant that decisions were delayed and the project of handing-over the Charity grain store to the college continued to carry over from year to year. However, the ability to appoint three 'additional trustees' meant that Dr Philip Draycott, with all his expertise on sugar beet production and experience of the Trust, could be reappointed despite no longer being a county councillor.

The seventh farm manager was Christopher Hayward. He was a 24-year-old farmer's son from Oxfordshire with an honours degree in Agricultural Business Management from Wye College. Tim left to take up a post as assistant manager to the Velcourt Group in Suffolk. Despite the problems for Christopher in settling into his new job, together with trustee and S&P changes, the farm was flourishing.

Set-aside Land and Conservation

During 1993, Monsanto had been running a series of articles on set-aside management, and used the demonstration farm as one of four targeted farms. This not only created great interest in the press, but the fact that the organisers of the trials regarded the standards of farming practice at the farm as far higher than any other farm in the survey gave the Trust a much-needed return to respect in farming circles. Tim Whitehead had been adapting the change in soil conditions as the

seasons progressed to produce a management strategy. He had mole-ploughed the land and the seed beds were prepared for following crops earlier than would normally be possible. For the first year of the scheme, 15 per cent (or 23 hectares) were taken out of production, but the accounts for the year looked healthy due to a combination of a fall in interest rates, Britain's withdrawal from the ERM and arable area payments given to support the introduction of set-aside. The farm staff, Tim, and then Christopher, together with Barry Quinton, were also undertaking contract farming which brought in welcome extra revenue.

In 1994, the rules changed again and the Trust was given the option of non-rotational set-aside instead of the 15 per cent rotational land of 1993. It was decided that 30 hectares would become set-aside in 1994.

The Trust was still engaged in lengthy negotiations to change the route of footpaths on the estate to the boundaries of the new fields. In 1993, this work was being partly funded by a grant from the Countryside Commission.

LEAF Farm – Linking the Environment and Farming

The Trust had been exploring the possibility of becoming a LEAF demonstration farm, and in December 1993 it was finally adopted as a member. The charity was run to promote environmentally responsible farming. 'It links farmers, consumers, and food businesses in activities and initiatives that build knowledge. It encompasses the whole-farm principle of Integrated Farm Management (IFM) to achieve a balance between the best of modern technology and sound traditional methods.'[1] The UK Agriculture website defines Integrated Farm Management as 'a whole farm system providing efficient profitable products that are environmentally responsible. Integrated Farm Management works by integrating beneficial natural processes into modern farming techniques and ensures that high standards of stewardship and environmental care are practised.'[2]

The Trust had prepared by carrying out an audit in June 1993 which proved a useful exercise in taking an overall view of the farming practices. In January 1994, an Environment Audit Workshop was held at the farm to share knowledge of this work with the farming community.

Morley Trials

The second coup of the year was the transfer of the Morley trials to the demonstration farm. As government funding had dwindled for agricultural research, the industry had had to fund its own trials, financed through Levy Boards, the Sugar Beet Research and Education Committee (SBREC) and the Home-Grown Cereals Authority (HGCA) and Development Committee. The Morley Research Group, founded in 1908, had become a major contractor for both the HGCA and SBREC. In East Anglia it had around 3,000 members who were estimated to produce around five per cent of UK winter wheat and 25 per cent of sugar beet. The Mid-Anglian Trials Group, established in 1985, needed a site with the highest environmental standards, and now that it was a LEAF member, the demonstration farm seemed ideal. Initial costs of the move would be at least £5,000 with extra travel and staff time as it was ten miles further than the existing Morley site, but the Trust were helping to fund the move. The Trust also offered another £5,000 in 1998 and a further £15,000 for the next three years.

Trials for 1994 were limited but, by the harvest of 1995, included fungicide responses, cultivar evaluation, Vician beans, the seed rate on variety Caspar of spring beans, weed control, broad-leaved weed control and fusarium seed treatments on winter wheat. These trials covered 8.2 hectares on 1,650 plots. This was a major achievement for the Trust: at last the farm would be fulfilling all its aims and objectives and becoming a centre of research and development for the area. As part of the new assessment process before the move, the Trust asked the Soil Survey of England and Wales to prepare a survey of the demonstration farm and to produce a large-scale plan suitable for teaching/demonstration purposes.

The pond which had been dug on the new Ashbocking land needed developing to provide good habitats for wildlife, and it was arranged that the new College Environmental Studies students would prepare a design for the project, with funding from the Trust.

As a further environment measure at this time S&P applied to the Hedgerow Incentive Scheme for a grant to put in two km of grass edging which would be kept for at least ten years. The public would be allowed access to the strips, and the Country Landowners Association came to Otley for their open day in May 1995 to see the new landscape changes.

Otley College Development

As mentioned above, the college had begun to teach degree courses in Environmental Conservation with a link to the University of East Anglia. As part of this development it needed a larger library and professional librarian to develop the stock. They asked for £18,000 or £20,000 in funding from the Trust but the Trust limited this to £10,000. However, they were also continuing to fund student study tours; in 1994 this amounted to a grant of £15,000 and the following year this rose to £20,000.

The new Suffolk Building College Library, 1993. The following year, as the stock grew, the library was given two of the adjacent classrooms for extra storage and study space. (R Thomas)

The library development also meant there was a need for an online broadband link to the UEA library, which meant upgrading the local telephone exchange to provide an optical fibre connection. For 1995, this was a pioneering development. The Trust granted a way-leave for the new optical fibre connections, and later in the year granted a small piece of land to house a new transformer kiosk to increase the college's electricity supply. The library rapidly expanded until it absorbed the classrooms on the upper floor of B block to include quiet study space for the degree students, a learning support centre and a computer room. So great was the demand for power during the winter of 1993–4 that periodically the supply failed, all the lights went out and computer screens went blank.

The Trust in action: Kenneth J Doran, chairman of the Felix Thornley Cobbold Trust, giving a cheque for £10,000 to Alexander Ferguson, college principal, to fund a computer link to the University of East Anglia.

The land agent was concerned with the college's change of direction and asked whether it should also change its objectives in line with the change to the industry. The college lease was also affected by this clash of objectives. It was agreed to seek the views of the Charity Commission and also to hold discussions to try to form a common business plan between Otley College and the Trust.

One complication in late 1995 was that the college now received funding from the Further Education Funding Council (FEFC) instead of the county council, and were thus forced to accept any opportunity for grants that might present themselves, in whatever subjects might attract students. They were also anxious to develop residential accommodation and asked for another ten acres of land for a residence and for sports

pitches from either West Middle or Charity Field.

In 1995, the college also wanted to build a new machinery workshop to accommodate the larger machines now being developed. Initially, they proposed a portal frame building of 145 feet by 120 feet and asked for funding. They were in a quandary as the site was becoming congested and there was little spare space. However, even if space was free, since the land was leased rather than owned, the college could not sell or lease land to raise funds, unlike many other colleges in the country. The Trust considered ceding the lease to the college, but this meant that the college might move away from agriculture completely and the Trust would have no control. This dilemma has continued until the present day.

Demonstration Farm 1995

In June 1995, Chris Hayward, the farm manager, decided to move back to his father's farm in Oxfordshire. The frequent changes of manager were causing a problem for the Trust as the job had become ever more demanding. Trustees debated therefore whether to employ a slightly older and experienced manager – perhaps someone who had already been a trials manager or assistant farm manager. The eighth appointee for the job was Matthew Ward, who was offered a slightly higher salary than his predecessor. He was a married man, so Stanaway Farmhouse was refurbished to bring more rooms into use.

In the summer of 1995, Morley agreed to move a member of staff to the farm to supervise the trials, and Ben Freer arrived on site. As a resident agronomist, his presence was of immense value to the farm and to the staff and students of the college.

In 1995 the set-aside rules were changed yet again, so that only 12 per cent of land needed to be withdrawn from cropping and the extra land was drilled with spring wheat and oilseed rape. By this time, the new grain store was in operation, but the old conveyor system was failing and needed replacing. Grain was moved by mobile auger and an adaptation of the bin system.

In the autumn of 1995, the draining of the Ashbocking land was also completed, with one large block of 65 acres of gently sloping land formed from old fields, which increased the value of the holding.

The Trust had paid for the satellite yield mapping of West Middle field, and the farm had been soil mapped, but to satellite map the whole farm would cost £2,500. At this point, Dr Ann Willington was consulted as to the way in which satellite maps might be used. Some of the problems were resolved when a seminar on Precision Farming was held at Otley College in March 1996 organised by Strutt & Parker and the Farming and Wildlife Group. The seminar used yield maps and soil analysis maps from the demonstration farm as study material.

At the March meeting of the Trust, the committee resolved to continue to research the new technology, and Dr Draycott asked for copies of all soil tests. A new soil map had also been prepared which gave clearer information on the uses of the results.

In 1996, the Trust made another land purchase – 65 acres of land adjoining Pear Tree Farm – so overall the farm now comprised 550 acres which was closer to the current average farm size for the area. The Trust was still searching for some light land in the area, but none became available.

Farm Environmental Improvements

At Stanaway Farm in February 1997 a Sentinel Plant was installed with the blessing of the Environment Agency to deal with the residues of chemical sprays from the sprayer trailer and accidental spills in the yard. The plant used a special agent which caused flocculation of the chemical particles resulting in one per cent residues which were dried and taken away, and 99 per cent residue of fresh water.

In 1997 also the Countryside Stewardship Scheme was extended to include managed arable field margins and hedgerow management, and the Trust adopted this scheme for the farm. Grass margins were good for conservation and also gave access in connection with the trials and general field operation. Some permissive paths were added and an additional payment was forthcoming for them. This was well-timed with the final end to disputes over the rerouted farm footpaths; an official opening day was held on 7 June 1997. The farm staff erected new way markers and signposts, and a leaflet was produced by Suffolk County Council and the Countryside Commission.

The margins of the pond at Red House Farm had now been replanted to encourage wildlife using students' designs. Bat boxes and owl boxes were installed around the farm.

Beef Unit

In 1997, the Trust agreed to a 50/50 partnership with the college in purchasing and rearing 40 calves. The calves were to spend 14 weeks at Otley and then move to Stanaway. They were then to be fed on Brewers' Grains until they were slaughtered in the autumn 1998 at about 550 kg live weight. The profits would be shared between the college and the Trust. Rumenco had been helping the college with a successful sheep unit trial, so they agreed to sponsor the calf trials also by providing the grains, minerals, laboratory analyses, barley and other feed stuffs. Stanaway Farm straw was to be collected by college labour and farm machinery used. Neil Ridley from the college oversaw the trial on a day-to-day basis, reporting to Jonathan West as head of agriculture, and the work was co-ordinated with Matthew Ward as farm manager and David Thornton of Rumenco. Twenty Herefords and 20 Continental cross animals were bought and RSPCA Freedom Foods standards of care were used to demonstrate a livestock system at a LEAF farm. The unit aimed to show a profitable unit with high levels of accountability and welfare, and it was hoped to generate media attention, and perhaps also some profit. The unit ran into problems with the first batch of calves, however, in June 1997 as three calves died of pneumonia.

In 1998 it appeared to be doing well, and the college gained a link not only with Rumenco, but also Tesco as a possible outlet for the meat. By the time the first batch went to slaughter a profit of £665.49 had been realised to split between the Trust and the college. One further animal had died which reduced the profit slightly.

Trust Committee 1995

The trustees changed slightly in 1995, with Kenneth J Doran in the chair, and H A Mitson re-elected as vice chairman. Other trustees were John Forrest, Joan Girling, John Gleed, Bruce N Hinton, C W M Penn and P F Bye. Dr A P Draycott was again appointed as an additional trustee and Dr D Mettrick was treasurer together with Peter Atkinson. William H Marshall was the appointed land agent with Chris G Story as his assistant and F G Fosdick as clerk.

In March 1996, however, Herbert A Mitson retired after 25 years as a trustee, and John Forrest became vice chairman in his place. The replacement nominative trustee was Michael C Evelegh.

In 1998 there were more elections, but Kenneth J Doran remained in the chair, with John Forrest as vice chairman. The other trustees were Michael Evelegh, Joan Girling, John Gleed, Bruce Hinton and Christopher Penn with Dr Philip Draycott as an additional trustee. The treasurer was Peter Atkinson and the land agent and valuer was William Marshall.

Otley College 1997

Plans for the new machinery workshop were proceeding, and the Trust agreed to contribute 40 per cent of the cost up to a maximum of £60,000 when it should be required. The college planned to demolish the old machinery workshop when the new building was completed, and to place a new dining block on the place. In its turn, the old dining area would become a student common room.

At the same time, the college was still finding it difficult to recruit agricultural students, so were forced yet again to widen their subject base. They joined in a consortium with three other colleges to form the Suffolk Business School with financial support from Suffolk TEC to provide management training for small and medium-sized businesses.

Three college tenants appeared at this time: Young Farmers' Club had an office on the campus to organise events for the students in 1997. The same year, Tastes of Anglia moved into an office in Charity Farmhouse and helped to market the college goat milk products. The following year, Otley and Orwell Training Group were created at the college; Matthew Ward was the secretary and Richard Garnham was the chairman.

The college was interested in developing a course on organic farming, including setting up a herd of organic sheep, and wondered whether the Trust would be able to provide some organic land. This proved not to be possible, so the college arranged for the students to work on an organic farm at Looms Farm, Burgh, about four miles away.

Demonstration Farm 1997–9

The farm was now attracting a large number of visitors. Apart from members of the Mid-Anglian Trials Group who visited the 14 hectares of trials five times a year,

other visitors to the farm were 50 German farmers, together with members of the NFU and three French visitors. In June 1997, members of the Suffolk Agricultural Association walked the farm and soil profile pits were dug to show the relation between the high and low yield soil and the results of the Precision Farming soil and yield maps were available, which showed the levels of pH, P, K and iron.

Appropriately, the farm was awarded first place in the Medium Class Farm Competition run by Suffolk Agricultural Association, and third place in the Suffolk Farms Competition run by the Farming and Wildlife Advisory Group (FWAG).

In March 1998, 20 teachers visited, organised by the Suffolk Farm Project Officer, Jane Ferris, and the following year 25 teachers came, many of whom had heard about the value of the event from previous visitors. It was planned to repeat these visits in the future and the Trust asked the Suffolk Farm Project (SFP) if they could help to produce a teachers' pack to provide additional information.

The work on the farm continued with undiminished pressure. Matthew showed a party of Ukrainians round the farm, the Suffolk WI, a group from the Doncaster branch of the NFU and representatives from Levington Agriculture, plus students from two middle schools in Suffolk.

In June of the same year, Matthew Ward announced that he was joining the staff of Strutt & Parker and leaving the farm. The ninth manager was James Molden from Leominster: James was half New Zealander and had an HND in Agriculture from Harper Adams Agricultural College. He had won an award for becoming the top industrial placement student in 1995/1996. Almost as soon as James started his job, he had to host a visit of Finnish farmers and French students. Power in Action was still visiting the farm every other year and these demonstrations continued to draw a large number of visitors to the site.

By now, the work on the farm was demanding a high degree of technical input, so the farm valued the on-site presence of agronomist Ben Freer from Morley; Matthew Ward had also qualified as an agronomist together with Gemmil from S&P. Nevertheless, so critical was the need for scientific information that S&P asked for an additional agronomist to visit the farm two to three times during the season to advise on sugar beet.

A Power in Action machinery demonstration during the 1990s from the (East) Suffolk Machinery Club. Demonstrations were held at first annually and then in alternate years on the demonstration farm from 1968 to 2006. (Brian Bell)

One trial which was suggested by trustee Dr Draycott was that of keeping beet in store for 14 weeks to see if the sugar content was affected. The result was that the sugar content fell, but only by 0.5 per cent. The crop yield this year (1998) had been ten tonnes an acre higher than in 1997, and the following year the farm was in the top five per cent of national performance.

Altogether the farm seemed to be prospering under this form of management. It was producing a good profit, which gave credibility to the farm but in 1998 the strong pound sterling affected profits, which fell from £65,858 to £62,049. The farm was still, however, slightly below the county average in size: at this point 222.5 ha were being farmed, but the average was 240 ha. In addition, they were leasing 22 ha to the college.

The environmental audit carried out each year demonstrated the possibility of producing a commercial return in conjunction with a caring approach to the environment. The Morley trials were going well,

and there was a good working relationship between the college and the farm manager. Matthew and James had been passing on details of the farm finances and management to the college, thus providing study material for the students. James Molden began writing about the farm trials for the *Farmer's Weekly* in 1998, which raised the profile of the Trust in the media. The Trust decided to adopt a logo and wondered whether to run a schools' competition to find a design.

At this point the trustees also began to consider setting up a visitor centre at Stanaway Farm to cater for the many visitors. Discussions in March 1999 highlighted the need for the provision of better toilet facilities for visitors and it was felt that a meeting space for about 65 people would be useful together with a small kitchen. An office might also be provided for the Morley agronomist in the building. Finally, a sub-committee was set up to further the proposals, which consisted of the chairman, the vice chairman and Mrs Joan Girling.

NOTES

1   See LEAF website (www.leafuk.org) for more information.
2   See UK Agriculture website (www.ukagriculture.com) for more information on Integrated Farm Management.

Chapter Fourteen

2000-2006
Decline of the Farm

International Political Climate

The first decade of the century witnessed world catastrophes that influenced the economic life of the nation as profoundly as the periods of the two world wars. In 2001, the attack on the World Trade Centre towers rocked confidence in trade in the immediate aftermath, but also led to the invasion of Iraq and then Afghanistan. The disruption of oil supplies and uncertainties over gas pipelines and population rise, combined with the rising fear over climate change and a series of natural catastrophes like floods and droughts, have all led to anxiety over food security and sustainability.

International Agricultural Measures

At the Berlin Summit in March 1999, the EU agreed to a new CAP reform policy, Agenda 2000, to cover the years 2000–2006. The statement said that 'By bringing the price of EU agricultural products closer to world prices, competitiveness on both domestic and world market will be enhanced'.[1]

This reform proposed a reduction in market support prices of 15 per cent for cereals, 15 per cent for milk and milk products from 2005, and 20 per cent for beef and veal. These reductions would 'be partly offset by an increase in direct aid payments, thus contributing to ensuring a fair standard of living for farmers'.[2]

The policy also laid emphasis on rural development and the stability of rural populations, by 'introducing a comprehensive rural development policy which recognises the multifunctional nature of agriculture and which promotes measures to support the broader rural economy. Measures have been brought together in one regulation which aims to contribute to the regeneration of rural areas and the promotion of diversification'.[3] It also emphasised the importance of environmental protection.

Animal Diseases

For agriculture in Britain, the decade began with two further epidemics: swine flu and foot and mouth disease. In August 2000 an outbreak of classic swine flu emerged on a farm at Sudbourne, near Woodbridge, and the same company owned a farm in Essex where a second outbreak was found a few days later. The emergency lasted until 30 December, but led to 53,000 pigs (which included infected farm animals and 'dangerous contact' animals) being slaughtered at a cost of £25 million for East Anglia.

The 2001 epizootic of foot and mouth disease was first detected at Cheale Meats abattoir in Essex and affected pigs from Buckinghamshire and the Isle of Wight. Since 1967, and the previous outbreak of disease, many slaughterhouses had closed, resulting in the transport of animals for slaughter over long distances. In the intervening years, a second change was that control passed to the European Community by directive 85.11; in 1980, a directive prohibiting farm burials of sick animals was passed unless the site was authorised by the Environment Agency. Thus, infected carcases were driven through the countryside and within a few days outbreaks of disease emerged in Devon, Wales, Cornwall, southern Scotland and the Lake District. However, at first MAFF insisted that culled animals could not be disposed of on site and must be taken to a rendering plant in Widnes, Lancashire, but this decision was quickly reversed with the evidence of so much contamination, and slaughtered animals were burnt on their farms. MAFF insisted that not only were animals on the infected site to be destroyed, but also all animals within three kilometres of known cases should be slaughtered. Two days after the emergence of the disease in Essex the EU imposed a worldwide ban on all British exports of livestock, meat and animal products. Several other countries were also affected, including the Netherlands, Ireland and France.

The effects on the countryside were disastrous: as the disease spread rapidly there was a ban on all animal movements and public rights of way in infected areas were closed, causing most of the countryside to shut down. Tourism was hit, animals suffered when kept on overgrazed fields and there was public horror at newsreel images of pyres of burning carcases. Regulations changed with Brigadier Alex Birtwistle being called in by the government to manage the situation. Animals were moved to the Great Orton Airfield for slaughter before being buried in mass graves. The pits were surrounded by 12-metre-deep walls to prevent contamination of the water supply as up to 93,000 animals were killed in a single week. The site has since been monitored closely.

Local elections were postponed while the emergency continued. The final cull was in January 2002, but some restrictions on livestock movements were retained until later in the year. It was estimated that over 4 million animals had been killed, at a cost of £8 billion to the British economy. It was also a public relations disaster; MAFF became a casualty, due to its failure to manage the crisis more quickly, and was merged with other departments to become the Department of the Environment, Food and Rural Affairs (DEFRA). Several public enquiries were also launched to identify lessons which could be learnt to prevent another disaster.

Trust Committee 2000

In 1999, Kenneth J Doran died and his place as chairman was taken by John R Forrest with B J C Moore as vice chairman. Other trustees were Mike Evelegh, Bruce Hinton, Dr Draycott, Mrs Joan Girling, John Gleed, L M Homer and Christopher Penn.

The agent reported at this time that he felt there were too few Trust meetings and that there were now substantial funds but too few projects. He was also concerned that there were so many people involved in running the farm that communications were difficult. He asked whether there could be up to five meetings a year with five pre-agenda meetings. He also urged the Trust to consider moving into the gap caused by the loss of ADAS involvement, and perhaps help to co-ordinate other agriculture-related trusts in East Anglia.

Demonstration Farm 2000

The farm in 2000 covered 549 acres, but the regional average had by now increased to 743 acres. The trend towards larger farm sizes was clearly moving so quickly that the Trust land always remained slightly below average in spite of their purchases. Farm income was falling and it seemed that the only way to increase income was to farm yet more land, or to cut activities – options which were not in accordance with Trust objectives. The farm was successful in gaining a contract to farm the Tuddenham Hall Estate, only three miles from the demonstration farm. This spread the costs as both soil and cropping patterns were similar.

Prices were low and CAP changes meant that income from grants would drop further. Indeed, profit for the year was £64 per ha, whereas the previous year raised £259 per ha. Break crops were less profitable and cereal prices were better, but a policy of sustainable rotation fulfilled the integrated farm management objectives. To counteract the falling price of cereals some were being sold forward, some at fixed prices.

A table completed in 2000 of average yields over a five-year period showed:

Crops	Yield per ha / acres	Ha grown / acres
Milling wheat	8.6 / 3.5	50 / 123
Feed wheat	9.2 / 3.7	70 / 173
Winter barley	8.5 / 3.4	20 / 50
Winter oilseed rape	3.7 / 1.5	30 / 74
Winter beans	4.1 / 1.7	20 / 50
Sugar beet	52 / 21.3	67 / 17

The joint college/farm beef trial sponsored by Rumenco and Tesco suffered a loss in 2000 as five animals died of bloat, so for the rest of the trial the animals were fed on a conventional diet.

There was a joint training day between the college and the farm in connection with the Eastern Region Development Plan scheme. Thus, throughout the winter and spring period 2000/1 there were over 340 visitors in all, from the Morley groups and others.

A group of college students were now working on an organic farm at Burgh, near Woodbridge, and the college again asked the Trust if they could provide organic land so that students would not have to travel away. Trustees asked Strutt & Parker for a report, who said that 21 ha could be converted over five years. There was, at present, a high demand and high return for organic produce, but the market was variable and the future uncertain, so they advised the trustees against the project. Indeed, the Government Organic Farming Scheme for 1999 had been oversubscribed twice, but no new funding had been announced and supermarkets were reducing the sales price of organic food. After consideration, trustees decided not to convert land.

Morley Trials on the Farm 2001

Morley trials were now covering 35 ha and, at the previous autumn visitor day, 57 visitors attended on one of the five scheduled visits for members. At the June Trust meeting in 2001 it was announced that Ben Freer was being promoted to a more senior post and would no longer be based on the farm.

James Molden, farm manager, succeeded in passing BASIS exams in 2001 and received the Bernie Orme Award as the year's most successful candidate. After this, he applied to take a three-year course run by the Worshipful Company of Farmers at Stoneleigh and asked for funding.

Morley now suggested that James Molden might become experiment co-ordinator in place of Ben Freer, although Ben would continue to oversee the project. Trustees agreed, with reservations, but wanted Molden's time working for Morley to be carefully recorded. They were also unhappy at the loss of a resident agronomist and asked for a replacement. However, James found that he spent less time away from the farm visiting Morley work at two other sites than had been anticipated – only 67 hours over three months as against an estimated five days per month – so the arrangement was allowed to continue for a further period.

Visitor Centre 2001

A sub-committee had been formed in 1999 to investigate converting the old grain store at Stanaway Farm into a visitor centre, and planning permission for the scheme was granted in 2000. At the same time, plans were made to convert the beef unit into a replacement grain store as soon as the college cattle were removed.

By 2001, some grant money had been identified and it appeared that conversion would cost £174,000. In November, however, the expected grant from MAFF was delayed due to the foot and mouth crisis; fortunately, additional money came from the East of England Development Agency. The situation changed with the demise of MAFF, but its replacement, DEFRA, offered a Rural Enterprise Scheme grant of 50 per cent of the costs, leaving the Trust to pay £115,000 after some adjustments. The architect for the project was David Pattenden from Ipswich.

Building work started early in 2002 as building regulations were due to change in March, which would have meant higher costs. The project was completed in September 2002. The centre was given the title of the Felix Cobbold Centre, with one room called the Thornley Room and the other, the Quinton Room, after Barry Quinton who had been working on the farm almost since its beginning in the 1960s. The opening ceremony was held on 21 November 2002, with local farmer, John Kerr, cutting the tape.

The Felix Cobbold visitor centre was constructed from the obsolete grain store at Stanaway Farm in 2002.
(Chris Lockwood)

The sub-committee realised that a separate manager was necessary to oversee the bookings and work of the centre, so in 2003, Rebecca Molden, the wife of the farm manager, was appointed. However, although a number of bookings were made in the first few months they were fewer than had been hoped, with many companies cutting back on outside events due to the financial climate. However, Strutt & Parker commented that they would expect a new centre to take two to three years to be established and produce a profit. The committee discussed a proposal to use the centre as a wedding venue, but this would mean new licensing and perhaps Charity Commission permission as this would not be agricultural use. It would also require a change in the facilities with additional soft furnishings – the idea was not pursued for the time being.

Rebecca also reported a number of building faults: the heating system was inadequate and noisy and visitors complained about the noise from the roof during rain storms. The kitchen was too small to permit 'in house' catering although external caterers were expensive, and there was also need for an office. Rebecca suggested that the garage might be converted to give the extra space.

College Cloven-hoofed Animals

At the outbreak of the foot and mouth crisis, the beef unit had already closed down after slaughter of the second batch of animals, with some loss due to the premature death of some animals. However, the college owned a herd of pigs and their presence during the outbreak threatened the closure of the college site. Due to the risk of contamination during the crisis, the scheduled teachers' day at the farm was moved to the Suffolk Showground.

The Trust agreed to house the college pigs as a temporary measure in September 2000 and in March 2001 all the college's cloven-hoofed animals – cattle, sheep and goats – were quickly moved to the farm as an emergency measure to allow the college year to carry on. The Trust were asked if they could keep the animals for a longer period, but any disease in the area would have closed down the demonstration farm as well as the college, so the trustees decided that they could no longer host any of the college animals and they were removed.

Conservation on the Farm

In 2000, there was an open day for LEAF, and in June of the same year, a Farming and Wildlife Group farm walk was also held. In 2001, the Trust arranged for a RSPB Volunteer and Farmer Alliance Survey of the farm. The RSPB were already providing management information on using set-aside land for bird conservation, and the survey found several red status species (threatened species), including quail, tree sparrows,

turtle doves, linnet, skylarks and song thrushes. There were also a number of amber status species such as dunnocks and goldfinches. In total, 55 species had been found.

James Molden suggested that the farm might be used for a shoot as a diversification project. However, after investigations it was agreed by trustees that only rough shooting might be allowed, and that any shooting would only be permitted if James took personal responsibility for the event. James found the project was not viable but decided to set up feeders on the set-aside land to encourage wild birds. After this, he organised rough shoots twice a year with a maximum of five guns to control the cock birds.

In 2001, the farm acquired a 24-metre trailed sprayer as liquid feed would give greater accuracy for trial work and Integrated Farm Management objectives. Spraying would be slower, but the spreader would cover more ground as it covered 24 metres instead of 18 metres.

College Lease 2000

After the retirement of Alexander Ferguson, the college had a new principal, John Pearson. The college governors were struggling with the finances after a period of exponential growth, and following substantial financial losses in 1999 they put in place a three-year recovery plan. Once again, the principal found that the leased land situation was a handicap and asked if the college might acquire the site and, once again, the trustees were unwilling to sell. They recognised that in the event of the college closure the site would go to its creditors and could be sold for purposes not compatible with Trust objectives. They noted, in addition that the existing lease did not cover the new buildings, such as the Food and Skills Building, an additional seven-acre field, or Charity Farmhouse, which had now been handed over for college use.

The trustees asked their lawyers to examine the lease. In the meantime, the existing rent was kept unchanged, but much of the money was being returned to the college in the form of grants for study tours, etc.

Trust Committee 2001–2002 and the Labour Group

The elections in 2001 were delayed due to the foot and mouth crisis. In March 2001, it was announced that the Labour Group had withdrawn from the Trust Committee, i.e. that Barry Moore, Michael Evelegh, Joan Girling, John Gleed and Christopher Penn had resigned. Their views were that whereas in the past the trustees had all been farmers or well connected with agriculture the county had now changed demographically. Thus, county councillors were now often from a non-farming background, and it was not appropriate for them to serve on an agricultural Trust.

The new committee did not meet until November 2001 as there was no summer meeting. At this meeting John R Forrest was in the chair, with Bruce Hinton as vice chairman. Other trustees were J Field, J Hore and D Thomas, with Dr P Draycott as an additional trustee. Apologies were received from C Barrow, S Sida-Lockett, L Homer and M More. Also attending were C A Monk and Matthew Ward from Strutt & Parker, Mr Mettrick and C Longden (for the treasurers to the Trust), J Gadsden (for the clerk) and Brian Prettyman (for the agent.)

William Marshall had retired as agent in November 2001, and Brian Williams took his place at this meeting. The committee heard that Suffolk County Council was being reorganised and that, in future, Brian Prettyman would attend meetings and would act as assistant to Brian Williams in Trust matters. The County Farms service was merged with the Operational Property Management under the Estates Manager. The County Farm policy was also under review: the size of the average holding had to increase over a 15-year period to remain viable in line with national trends.

In 2002, discussions with Suffolk County Council were held with regard to the composition of the Trust committee. The council was finding it difficult to appoint seven nominative trustees with agricultural links, so it was agreed that, in future, only four trustees had to be county councillors, and that three additional trustees might be appointed to make up the numbers. In June 2002, therefore, the Trust committee included John R Forrest, Bruce Hinton, Colin Barrow, John Field, J Clover and Dr Draycott.

In November, another proposal was discussed as the Labour Group were unwilling to stand, A Gillespie, principal assistant county solicitor, proposed that in future some trustees might be appointed from outside the council – Suffolk Agricultural Association (SAA), for example, might provide nominees. This would provide a new membership of three trustees from the county council, three from SAA and four others to be co-opted. The suggestion was accepted and the solicitor was asked to write to the Charity Commission to commence the process of change. At this meeting there had, in fact, been another change as Selwyn Pryor had replaced Colin Barrow.

Suffolk Agricultural Association was happy to be involved with the Trust, and three farmers of some standing in the community – Robert Baker, Bruce Kerr and George Harris – were invited to the June meeting in 2003 to meet what remained of the old committee, but Bruce Kerr then withdrew and was replaced with Stephen Cobbald.

Demonstration Farm 2001–2003

Work was continuing on precision farming, with a soil structure report on the Swiss Farm area completed in May 2002 by Bryan Davies, a soil management consultant from Cambridge University. It was a difficult year for farming as it became the wettest year for 250 years. On the farm, three barley fields were flooded, one of them experiencing a complete crop failure.

In June 2001, Strutt & Parker announced that Matthew Ward was moving to work in the Norfolk, Lincolnshire and Leicester area. This was a real loss to the farm; Ward's initial work as farm manager and his continued support for James Molden after his move to Strutt & Parker were invaluable.

In the autumn of 2002, John Pearson from the college gave a presentation on the plans for the improvement of the college site which was to be developed by the Derek Lovejoy Partnership. This showed the need for a large new car park to the west of the present site with parking for 480 cars and provision for buses. The college also wanted an area of field adjacent to the eastern boundary to be used for a residential block and sports field, and substantial funding for a new food research building to be built as part of Food (East Anglia) Skills and Technology (FeaST) initiative. They also asked for their lease to be extended to 150 years.

The trustees were sympathetic but proposed planting a buffer zone of trees between the sports field and Stanaway Farm. The problem of the lease was still outstanding and the trustees were still concerned that the college was developing away from their own core objectives.

In 2002, it was announced that James Molden had been successful in his Fertiliser Advisory Certificate and Training Scheme (FACTS) exam. James and Barry Quinton were now not only farming the demonstration farm, but also the Tuddenham Hall land. The first year of this contract achieved poor yields, so a lime analysis was carried out and the soil was found to be very acidic. In the second year, lime was applied and yields began to improve.

In 2003, it was agreed that Strutt & Parker should now manage not only the demonstration farm, but all the Trust properties. Suffolk County Council were to continue to provide legal and property advice and would appoint consultants. However, the provision of accounts and timely financial updates was proving to be delayed by a system whereby Strutt & Parker passed information to the county treasurer. A new computer system at the council offices helped for a time, but by 2003 there was a delay in auditing as the information was not collated in time. To remedy the situation, Strutt & Parker were asked to complete all the farm accounts in future, but the council were to continue with non-farm book keeping until April 2004.

At the end of 2003, James and Rebecca Molden announced that they would be leaving in February 2004, which meant that the Trust needed to find not only another farm manager but also a manager for the visitor centre. Rebecca had been working hard to publicise the centre, and having a centre manager on site was useful, but bookings were still below those hoped for. The existing sub-committee gained two new members, John Field and Robert Baker, to recruit a new manager and to examine the future of the centre. Barry Quinton was also concerned at losing yet another farm manager, and it was agreed that he should be involved in the recruitment process by showing candidates round the farm. Once again, discussions took place on whether to recruit someone young and keen or older and mature and possibly 'set in their ways'.

Profitability and Management of the Farm

At the end of 2003, the farm had a trading profit of £3,250, but the visitor centre had lost £12,339. Fixed costs for the farm were higher than for any ordinary farm due to the trial work and the need to employ two full-time workers. Thus, on other farms fixed costs

would be £350–£400 per ha, but the demonstration farm had costs of £750 per ha. The Tuddenham contract land gave a surplus of £3,800, which meant a profit to the Trust with no fixed costs. The current exchange rate meant an increase in area payments, so the cash balance for the year was £17,500, which was above budget.

In January 2003 the accounts were ready and examined. The overall picture was that investments had fallen from £745,000 to £560,000 largely due to the stock market and a fall in interest rates, so a year-on-year valuation was instituted to monitor the situation. By June the following year, the Agenda 2000 reform of CAP would mean that payments from the Single Farm Payments Scheme were due to go down, but the Entry Level Stewardship Scheme, which would be run by Natural England, would provide payments of £12 per ha.

The Trust deed of 1966 had not been amended to include the changes in management and as part of the general 'tidy-up' the Charity Commission were asked for investment advice due to the poor performance of the Common Ordinary Investment Fund (COIF).

Birketts Solicitors, in Ipswich, had already been appointed by the trustees to negotiate the new college lease, and it was decided to ask them to become the Trust's legal advisors to replace the county council solicitor. A meeting was held with them to arrange for a legal health check. As the county council was no longer managing the legal work of the Trust, Birketts recommended that the archives should be recovered and held securely by the Trust.

By January Paul Creasey had been appointed as farm manager and he was introduced to the trustees at the meeting in February 2004. Priscilla Clayton-Mead had been appointed as the new manager of the visitor centre. Once again the trustees discussed the possibility of widening the usage of the centre to include commercial bookings or weddings.

One of Paul's first problems was to carry out an asbestos survey in line with Health and Safety policy and an HSE requirement. Strutt & Parker were not licensed to help, so Paul attended a course to qualify him for the task.

To investigate the reported problems with the heating of the visitor centre, the committee called in a heating consultant who reported that the existing boiler was too small for the area and the overall system was not right for a conference centre. In June 2004, therefore, a new boiler and pump were fitted and extra fans placed in the Quinton Room. The roof was lined with fibreglass and plasterboard to reduce noise. In order to carry out all the renovations, the centre had to be closed for three weeks, with a loss of bookings. The total cost amounted to £15,000 for the work. Overall, by June 2004, the centre had had an income of £41,000 and expenditure of £67,000, although the actual trading loss was only between £14,000 and £15,000 after building changes were accounted for. The committee discussed installing folding doors between the two rooms and explored the costs involved in adjustments for weddings and corporate hospitality as a way of raising income. However, bookings for the future still totalled only £6,000.

College Lease 2004

Birketts' initial report on the situation, prepared by James Hall, confirmed that the college was in breach of the existing lease due to the extensive redevelopment of the site. Sub-letting arrangements should be negotiated, and some rent adjustment for 'tenants' improvements'. A rent of £30,000 was suggested, which was almost double the existing rent. However, it was agreed that Suffolk County Council should be responsible for finalising the new lease.

It was agreed that half a hectare of land from Middle Field should be handed over to the college after harvest, and trustees would be responsible for the new frontage land along the highway beside the new car park.

In 2004, John Pearson retired and the college had a new principal, Philip Winfield, who had moved from Plumpton College in Sussex; he was invited to attend the Trust meeting in June 2004. The lease problem was still unresolved, but the Trust agreed to reduce the rent for the next five years as Charity Farmhouse, which had now been handed over to the college, needed extensive repairs. Philip told the trustees that he was making efforts to increase numbers of agricultural students from the present eight to around 30.

The problems dragged on into the autumn. A lease had been signed at the November Trust meeting, but there were still unresolved issues. Stephen Cobbald had been a governor of the college, but had now left the board, meaning that an important information link

had been lost. The chairman of the college governors, Robert Black, was about to retire, to be replaced by John Clement, and it was agreed that several trustees, including John Forrest, should attend Robert Black's leaving party.

Residual Estate

At Hope Farm in Sproughton the elderly tenant was relying on his brother-in-law for help with the work. Birketts noted that his rent had not been raised since the review of October 1997, and the Trust had a duty to obtain a fair rent from their property. Similarly, the allotments rent had not been raised. The Trust were charging £125 pa for the site, but Sproughton District Council were charging £4,114.50 pa for allotments. Birketts also reminded the Trust that both parcels of land must be registered so that payments might be received for them, and this meant retrieving the deeds from the council. Far South Field on the demonstration farm also needed registration, but the land reserved for future college use did not.

The Hope Farm tenant was served with a Section 12 notice that the rent would be raised, but as he was ill his daughter appointed an agent to deal with the problem. He was still reluctant to leave the farm and wanted to find a way of staying on.

In June 2004, the Trust were reminded that a statutory declaration should be made for footpaths on the residual estate. The deeds had still not been received, but C A Monk from S&P had begun mapping Hope Farm and boundary checking before registration. He was also staking out the boundaries of the land to be given to the college.

Morley Research Centre, TAG and STAR

In 2003 Morley became part of The Arable Group (TAG). The initial sponsorship by the Trust was due to end in 2006, but this was a moment for reassessment. TAG said that they wanted more grassroots-orientated demo work. Soil and plant science workshops were always well attended and more should be held. In 2005, TAG asked if they could continue trials for another five years and for a donation of £20,000 or £25,000. They said they would also like to make use of the Felix Cobbold Centre. The Trust agreed – the trials raised the profile of the farm and the work would help to develop the new manager, Paul Creasey. Ten hectares were set aside for the new trials.

At the June 2005 trustee meeting, it was announced that Paul was very happy to carry out the trials, and a steering group was set up to assist him as he was still new to the farm. The Trust made a donation of £20,000 to TAG, and was willing to give another £5,000 if additional help was required. Thus, in the autumn of 2005, the Sustainable Trials of Arable Rotation (STAR) began. Rothamsted Research had been asked to look at the layout and was happy with the site. It was agreed that aerial shots would be taken, and the beginning was well publicised in *Farmers Weekly* and *Crops* magazine, ensuring that FTCAT was mentioned. At the open day, Paul and his wife worked hard to represent the Trust.

The objectives of the trials were:

1. To examine different cultivation systems for sustainable arable production;
2. To examine different rotation systems and how they interact with the required cultivations and inputs;
3. And to demonstrate to Suffolk farmers alternative systems of cultivation on a Beccles/Hanslope series clay soil throughout a five-year rotation.

The rotations were:

1. Winter cropping,
2. Spring cropping,
3. Continuous winter wheat,
4. Alternate fallow.

The establishments were:

1. Annual plough,
2. Deep non-inversion,
3. Shallow non-inversion,
4. Managed approach.

This programme thus gave 16 treatments times three replicates.

Felix Cobbold Centre 2004

At the end of 2004, Priscilla Clayton-Mead left the centre and moved to Portugal. Like Rebecca Molden, she had worked hard to get bookings for the centre and had been doing some catering herself to keep costs

down. Trustees realised that sensitivity was needed over the appointment of a new supervisor for the centre and Paul would be given a management role for the centre, which would be good for his career.

The centre had been used as a base for visiting farm groups and Paul reported that there was a need for a trailer to carry disabled children round the farm. Schools also needed £1,000 assistance for bringing the disabled children to the site and a Trust donation to the 2005 School Farm Fair to be held at the Suffolk Agricultural Association showground, Trinity Park, was increased to £1,500.

The new centre manager appointed was Louise Whitehead. In June 2005, it was reported that she had been working hard on marketing the centre; however, results were still disappointing in the difficult trading situation, and by November 2005 it was reported that the centre continued to lose money and was proving to be a drain on the farm resources. The committee were concerned, as they had hoped that after three years the centre would have established itself and be making a profit. However, other countryside conference centres in the area were also doing badly – the future looked bleak.

Trust Reappraisal 2006

At the November 2005 meeting it was reported that while the investment income had improved slightly, the farm had a net loss of £11,882, while the Felix Cobbold Centre had incurred a loss of £46,222 due to rebuilding costs. The Tuddenham Hall contract farming was bringing in a return of £120 per acre, but a new contract being negotiated would bring in a slightly lower income.

It was also announced that 100 acres of land adjacent to Stanaway Farm were available for purchase. It was an opportunity too good to miss – a larger estate would produce higher profits – so the agent was asked to make an offer and by the February 2006 meeting Potash Farm had been bought. The fields of this new farm were renamed after members of the farm staff – Molden, Quinton, Creasey, etc.

At the November meeting, John Forrest reported that the Perry Foundation in London had invited him to a meeting to try to establish a forum for agricultural charities; the meeting had gone well and a new committee had been formed. John had been asked to approach the Chadacre Trust and Suffolk Agricultural Association to seek a way forward for the new group.

By the February meeting, the trustees were clearly deeply unhappy about the demonstration farm finances and were questioning the future of the Trust as a whole. In the present climate was there an actual need for so many demonstration farms? Trustees had been meeting with representatives of other charities and it was clear that the unease was not limited to FTCAT. The accounts showed a loss of £32,000 for the farm after financing the STAR project. This meant that the farm was unrepresentative of a commercial farm, with a profit variance of £30,000 or £40,000, although it was trying to provide a model of the best methods of commercial farming.

One of the best clients of the visitor centre, Change Consultancy, had decided not to use the centre due to changes in NHS funding. Louise was now working part-time for the college in the new food skills centre, but a budget forecast showed that with an estimated 30 per cent occupancy rate in the next year the centre would lose another £14,500 in 2006. As an emergency measure, it was decided to let the visitor centre as office accommodation, and to investigate the problem of repaying grants provided for its establishment. It also seemed that it would be necessary to make Louise redundant.

A sub-committee was formed to look at the options for the future of the Trust.

NOTES

1 European Union Statement. *Agenda 2000 – A CAP for the Future*, 1999, Brussels.
2 Ibid.
3 Ibid.

Chapter Fifteen

Otley College – 40 Years of Suffolk Agricultural Education

Since 1970 the organisation now known as Otley College has been situated on part of the Felix Cobbold Agricultural Trust land, and therefore its history has been tightly bound with that of the Trust. Despite this, they are two separate organisations and each has its own history and agenda. This chapter traces the history of the college from its own perspective up to 2010, when it celebrated its 40th birthday with a reception and reunion of staff, old and new.

Agricultural Education in East Suffolk

Agricultural education in the area began during the Second World War with five-day courses at Wickham Market to teach farm staff to use tractors. With the present Suffolk County still divided into East Suffolk and West Suffolk there were two Education Organisers – Graham Boatfield in East Suffolk and H Redvers Clayton in West Suffolk – and the courses were set up with the additional help of the Advisory Officers from the National Agricultural Advisory Service (NAAS).

In 1956, Graham Boatfield began day release courses in Ipswich to teach agriculture to a group of about ten students at a time and two years later, Brian Bell joined him, specialising in farm machinery. Day courses were also run in Bury St Edmunds, Halesworth and Lowestoft and evening classes were held in Ipswich, Saxmundham and Halesworth, so it was a heavy workload.

The classes moved to the school at Witnesham in 1960 when two classrooms and an adjacent wood-working room had become vacant after the school stopped catering for children from five to 15 and became a primary school. A third member of staff, Alan Porter, was taken on. At first the centre was named the Agricultural Education Centre at Witnesham, but it later adopted the name of East Suffolk Educational Institute. Between 1960 and 1970, numbers gradually climbed from 50 students to 300, and the

staff offered a three-year day release course studying agriculture and farm machinery for the first two years, with third-year options of studying pigs, cattle or arable farming. The students attended Suffolk College in the morning for theoretical work and moved to Witnesham in the afternoons for practical work. By 1968, the staff had grown to six, with a number of part-timers as well.

The importance of the East Suffolk Educational Institute to the farming community of the area is illustrated in Ronald Blythe's *Akenfield*; in his village, there lives not only two of the staff members, but also the character 'Brian Newton' who is a young farm-worker attending day release classes as well as 'Terry Lloyd' who became a pig farmer after spending two years at the institute. The interviews with these men shows the difficulty in teaching young village boys with poor elementary education who are entering an industry that is becoming far more technical than it was at the turn of the century. One of the teachers complains that they are not able to give the boys a wider education and teach them to be critical. He also complains about the difference between the farmer's sons and the farm-worker's sons – the former talking about buying tractors and the right choice of fertiliser, and the latter completely uninterested in the administrative side of the farm.

The Move to Otley 1970

In 1970, the Felix Cobbold Trust offered the East Suffolk Agricultural Education Centre accommodation at their new demonstration farm at Otley, and a new education centre was purpose-built for them at a cost of £80,000. This consisted of a reception centre, several classrooms, a canteen, a library area and administrative offices. There was a large barn nearby which housed farm machinery on one side and a milking parlour, milk room, pig sties, and a bull pen on

The Witnesham tractor fleet. From left to right, Alan Porter on a Massey Ferguson 35 with manure loader, John Price on a Fordson Dexta, Brian Bell (head of machinery section) on a 'new' Fordson Major. Beyond Brian can be glimpsed a Ferguson 20 and an 'old' Fordson Major. (Otley College)

the other. In addition, the students had access to the demonstration farm and could study the techniques being used.

The grand opening at Otley on 4 July 1970 was performed by Lord Netherthorpe, the chairman of Fisons, and Captain the Honourable C A B Bernard, chairman of the county council, was also present. Graham Boatfield became the first principal. During the day, visitors were also able to view the demonstration farm under the guidance of Roger Leggett, farm manager. (See Chapter 10 for more information on Roger Leggett.) Brian Bell became head of farm machinery, and Bob Hainsworth was head of agriculture; there were five other lecturers. In addition, there was one secretary, Mrs P Fordham, along with a clerical assistant, a cook, one cleaner, a stockman, caretaker and a farm machinery technician – 15 staff in all.

During the 1970/1 session, apart from running the courses transferred from Witnesham, the staff organised a number of new practical farming courses, including a refresher course on farm machinery for the recently appointed farm safety inspectors to the region. In all, 486 people attended the courses and several part-time instructors were taken on, at a rate of £2 5s an hour, to supplement staff numbers.

During the first year, an apiary was installed on the nearby Bee Field by John Izzard to teach beekeeping. John was instrumental in setting up a spray warning scheme for beekeepers in the region, which continued until 1987. (A sign naming the field is still attached to the nearby building, although the bees have disappeared.)

The college had to expand fairly rapidly, due not only to local demand, but also because of the recommendations of HM Inspectors in February 1973 as they thought that the location of the institute had great potential. They recommended setting up a commercial pig herd and doubling the size of the sheep flock to 100 ewes. Courses at this time included general farming, mechanised arable farming, cattle or pig production, gas welding, electric welding, animal health, barley beef production, farm office training, horse and pony management, beekeeping and pollination.

At the prize-giving ceremony in 1974, Graham Boatfield announced that there was another name change to reflect the transfer of horticultural education from Witnesham to Otley – East Suffolk Agricultural and Horticultural Institute.[1] Horticultural education had started at Witnesham in the late 1960s with classes run by June Bowry using the large school gardens for teaching purposes. She also held classes at local Women's Institutes. When the Agricultural Institute moved out, John Pearson joined June in providing more classes at the Witnesham site in the vacated classrooms.

When the horticultural staff moved to Otley in June 1974 the total increased to 11 lecturers, three technicians and 11 office, caretaking and kitchen staff. By this time, Brian Bell had become vice principal. With the staff numbers growing, the buildings also needed to expand so in June 1975 the workshop area was almost doubled with the erection of two new workshops on the original car park. Roger Leggett and his farm staff had to lay a new car park in 1974 to replace the lost area. The move was a success: in 1975 the new horticulture department was teaching courses in commercial, decorative, nursery, amenity or private horticulture. The first City & Guilds course in professional floristry began at this time.

By 1976, the institute had a total of 688 students including local school link students, day students, block release and evening classes, after a report by the Careers Service that 80 per cent of school leavers had expressed an interest in entering agriculture or horticulture. In the same year, the students joined with West Suffolk students studying at the Chadacre Farm Training Centre in the old West Suffolk area[2] on a study tour of southwest France. The Felix Cobbold Trust has continued to support overseas trips for students and many useful contacts have been made in this way.

Another event in 1976 was the arrival of the Black Bull of Otley. Rintoul Booth, its creator, had been agricultural editor of the *East Anglian Daily Times* and

was a friend of Graham Boatfield. He became interested in producing models of animals using pipe cleaners sprayed black. Graham suggested that he should come to the institute for a short course in oxy-acetylene welding under the guidance of master welder, Frank Ager. Rintoul's skill improved to a point where he felt able to undertake larger work and produced a small model of a Holstein Friesian bull from the Sutton Hoo herd, which was then turned into a three-quarter life-sized model in 1976/77, complete with large ball bearings as eyes. Rintoul died suddenly in 1978 so this was his only full-size sculpture. Some years later, the ball bearings became rusty and needed some work. Frank Ager undertook the repairs but had a strong impression that Rintoul was overseeing his work and complaining about the changes, so Frank decided never to touch the animal again.

In 1976, it was also decided to set up a Youth Opportunities Training Programme (YOP) at Otley in farm machinery repair and horticulture, in conjunction with the Agricultural Training Board. The college was involved in the Training Opportunities Programme (TOPs) adult retraining scheme. One of the trainees was Chris Opperman, who in 1991 became a presenter on BBC Radio Suffolk. In 1977, the Agricultural Training Board approved a number of one-day practical courses on a wider range of subjects, including sprayers and combine harvesters.[3]

In 1977, the first chairman of the governors, E J W (Jack) Fiske, died. He had been chairman of the Felix

Graham Boatfield and Rintoul Booth pose for a publicity photo of the newly created Black Bull of Otley.
(*East Anglian Daily Times*)

Cobbold Agricultural Trust at the time of their transition from a smallholdings trust to owners of the demonstration farm at Charity and Stanaway Farm, and had thus had great influence on the decision to bring an educational establishment to the farm. As a tribute to his work the institute decided to establish a memorial plantation in his name. Donations were invited from many people and organisations linked with the institute and the Fiske Memorial Plantation was opened in November 1979.

From the late 1970s, the college began to have its regular open days in spring and early autumn, which served to showcase the work of the college and provided useful opportunities for student recruitment.

1980s Developments

By the merger of east and west in 1974, Suffolk County Council had inherited two agricultural training centres – East Suffolk Institute and the West Suffolk Farm Training Centre at Chadacre. East Suffolk Institute, however, then changed its name to Otley College of Agriculture and Horticulture and continued to experience growth due to its large number and varieties of courses.

A new variety of course was introduced in 1981 – the Unified Vocational Preparation scheme (UVP) – through which young people could attend on a regular basis for six months while working on a farm or holding. Further government initiatives followed, such as the Youth Training Programme (YTS) operated by the Manpower Services Commission.

In 1984, Frank Ager retired. He had joined the staff as a farm machinery technician in 1972 and his welding skills had become legendary – it was said that he could weld together two pieces of silver paper. His tuition of Rintoul Booth and his later repairs to the bull made him an important part of the story of Otley College. The following year, Ken Miller retired. He had joined Witnesham in 1968 and later became head of machinery at Otley. In this post he had been greatly involved in the apprenticeship training schemes, and also assisted Brian Bell with the Suffolk Farm Machinery Club Power in Action demonstrations on the demonstration farm.

A third notable loss to the staff was that of Graham Boatfield, first principal of the college, in 1986. Graham had made a vast contribution to agricultural

education since 1956 and his retirement was marked by the opening of the Boatfield Barn on 11 October by John Gummer, a Suffolk Coastal MP and Minister of Agriculture. On the same day, John Gummer opened the Philip Jolly glasshouse to commemorate the death of a man who had supported Otley as a governor. Philip's family presented a rose bowl in his memory which is awarded to the top floristry student each year.

By 1986, the total number of employees had grown to 41 regular staff. Ivor J Santer was head of agriculture, John Pearson was head of horticulture and Alexander Ferguson was the new principal replacing Graham Boatfield in July 1986. Student numbers had topped 700. Ivor then left in 1986 to become vice principal of a Scottish agricultural college and his place was taken by Keith Broomer.

Keith decided to establish a goat unit and travelled the country to find likely milking goats so that the unit could teach not only goat husbandry but also goat dairy milk production. This required the conversion of a horticultural storage area into a goat housing area together with milking parlour and milk room. The work was completed in 1988 and Lord Tollemache performed the opening ceremony, while an ex-Otley student, Ann Meadley, took charge of the unit. The food developed by Dengie Feeds for the goat herd was sold nationally as the Otley Goat Blend.

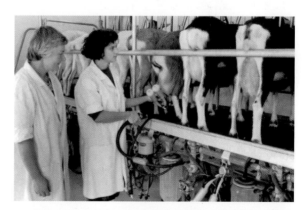

Otley-trained Ann Meadley (left) supervises a student milking goats in the new dairy unit. (Otley College)

Also in the summer of 1986, Otley gained status as an Approved Training Organisation by the MSC and began a two-year Youth Training Scheme, increased from the one-year courses introduced in 1983. Farmers were asked to pay £11 per week for the first year to support their trainees and £14 in the second year. The following year, in conjunction with Suffolk College and the Ipswich and Suffolk Chamber of Commerce, they set up Suffolk Training Opportunities to train the long-term unemployed.

By 1988, the buildings were again becoming too small and a reception area, dining hall and floristry hall were constructed and opened in September 1989 by Sir Simon Gourlay, NFU president. As a consequence, the Otley Bull had to move into a new resting place in the visitor's car park.

In 1989, Chadacre Agricultural Institute finally closed its doors due to the decline of demand for residential courses. It had been endowed in 1920 by the first Lord Iveagh to provide free residential education in agriculture for 25 students. The sale of the institute and estate in 1990 provided funds to found the Chadacre Agricultural Trust, which has the present Lord Iveagh as its chairman. The Farm Training Centre at Chadacre also had to leave its home when the estate was sold but students who were due to complete courses were able to transfer to Otley. Simultaneously, Otley was offered Bransons College at Playford, previously a private sixth form college, as a student residence.

1990–1999 and Continued Growth

As Chadacre closed, Otley grew and the number of courses widened to include new subjects such as week-long courses on 'Working the Heavy Horse'. The staff numbers by 1990 had climbed to 74 to deal with the rising number of students, and the overcrowded dining hall and the Fersina Vaughan conservatory provided extra space.

In 1991, Robert Black became chairman of the new governing body of Otley College, under the Education Reform Act (1988) by which funding came from the Further Education Funding Council instead of Suffolk County Council.

Agriculture itself had begun to change and Otley was fortunate in being offered the use of Looms Farm, Burgh, for practical instruction in organic growing in the winter of 1992. The college asked the Trust whether they could provide organic land on the demonstration farm, but the Trust's agent thought it would not be economic. Also in this year, the Otley Training Group

merged with the Orwell Training Group and settled into an office at Otley. The Group presented Otley with £5,000 to help furnish and equip a new library, a facility which was becoming ever more necessary as Otley established a master of horticulture course in addition to postgraduate degrees in conservation.

Once again, the builders moved onto the site and by the summer of 1993, the Suffolk Building was completed with a new library on the upper floor. However, while the building had still not reached completion, the decision was made to construct the two Eastern Electricity blocks across the courtyard to house the new environmental studies department and additional space for floristry.

On 1 April 1993, Otley was incorporated, severing its final links with Suffolk County Council. A further change was that Brian Bell retired as vice principal in July 1993, and was replaced by John Pearson. In December 1993, however, Brian was asked back to meet the Duke of Kent when he came to open both the Suffolk Building and the Eastern Electricity Management Centre. The new facilities comprised 2,000 square metres of space, including new classrooms and the library. Not only were there now 2,000 students enrolled, but for the first time the college offered first degree and postgraduate courses in conservation management, which were linked to the University of East Anglia. The student body thus comprised students of all levels of attainment, aged 16 to 86.

The degree courses necessitated linking the library at Otley to the UEA library by STD line which meant the local telephone exchange had to be upgraded to cater for the service. A website was created by the librarian, at first using a company in Ipswich as a server. This was one of the first agricultural college websites in the country, and it meant that a search for the term 'floristry' on the internet resulted in three hits – two florist shops in California and the Otley College floristry department.

The pace of expansion continued: in September 1993, the college began a full-time small animal care course, which required yet another new block. Work began in the summer of 1993 to be followed a year later by a second block for exotic animals and then a kennel and grooming parlour which came complete with a hydraulic table to raise heavy dogs to a suitable height for treatment. With each new building, the range of animal care courses also could be increased from the first NVQs in animal care to a pre-veterinary nursing certificate by the end of the 1990s. Much of the work in constructing these buildings was carried out by teaching staff who spent the summer 'breaks' laying concrete paths and building walls.

In 1994, another teaching block went up beyond the Suffolk Building to house business studies and information technology, complete with a lift in the atrium. At the same time, the library expanded into two classrooms on the upper floor of the Suffolk Building to provide study places. A third room was filled with computers for student use.

At this period the college faced a dilemma: with an increase in farm sizes fewer students were entering agriculture at the level that the Felix Cobbold Trust had been formed to encourage – that is, at the level of farm labourers rather than farmer's sons or managers. Farms were not only becoming larger, but mechanisation was becoming more complex with satellite-guided field management. The courses had to be changed to meet the new needs of the industry, and this included teaching computer technology to farm managers as well as the advanced engineering skills necessary to service huge combine harvesters. Traditional skills – game keeping, arboriculture, turf management, carpentry and bricklaying – had to be augmented by an ever increasing range of additional courses to recruit students. These included business management, leisure and tourism – even interior design.

In 1999 with Ian Miller as project manager, Otley opened a new engineering centre to teach agritronics. The centre included state-of-the-art simulator equipment for fault diagnostics and the coveted status of Centre of Excellence was awarded shortly before it opened in March. The department also provided a mobile unit which could be taken out to schools.

Horticulture at this time included commercial crop management, so for weeks every spring the Jolly building might be filled with a fragrant crop of freesias or alstroemerias, and each afternoon bunches of cut flowers were brought to reception for sale. Additional glasshouses were filled with a vast range of pot plants

throughout the year, while a plantation of sapling trees grew on a plot to the rear. An aerial view of the site shows the huge extent of the glasshouses, polytunnels and plantations and the importance of horticulture to the college.

Aerial shot of Otley College around 1995. Bordering the road at the front can be seen the new red-roofed Suffolk Building containing classrooms below, and the new library on the upper floor. Adjoining is the IT centre completed the following summer, with additional classrooms on the ground floor. Next to the Suffolk Building, also with a red roof, is the Eastern Electricity Building containing the new Environmental Conservation Department and Floristry. At the top right of the campus are the other new additions: two new animal care houses and the kennels and grooming parlour. (Otley College)

One course introduced in the mid-1990s that was typical of the innovative nature of the Otley programme was Holistic Horticulture. The only comparable course in the country was at Dartington Hall in Devon, so students came from all over the country to take part. The syllabus included a study of biodynamic agriculture following the principles of Rudolph Steiner, and it was thus possible to find a group of students at a far corner of the campus taking it in turns to stir a huge tub of fertiliser prepared to Steiner instructions, and testing its potency by use of divining rods.

The campus was crowded and yet vibrant. A short distance from the staff canteen was the pig unit of 80 sows. These intelligent animals had been given computerised collars to control the amount of feed given to them when they passed through a set of metal doors. However, a number of pigs found that they could win additional feed by reversing back through the gates, and the system had to be changed.

Not far from the pigs was the goat unit containing 48 milking goats, with the kids in a shed the other side of the pathway. Milk used in the staff canteen was sent from the dairy at the side of the goat shed in large jugs, and occasionally someone going to fetch additional milk retrieved the wrong jug and brought milk intended for the kids still full of colostrum. Apart from goat milk, the dairy produced prize-winning soft goat cheese flavoured with herbs or walnuts which were marketed through the marketing group Tastes of Anglia.

The floristry department produced exotic flower arrangements which were displayed all over the college and a small flower shop was opened to teach shop management to the students. This enabled college staff and students to order bouquets of flowers for special occasions. Indeed, flowers were everywhere – in reception, on landings, in the library, growing in the glasshouses and blooming in herbaceous borders throughout the site. However, by the end of the century Otley had trained many of the florists working throughout East Anglia and demand for further tuition declined.

During this period, landscape design courses became very popular – often adopted as a second career by mature students. The college also offered part-time courses in leisure gardening, making good use of the opportunities for extensive plant-identification resources on site.

The problems of space became more acute as the decade progressed, with few leisure facilities for students on site, a crowded canteen and ever-increasing pressure on parking space. However, it was a college full of energy and surprises: where else could you pass a man in a corridor carrying a Stone Age axe over his shoulder, or meet a large group of ladies carrying spinning wheels? One shed might be filled with a Chelsea Flower Show stand under construction and another might be full of young students learning to drive tractors. The Inspectors' Report in 1997 recorded high levels of retention and attendance levels throughout the college and, by this time, student numbers had risen from the 2,000 enrolled in 1993 to 878 full-time students and 5,180 part-time students.

Otley College 2000–2010

After this period of rapid expansion, the new decade opened with a period of reassessment and consolidation.

Government funding moved into new areas and demand for agricultural courses continued to decline, as did horticultural work. After the retirement of Alexander Ferguson in 2000, the new principal, John Pearson, undertook a major reorganisation of the college and as a result, there were many staff changes.

Suffolk suffered from various animal diseases, including the foot and mouth outbreak in 2001, which threatened to close the college due to quarantine restrictions, and also resulted in the pig sties and the goat herd having to be moved to the demonstration farm. The goat herd was finally sold shortly after. Floristry continued to decline, partly because of the success of the previous courses in fulfilling demand. Information technology and business studies courses, which had seen a rapid growth in the 1990s, faced fierce competition from every other college in the area, and so were wiped from the Otley curricula, although information technology remains a core part of many other vocational courses. Even the pioneering move into environmental education degrees, which took place in the 1990s, has been affected by the growth of similar courses in other colleges.

Philip Winfield became principal in 2004 after the retirement of John Pearson. Under his guidance and the guidance of the vice principal, David Milligan, the college site was totally transformed once again. The college, which celebrated its 40th anniversary in 2010, is almost unrecognisable from the institute that arrived on the Otley site in 1970, although parts of the old buildings remain imbedded in the new. The large new car park on the east side caters for the first time for the huge numbers of people that visit the site for demonstrations. The new reception area in the Millennium Building, which also houses classrooms and a laboratory, is on the site of some of the old glasshouses, and the college has thus turned to face east instead of west. Even the Otley Bull has made its third move to the middle of the campus.

In the difficult agricultural climate of the new century the college has adapted to meet the challenges of the present, and will no doubt continue to support the land-based industries in Suffolk and the wider community. It can now offer foundation degrees in conjunction with the new Suffolk University College, which opened in 2007, with a higher education centre on the Otley site.

The new food centre, another centre of vocational

In the summer of 2010, Otley College celebrated its 40th birthday with a gathering of friends old and new. From left to right: Brian Bell (former vice principal, Otley College), Professor Peter Funnell (Suffolk New College), David Lawrence (principal, Easton College), Alex B Ferguson (former principal, Otley College), Philip Winfield (principal, Otley College), John W Pearson (former principal, Otley College), Professor David Muller (principal, Suffolk New College), Simon Summers (principal, Lowestoft College), Richard Lister (deputy provost, [Professional Services], University College Suffolk). (Otley College)

The national need for skilled construction workers is now being met in new and enlarged teaching areas, which includes some emphasis on conservation building work. Similarly, the enlarged engineering section, which has developed from those wartime classes in tractor maintenance, now equips students to maintain not only heavy plant and machinery but also plumbing and electrical installations.

Animal care, started in the 1990s, continues to be popular on the site. Equine studies have been transformed with newly installed on-site stables and paddocks, meaning that unlike in the 1990s, students do not have to travel off site for their practical work. An indoor arena encourages the tuition of dressage in even the most inclement weather.

The facilities for staff and students have improved in this decade. The dining hall, in its third incarnation, is large and airy and the site also includes two cafés. Students have a number of lounge areas and sports facilities – both lacking during the 1990s. Young Farmers have an office on site, near Charity Farmhouse, to encourage social links.

excellence, offers an industrial kitchen facility at which companies can test new recipes, and courses are also offered in cookery and food processing. Nearby is a new fisheries centre that was opened in 2008 under the guidance of Steve Coghill, offering courses on fish husbandry – a useful sideline for farmers who wish to diversify. Another new subject area introduced this century is sport, and the college is fortunate in having acquired additional land, including a new sports field, from the Felix Cobbold Trust to facilitate this.

As rural Suffolk changes in the coming decades Otley will no doubt continue to modify its facilities and courses to meet the needs of the county. It is a college that the county can be proud of and in the words of Graham Boatfield at his retirement in 1986, in spite of being told year after year that there was no money and that progress would be hard 'we have tried to make this college of the countryside at Otley into something which matches the needs and the rural realities of this county'.

NOTES

1   East and West Suffolk merged to become Suffolk County in 1974.
2   The West Suffolk Farm Training Centre had been set up in the grounds of the Chadacre Institute in 1967 and included two lecture rooms, a tiered lecture theatre, a common room, three workshops and offices.
3   The Agricultural Training Board for the county was at this time organised by Kris Miscewski from his own home.

Chapter Sixteen

2006–2010
End of the Demonstration Farm and a Third Stage

National Situation 2006–2010

The last few years of the decade have seen a crisis in the banking systems of the USA and Europe, triggered by lack of regulation over speculation and debt. The 2008 sub-prime mortgage collapse in the USA was followed by a lack of confidence in banks, prompting many governments to take emergency action to support their national banks by pumping in money from reserves. Towards the end of the decade, these actions have led to a number of Eurozone countries – Greece and Ireland in particular – seeking support for their currencies through emergency loans from the International Monetary Fund. In Britain, the near collapse of Northern Rock was followed by crises in the Royal Bank of Scotland and the other major banks. For two years the government borrowed heavily to bail out the banks, and the Bank of England reduced interest rates to 0.5 per cent, which led to hardship for those sectors – including pensioners and charitable trusts – relying on income from interest rates.

In Britain, the election of 2010 saw the formation of a coalition government by the Conservatives and the Liberal Democrats who are implementing economic change in order to reduce national debt. The consequences of these changes will be far reaching and, as yet, unknown. The outlook appears to be bleak in Britain: each government department has been asked to cut its budgets, universities are being asked to fund themselves from student fees rather than state subsidies and many research programmes are being cut.

For industry, the situation poses an enormous challenge. The balance of economic power is slipping eastwards to China and India, so companies in Europe must cut costs to remain competitive. At the same time, the realities of global warming must be faced and green sources of power explored. Bio fuel production, wind farms and solar energy systems – all are affecting the countryside and changing the balance of crop choices and food production.

Farming in Britain has diminished; in 2010 only two per cent of the population were engaged in the agricultural industry with many of the permanent jobs demanding high degrees of skill and knowledge. Casual labour, on the other hand, is often supplied by immigrants, usually working for gang masters. Since the recent changes in the composition of the EU, many of these workers are from Eastern Europe, and not all are working legally.

Towards the end of the decade there were more signs that the industry was in trouble. Low milk prices forced many dairy farmers, who struggled to rebuild their herds after the foot and mouth outbreaks, to leave the industry. Bovine TB hit both dairy and beef farmers, while the solutions of either culling badgers or vaccinating the National Herd were debated. One of the solutions is a form of intensive farming that would be applicable to both dairy and beef cattle. In fact, one producer sought permission to open a vast 'factory farm' in Lincolnshire with cattle being kept almost entirely within sheds, following American models. The method would cut costs, but welfare issues are still being discussed and permission has not been granted.

For pig farmers raised welfare standards in Britain introduced after the various epidemics are pricing British pork and bacon products out of the market as foreign farmers are not subject to the same restrictions. Chicken farmers face similar problems as increased welfare restrictions mean that battery hens will shortly be produced at a lower stocking rate. Organic eggs and chicken meat are becoming more popular, and any label such as 'barn eggs' or 'free range' which suggests that the most extreme forms of battery hen farming have been avoided are popular in supermarkets, albeit at increased cost to the consumer. However, at the beginning of 2011 there was a new move to introduce factory farming of rabbits to provide another source of cheap protein. Predictably, animal campaigners have been unhappy about the proposed cage sizes.

Farmers throughout this period have sought alternative methods of using their land. For livestock breeders, llamas, alpaca, ostriches and deer are farmed in Suffolk, along with rare breed specialists. The Rare Breeds Survival Trust was founded in 1973 to support native breeds, but many farmers outside the Trust are rearing unusual animals – like Jimmy Doherty of television fame at his Wherstead Farm. Niche markets for these special meats have been found in farm shops and farmers markets, which appeal not only to consumers looking for high quality and unusual products, but also to those worried about 'food miles' – the distances from which British food is sourced. Close to Trust land is an example of this trend: the Swiss Farm Shop off the B1078, which is certified by FARMA – the National Farmers' Retail and Markets Association.

Local fruit farmers have resorted to offering 'Pick Your Own' as a way to overcome the difficulties of finding good pickers, but towards the end of the decade many Suffolk fruit trees and bushes have been grubbed out as foreign produce has flooded supermarkets. Box schemes – weekly deliveries of fresh produce to a regular clientele – are also offered by vegetable producers like Great Tey Farm, North Essex.

Otley College has opened a fish farming centre, teaching local farmers how to farm trout and other fish. The fish may then either be sold locally, or offered as a sporting resource for fisherman. Golf courses created on farmland also cater for the local leisure market.

One local enterprise, the Boxford Group, illustrated this move towards diversification. Bill and Devora Peake started an organic fruit farm at Stoke by Nayland in the 1940s with 900 acres, and were founder members of the Soil Association with Lady Eve Balfour. When the fruit market suffered, they began to produce Copella juice from their orchards to add value to their products, but also opened two 18-hole golf courses in 1972. The family firm continued to suffer financially so took advice from John Harvey Jones, and then opened a 30-bed hotel in 1998, which has been expanded to 80 rooms. The site also has a conference centre and a spa health centre, together with the Pippin Shop selling local produce. Their organic fruit is still being produced, but it is the other enterprises that are producing the finance.

Paintballing, shooting and riding – all are offered locally as leisure pursuits making use of farmland in an effort to increase profits. One of the Trust tenants in Sproughton, for example, is running an equine centre and providing storage for 100 caravans.

Above all, farm land is under threat of development for new housing. As Steve Coghill of Otley College says in *Return to Akenfield*, 'they are not growing crops in this area, they're growing houses.'[1]

Trust Committee 2006

At the crucial Extraordinary Meeting of 21 April 2006, the committee consisted of John R Forrest in the chair, Robert J Baker as vice chairman, Bruce Hinton, Jeremy C P Clover (who had now become chairman of Suffolk County Council), Selwyn Pryor, Dr Philip Draycott, and M G Harris. J D Field and Stephen Cobbald apologised for their absence. Also attending were C A Monk and Mark D Hall, from Strutt & Parker, and C Prior, clerk to the Trust.

Options for Change

Mark Hall reported that the sub-committee had met with Strutt & Parker on 17 March to discuss options for the Trust. The options were:

1. To continue as at present;
2. To arrange for Stanaway Farm to be contract farmed – under this arrangement the Trust should get a return of around £53,000. In addition, Stanaway Farmhouse, the visitor centre, the Tuddenham Store and livestock sheds could also be rented out, so the total profit might be estimated at around £110,000.

The advantage would be that the Trust would still be involved with the cropping and cultivation and some trials could continue. There were disadvantages in that the Trust would still need to keep an agent, and in a bad year the contractor's charges would still have to be paid, so that the Trust would have higher overheads and possible losses.

3. A Farm Business Tenancy (FBT) – The farm could be let for a three-year period, with Stanaway Farm and the visitor centre rented out. The remaining buildings, such as the

grainstore and chemical store, would be included in the FBT. Income would be certain, management fees would be less, and there were few risks. The Single Farm Payment entitlements could be let with the land, thereby enhancing the rent.

The disadvantages would be that the Trust would have no influence on crops grown or input to existing trials and demonstrations. VAT could not be reclaimed on professional fees, and the stewardship schemes would be passed to the tenant to manage.

4. Sale of the estate – The Trust could consider selling all the land and reinvesting the funds to meet the Trust's objectives in an alternative manner. At the present rates of interest in 2006 this might produce an investment income of around £104,000 pa.

The sub-committee recommended a mixture of options three and four. Some outlying land could be sold, but the strategic area around Otley College and Stanaway Farm could be kept and let for a FBT. At this point, it might be possible to allow Otley College to buy their freehold, as they had long wanted. Bruce Hinton commented that the option had been discussed with the college and was being considered by them.

Estate Division

Strutt & Parker had examined the Trust land and divided it into ten potential sale lots, and also compiled estimates of current market values. The ten lots comprised 617 acres, but excluded the college site. C A Monk advised that the Trust should retain the first four lots, but sell Lots 5–10.

The lots to be retained included the arable land surrounding Stanaway Farm and Potash Farm, the newly acquired fields which had, incidentally, now been renamed with the names of Trust Farm managers – Leggett, Molden, and Quinton, etc. The third lot was Charity Field, which

might in future be acquired by the college in any future expansion, and Lot 4 was Nelson Field, on which the STAR trials were being conducted.

The lots which C A Monk recommended might be sold thus included all the other parcels of land acquired throughout the area, of varying quality and value. The market for land was fairly positive, and C A Monk suggested selling either in June or September.

After lengthy discussions, the trustees finally agreed that no land should be sold at present, apart from small parcels which could be sold at premium values: several plots had already been negotiated as possible garden land for houses bordering the demonstration farm and good prices were being achieved for each.

The Trust would, however, cease farming operations at the end of the harvest in 2006, and the farm would be offered for a Farm Business Tenancy for a three- to five-year contract. This contract would include the grain store, but for the other buildings the Trust would apply for a change of use. The ill-fated visitor centre would be offered to the college as a conference centre and office location at a commercial rent. Alternatively, it could be converted into offices.

Sadly, the three employees of the farm would be

The large square campus of Otley College in 2006. The new car park is in place to the left of the site, but the adjacent reception, learner services and animal studies block is yet to be built. On the top corner is the equestrian centre, and below it can be seen the engineering and construction buildings. Beyond the square site above right is the new sports field and, beyond the sports field, the lane leads to Stanaway Farm and the visitor centre. Along the right-hand border of the square is Charity Lane and the Fiske Memorial Plantation. The two large commercial greenhouses were demolished in 2011. (Otley College)

made redundant. As the farm manager was living in Stanaway Farmhouse any decision over its future had to be delayed until it became vacant. Barry Quinton had been working loyally for the farm since it had been acquired by the Trust, a total of over 36 years, and had helped all of the new farm managers to settle into their posts with patience and tolerance. Further, it might be hard to find alternative work at his age. Trustees had to arrange redundancy packages for the three bearing in mind their various situations.

James Hall of Birketts Solicitors was to be asked to approach the charity commissioners to arrange for a revision of the charitable objectives of the Trust. The commission also needed to be told of the recent purchase of Potash Farm so that the land could be vested with the Official Custodian for Charities.

Steps towards Change

Once the decisions had been made, action followed swiftly. The owner of Tuddenham Hall Estate was told that the Contract Farming contract would cease after the harvest of 2006. Strutt & Parker were also asked to arrange a machinery sale of the farm equipment after harvest. Planning consent had to be sought for change of use on the farm buildings, and TAG notified urgently about the farm changes. The STAR project had already attracted wide attention, and trustees hoped that the trials might be allowed to continue in some way and would continue to offer financial support.

Further, all the other organisations benefiting from the Trust needed to be acquainted with the changes – Suffolk Agricultural Association, Otley College, LEAF, School Farm Visits, and Suffolk Farm Machinery Club which had been holding biennial Power in Action demonstrations on the farm for nearly 40 years.

The most important task, however, was to find a new tenant for the farm and a tender document was drawn up to go out in early June.

June 2006 Meeting

Matters were still moving quickly. The three employees had been informed of their redundancies: the centre manager would be leaving on 31 July and Paul Creasey and Barry Quinton would leave on 30 September, but Paul would continue to live in Stanaway Farmhouse until the end of the year. Clarke &

Simpson would auction some machinery and equipment on 26 September, and tender documents were about to be sent out to find a new tenant, with a viewing date on 16 June.

The Arable Group's Suffolk committee chairman, John Taylor, had expressed a hope that the STAR trials could continue, and asked if the Trust could replace the supply of labour and machinery with financial support. One problem was that the trial occupied only 11 ha of the 15 ha Nelson Field, so costs for maintaining the spare 4 ha had to be considered.

A meeting had been held with the college governors, principal and vice principal to discuss future plans for both the Trust and the college. The Trust wished to continue to support agricultural education at the college and wanted suggestions as to how this might best be achieved. The college was interested in acquiring part of Charity Field, which would be used for development of their sports programme, and also Middle Field which would be used for grazing horses and alpaca.

One other result of the announcements to interested organisations was a letter from Brian Bell, secretary of the Suffolk Farm Machinery Club, announcing his decision to retire from the post after 21 years, as Power in Action demonstrations would, in all probability, no longer be held on Stanaway Farm.

The contract with Strutt & Parker would also change after a considerable amount of work spent in restructuring the Trust property, and it was noted that the situation would need to be considered after the end of farming operations at Stanaway Farm.

One further important item on the agenda was the news that the tenant of Hope Farm, Sproughton, had finally agreed to surrender his farmland and buildings, but wanted to keep his house and garden through a five-year assured tenancy.

The Sproughton allotments were still being run by Sproughton Parish Council, but they wanted to use part of the land as a car park and also hoped to build some affordable housing. As these changes were not agricultural, usage negotiations continued between the Trust and the council.

Stanaway Farm 2006

The new tenant for the demonstration farm was John Taylor, a partner in F G Taylor & Sons of Grove

Farm, Clopton. John had agreed to take on the Countryside Stewardship Scheme, was a LEAF member and had also agreed to work on the STAR project so that Nelson Field could be included in the FBT. He also took over the two grain stores, the chemical store and the sentinel shed. The Single Farm Payment entitlements were transferred to John for the 2007 claim year, but it was arranged that they would revert to the landlord upon termination of the tenancy.

Of the other buildings, it had now been confirmed that grants for the visitor centre did not need repayment if changes did not take place until after January 2007, so the building would not be let for the time being.

For the Hope Farm land, the 65 acres had been let on a three-year FBT to J Williamson and son, the same farmer that had been working the land for the old tenant, who in turn had been given a short-hold tenancy for the farmhouse and garden.

Trust Management

A second extraordinary meeting of trustees was held in November 2006 to examine potential models for managing the Trust, using information from Morley Agricultural Foundation, Chadacre Agricultural Trust and the Perry Foundation for inspiration. Chadacre had an administrator – Dr Helen Smith – who impressed the trustees, and the chairman and vice chairman felt that they should find a 'Dr Helen Smith look-alike' to manage their affairs. Morley also had an administrator, which confirmed trustees' thoughts that this was a good model to follow. However, if an administrator were appointed, then Strutt & Parker would no longer be necessary for most of the work. Although, due to the varied nature of the Trust holdings, a land agent would still be needed for the Sproughton lands, the farm tenancies and the Otley College lands, for example, so a tender would be put out, for which Strutt & Parker might wish to apply.

By March one problem had been solved. Dr Helen Smith's husband, Colin, was available for the post of administrator and was appointed, thus ensuring close future co-operation between Chadacre and FTCAT. Thus, by the May meeting, the Trust transformation was almost complete. The trustees agreed a new working title of Felix Cobbold Trust and the new aims and objectives should be 'to advance and improve agriculture and related industries, in particular to educate

and inform farmers, trainees and the general public by supporting training, demonstrations, research and development'.[2]

Many of the administrative problems had now been solved – the new administrator was given a mandate to manage the COIF funds and a new bank account was set up. Several requests for funding had also been received for consideration and were approved during the next few months. Work was put in hand to produce a new logo and this was completed by the July meeting so that the new stationery and website could be designed.

The trustees also considered the appointment of new trustees. Suffolk County Council confirmed that they would continue to make appointments, but as both the council appointments and the Suffolk Agricultural Association appointments were made at the end of a four-yearly cycle it could happen that all trustees might be appointed on the same day, resulting in a loss of continuity. The four additional trustees would then be appointed by the new trustees, rather than remaining in the post from the previous session.

In July 2009, an agreement was made to safeguard the Trust, partly because the Charity Commission asked that trustees should have no other interest than to act on behalf of the Trust, and they should be selected according to their experience and skills. The solution was that the Trust itself should now accept responsibility for appointing all trustees as independent trustees, and continuity would be achieved by a rolling programme of retirements. Each trustee would serve for three years and then retire in rotation, but would be eligible for re-election. Thus, there would be nine trustees, with up to three retiring each year. In changing the method of appointment, it was decided that new trustees should be recruited with particular expertise. Hence, Alan Hawes is an accountant, Mike May is a scientist, and James Forrest is a farmer. At last, almost a hundred years since the establishment of the Trust, the problem of maintaining continuity among trustees was finally resolved.

Estate Matters

In April 2008, Lacy Scott & Knight took over from Strutt & Parker as the property management agents for the estate, with Rowland Beaney and Philip Scarff providing overall and day-to-day supervision respectively.

Also in April 2008, a new lease was created for Hope Farm House, which was granted to Simon and Nicola Bloss, who wished to re-establish a caravan storage business and set up an equine business.

Of the Stanaway buildings, a new tenant moved into the old piggeries and grain store to operate a chauffeur and car hire business, and the former farm workshop was let to a fitness equipment company. A few months later in 2008 a tenant was found for the visitor centre. It was also decided that a derelict concrete and asbestos barn should be replaced by a new portal frame building 20 metres by 18 metres, and this was finally completed in January 2010. When Paul Creasey vacated Stanaway Farmhouse in January 2009 a programme of damp proofing and renovation was carried out on the building prior to its being re-let. Additionally, as Lacy Scott & Knight had now taken over the property management work from Strutt & Parker a storage unit was bought and installed in the farmyard to house the archive files.

On Stanaway Farm, John Taylor was finding rabbits a problem so additional fencing was installed around three sides of Nelson Field. Rabbit fencing was also installed at Hope Farm, where a similar problem existed.

The STAR trials continued and began to produce useful agronomic information. It was agreed that Dr Philip Draycott would be involved in producing the final report. By 2008, the project had attracted a high level of interest across the industry and results had been considered at a number of industry events, such as the Oilseed and Pulse Conference 2009, and were featured in the agricultural research press.

In 2009, it was announced that The Arable Group (TAG), who were organising the STAR trials, had decided to merge with the National Institute of Agricultural Botany (NIAB) and would in future be known as the NIAB/TAG group. The new chairman of the group would be Tony Paxton OBE, who currently also chaired the Nuffield Farming Scholarships Trust and the Sustainable Arable Link R&D Programme Management Committee for DEFRA. The new group would thus have greater resources to 'support the development of improved crop varieties and inputs, to evaluate their performance, and – through applied agronomy research and farmer communication – to ensure the benefits are transferred effectively into practical agriculture'.

FTCAT had been helping to sponsor the TAG Professional Development Training scheme, and they decided to continue to offer help to the new NIAB/TAG programme.

Also in 2009, the Trust purchased an additional 33 acres of Pear Tree Farm and this land was added to the tenancy of John Taylor. In January 2010, it was also agreed that a long-standing problem of access to the field behind the White Horse pub should be resolved by asking the adjacent farmer to undertake all cultivations.

Death of John Forrest and Jeremy Clover

The chairman, John Forrest, died unexpectedly in April 2008, and his place was taken temporarily by Robert Baker, until October, when Stephen Cobbald was elected as chairman and Robert Baker returned to his post of vice chairman.

John Forrest's family asked whether a memorial fund could be set up in his name, which would be administered by FTCAT. John had worked tirelessly during the difficult time in which the Trust had been reshaped, and his loss was keenly felt by the trustees. By January 2009 plans were drawn up and a meeting of the newly formed John Forrest Memorial Award committee was held at Bury St Edmunds Farmers Club to discuss funding and objectives. It was agreed that the main objective should be 'to further the personal development of young agriculturists for the wider benefit of the industry'.[3] It was also agreed that the first award would be 'to provide training for young scientists in communication skills'.[4] Visitors to the funeral of John had contributed £5,005, which was now available as funding for the new Memorial Award, and it was agreed to seek additional funding from major industry firms and charities. By October 2009 a total of £8,091 had been raised, and the Memorial Award made plans with WRENmedia for the first course (5–7 January 2010) for a possible eight students funded. However, due to adverse weather this very successful course was postponed to 28 30 June.

A second loss among trustees occurred in February 2009, when Jeremy Clover died. Jeremy had been a trustee appointed by Suffolk County Council for 20 years, thus serving during the critical years in which the Trust was reformed.

Otley College 2008

During 2008, Otley College again began negotiations to buy their site, this time because it was possible that funding might be available from the Learning and Skills Council. By January 2009 a firm offer was received by the trustees for the 60.7 acres of the site.

The trustees had always been reluctant to sell this land, but after long discussion they now agreed to the plan. Completion needed to be before the end of March 2009 when the LSC were being closed. However, by April the college reported that their possible funding was not forthcoming and they were having trouble identifying alternative sources. A rent review was now overdue, so Lacy Scott & Knight were asked to initiate one.

At this time Otley had also asked for funding for a new Agricultural Link Co-ordinator for Suffolk as a way of increasing the number of good candidates entering the industry via further and higher education. The successful candidate might be incorporated onto the staff of the college. The Trust agreed with the provisos that they should be invited to sit on the appointment panel, and that the Chadacre Agricultural Trust should also be asked to provide funding.

AgriFood Charities Partnership

The AFCP was formed in 2006 at the instigation of the Perry Foundation as an initiative to co-ordinate research grant awards between agricultural charities, with Dr Paul Biscoe as CEO and Philip Richardson of TMAF on the committee. Colin Smith attended the first meeting in East Anglia in October 2009 to discuss best practice for grant-awarding agricultural charities in the region. Paul Biscoe had conducted a survey of the work of 17 trusts, which was used for the basis of discussions. The meeting was to be followed by similar gatherings in the southwest and north-east of the country.

Grant Awards

By 2009, trustees had begun to discover for themselves the most useful way to distribute grants, and these varied from grants to individuals to local events and a variety of research programmes. The formal structure adopted was to make awards in six categories: Education and Training, Research and Development, Promotion and Publicity, Capital Works and Equipment, Production and Marketing, and Environment and Wildlife. Thus, 37 farmers were sponsored for The Arable Group Professional Development Training, as part of the education and training element of the grants, and research into phoma stem canker in winter oilseed rape was supported. For industry promotion, Writtle was given a grant to support the Essex Schools Food and Farming Day in June 2009, with just under 3,000 primary school children attending an event held at Writtle College. The Trust had also decided to support some environmental and wildlife projects and in 2008 sponsored a research student for a year working with the Game and Conservation Trust. For many projects funding came from a variety of sources, such as the Chadacre Agricultural Trust.

Trustees 2010 and Governance

At the January 2010 meeting, the newly composed and constituted trustees group first met. The Charities Commission, Suffolk County Council, and Suffolk Agricultural Association had all agreed that the change

Trustees of the Felix Thornley Cobbold Agricultural Trust, 2011. Back row, left to right: James Forrest, Mike May, Alan Hawes, Bruce Hinton, John Field. Front row, left to right: Robert (Bill) Baker, Stephen Cobbald (chairman), Dr Philip Draycott. (Colin Smith)

should be made to a committee composed of trustees appointed by trustees, and retiring in rotation – a change that had been one of the final concerns of the late John Forrest.

Thus, at the January meeting, the trustees were Stephen Cobbald, chairman, Dr A P Draycott, J D Field, Alan Hawes, Mike May (who had recently retired from Broom's Barn Research Station), and Bruce N Hinton, with apologies from Robert Baker and M G Harris. At the next meeting in April 2010, the trustees elected a further trustee, James Forrest, the son of the late John Forrest, who had taken over the family farm business in Stonham Aspal.

In the summer of 2010, the Trust suffered another loss when Philip Scarff, the land agent working for Lacy Scott & Knight, was killed in a road accident while cycling. His place was taken by Chris Philpot.

Grant Awards 2010–2011

By the end of the final financial year of the Trust century, the Trust had agreed 34 awards to a value of £130,819. Grants were no longer confined just to Suffolk, but included East Anglian region projects, such as help for the Essex Schools' Food and Farming Day held at Writtle College mentioned previously. Of the total for the year, £61,094 remained unclaimed, but of the £69,725 distributed, 54 per cent went to research projects, 27 per cent to education, 14 per cent to public education and four per cent to environmental research. The unclaimed grants were due to unavoidable delays in starting research (among other things) but meant that the earmarked funding was thus unavailable for alternative projects.

Two projects requiring grant awards – both of which fell into the research and trials category – approached the Trust for help and/or advice in the final year of the Trust's first century. The first was a plea to assist in keeping Saxmundham Experimental Station operational and the second was a request made by Dr Belinda Townsend for a grant for a research student for Broom's Barn Research Station.

The first project concerns the Saxmundham Experimental Station approach and it is interesting for several reasons. Harry Fiske, ex-chairman of the Trust, had worked at the station when it first opened in 1899. It had been set up by East Suffolk County Council with 'whisky money' applied to agricultural education. The

original objective of the station was to demonstrate that farmyard manure could be replaced by 'artificial' fertilisers and other experiments were aimed at improving grassland. All that remained of the original station is Harwoods Field, approximately 2.8 ha, which constituted the old Rotation 1 site. Work at the station had carried on for much of the time although it was mothballed in 1986 until 1998/9 when Rothamsted Research, Levington Agriculture and Norsk Hydro put the field back into cultivation to celebrate its centenary. With the demise of Levington and changes in the fertiliser industry, the work was taken forward by British Sugar who carried out a rotation of beet on the four blocks of Rotation 1. In 2003, Edmund Brown was asked if he could keep Rotation 1 going after British Sugar withdrew, and it was cropped and fertilised and the plots taken to yield from harvest 2004 until 2010.

In 2008, Natural England's Catchment Sensitive Farming (CSF) team used the site for a demonstration called 'Getting the Balance Right' which attracted around 100 farmers to the site.

Currently the site deeds are held by BBSRC and leased to Rothamsted Research, under an agreement which will last until 2030, although Rothamsted has currently no use for the site, so it is being leased by ADAS for two years of phosphate experiments. The Trust was approached to see if support could be raised to prevent this historic site being lost to agricultural research. After careful consideration of all the factors, the Trust reluctantly concluded that the costs of maintaining the site were disproportionate to the likely scientific benefit to the industry.

The second project, the Broom's Barn Research Station application, is important for its significance to the current state of agriculture and its relationship to global warming. The station plans to research the genes that influence the cell wall structure of sugar beet roots. Sugar beet is an attractive feedstock for bioprocessing to produce novel by-products; it is also ideal for second-generation bio fuel production using waste pulp instead of extracted juice. This will become an important part of sustainably managed industrial projects with reduced reliance on fossil fuels for transport and industrial projects. Diversifying the market opportunities for sugar beet will help to secure the future of this crop for the East of England.[5]

The waste pulp generated as a result of sugar

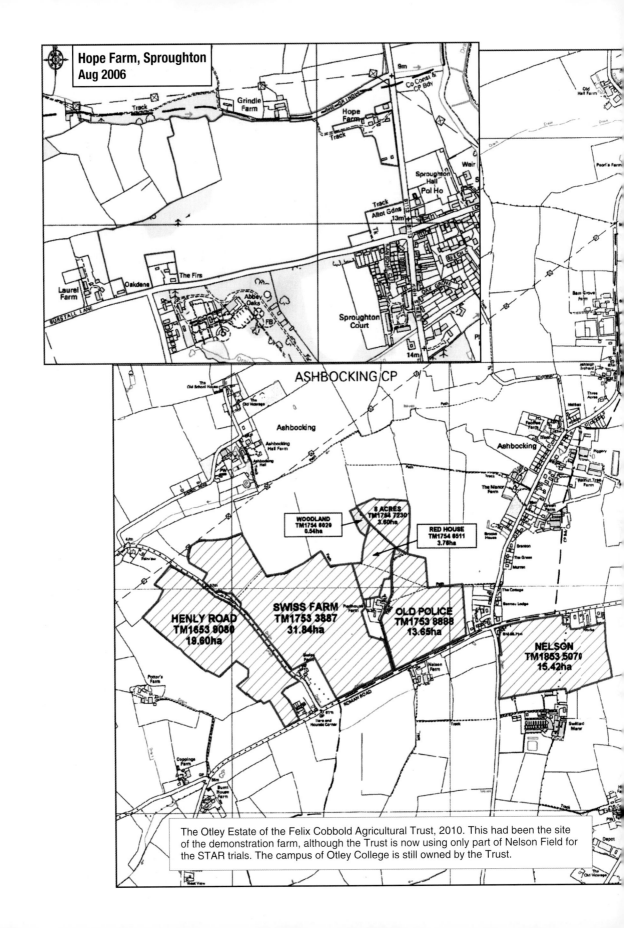

Hope Farm, Sproughton
Aug 2006

ASHBOCKING CP

The Otley Estate of the Felix Cobbold Agricultural Trust, 2010. This had been the site of the demonstration farm, although the Trust is now using only part of Nelson Field for the STAR trials. The campus of Otley College is still owned by the Trust.

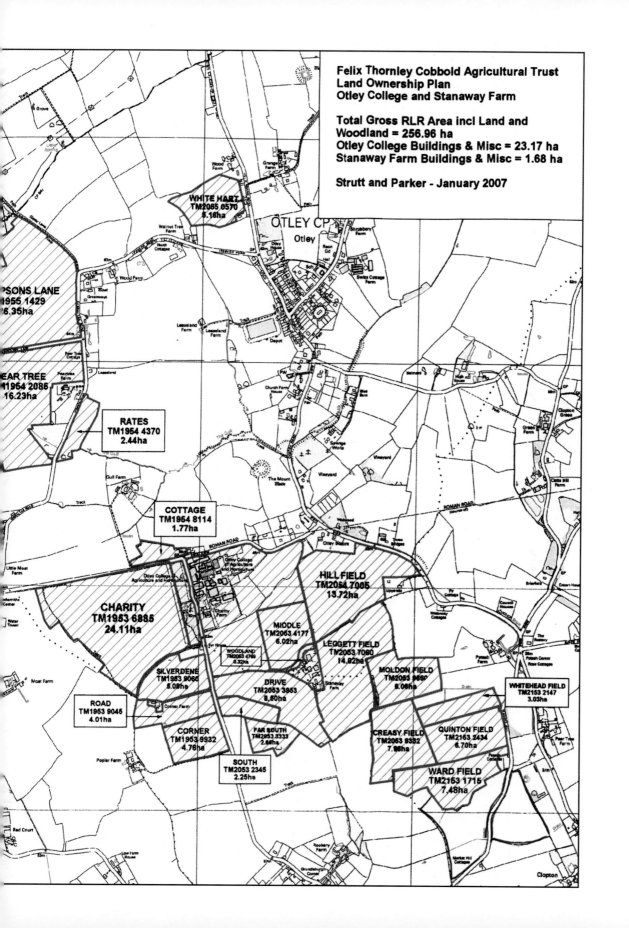

Felix Thornley Cobbold Agricultural Trust
Land Ownership Plan
Otley College and Stanaway Farm

Total Gross RLR Area incl Land and
Woodland = 256.96 ha
Otley College Buildings & Misc = 23.17 ha
Stanaway Farm Buildings & Misc = 1.68 ha

Strutt and Parker - January 2007

extraction from whole roots is mostly dried for sale as a high-energy animal feed. Pulp contains some residual sugar but is mostly composed of the cell walls of the plant – a mixture of cellulose, hemicelluloses and pectin which are made up of a complex network of different sugars which could be further exploited. The research will use molecular genetics and biochemical approaches to identify key genes that impact the structure of the cell wall in sugar beet roots so that breeding targets can be set up to produce beet for sustainable and efficient bioprocessing.

This project was also supported by the Chadacre Agricultural Trust and demonstrated further the way in which the trusts are now co-operating to support agricultural research. Sadly, this project was axed in the revision of research objectives at Broom's Barn, the sugar beet research station.

STAR Project

In 2010, the NIAB Sustainability Trial in Arable Rotation (STAR) research project – begun in 2005 as part of the work of the demonstration farm – held a successful open day on 6 July attended by over 60 people. Although the original plan was to end the trial in 2010, it is proving so successful that the Trust agreed that Ron Stobart, head of crop research communication at

2010 photo of the Sustainability Trial in Arable Rotation (STAR) research project on Nelson Field, Trust estate at Otley. (NIAB)

NIAB/TAG, should continue until 2014 and then have a further grant for six months to write up and present the results.

In July 2011, Ron reported that the project shows the importance of ploughing to manage grass weeds in wheat. Thus, growers who establish wheat using non-inversion cultivations should reduce grass weed populations with a range of techniques, rather than relying on high input herbicide programmes and for some rotations a return to the plough may be the most profitable option.

The Felix Cobbold Agricultural Trust and a New Century[6]

At the end of its first century, the Trust has shown that it is now perhaps even more relevant to agriculture in East Anglia than it was when it was created by East Suffolk County Council in 1910. At a time of economic uncertainty, government funding for research is being cut to the minimum and the work of agricultural trusts has taken on an urgent new significance.

We have seen over the last hundred years the ways in which central control exercised both through 'the stick' of legislation and 'the carrot' of subsidies, has shaped the face of British agriculture, but in the present situation the coalition government is seeking to pass power back to the community.

Power over decision-making has returned to the roots of the industry, and although there are few philanthropists – such as Felix Cobbold, Lord Iveagh and Harper Adams – to carry forward the work of educational research and training, the trusts formed from their bequests are now filling the void caused by the withdrawal of central control. On the Rothamsted Research project – a project that explored the risk of severe phoma stem canker on oilseed rape – 16 'industrial partners', including FTCAT, are funding the work. This project was subsequently transferred to the University of Hertford. Similarly, the Broom's Barn project discussed on page 127 is being supported both by FTCAT and the Chadacre Agricultural Trust. Agricultural research like these projects is increasingly influenced by part-funding from industry in LINK projects with government funding agencies, and thus agricultural charities have become a vital extra source of such funding packages.

Early in 2011, the trustees invited a small group of people with expert knowledge and from key organisations in East Anglia to join them for a forum to discuss the future work of the Trust and identify areas of need. This group included Mike Appleyard, the regional partnership manager of Lantra; Dr Tina Barsby, the chief executive of NIAB TAG; Dr Paul Biscoe, the chief executive of AFCP; Ian Campbell, Unitron UK Ltd; Stephen Fletcher, the chairman of the Suffolk Agricultural Association; Jim Godfrey, vice chairman of the Practice with Science Group, RASE; the Earl of Iveagh, Elvedon Farms Ltd and chairman of the Chadacre Agricultural Trust; David Lawrence, principal of Easton College, and Tim Schofield, Suffolk FWAG. It was a useful conference which focused primarily on research and education, identifying several areas in which the Trust could target resources, such as:

1. The Trust should consider working more closely with other agricultural development charities in East Anglia to provide substantial funding for major projects, which would also increase their influence on local research. At a national level, this will enhance the negotiating power of the AgriFood Charities Partnership when discussing research priorities with official bodies.

2. The group considered that Trust support would be beneficial in generating more awareness of agriculture as a rewarding career. Schools at present do not appear to feel that agricultural work is a suitable career, and the appointment of a schools liaison officer at Otley College was regarded as an important step, along with providing support materials for the National Curriculum 14+ age group.

3. In the field of tertiary education, Otley College has found it difficult to maintain its agricultural education courses partly due to the lack of interest from schools noted above. However, on-farm basic training is not sufficient to provide the high level of technical skills required, and health and safety legislation coupled with a lack of colleagues with time to teach means that much practical training must be off-farm. To

meet these needs, Easton College is evolving into a College of Contemporary Agriculture, offering BSc and MSc degrees in association with the University of East Anglia, and the Trust will be able to support this development of high-level agricultural training in the eastern region.

4. One other traditional means of providing skills training, the Young Farmers Clubs, appears to be in difficulty at county organisational level. Increased funding is required for organisation, recruitment, leadership and training, so that the YFCs can become a major force in attracting young people into the industry.

5. Since the withdrawal of the free farm advisory services, there has been a problem with the dissemination of research knowledge for the last decade. Regional training groups organised by NIAB TAG reach mainly elite groups, and the work of other freelance and crop-specific agronomists is available to narrow client groups only. The group identified a need for the Trust to fund and promote internet-based dissemination of information about new technology, innovation and research.

Agricultural research has traditionally adapted and applied techniques developed in other fields. This is expected to continue, particularly in plant and animal breeding, disease control for crops and livestock, response to climate change, effects of agriculture on soil structure, water conservation, bio energy production and energy generation, and managing the effects on wildlife and the environment. The Trust expects to participate in funding large and small projects in all these important fields.

Conclusion

For assets and finance, the Trust started the twentieth century with 861 acres, 25 perches, together with very little money after duties had been paid. At the end of the century, the Trust has assets totalling £6,000,000, including 790 acres of land, the site of Otley College, two let farmhouses and three industrial units. In addition, trustees have been investing money throughout the century and, despite recent falls in interest rates and money being distributed in grants each year, the total held in equities and cash is now £990,000. It is an astonishing record of good husbandry. Despite guiding the Trust through a century of wars, pestilence and turbulent money markets, the trustees have survived with assets and the financial power to carry on the intentions of their founder, Felix Thornley Cobbold, into an uncertain future.

At the beginning of a second century, the Trust will strive to ensure that the resources at their disposal are used to advance and improve agriculture, and, in particular, to educate farmers and young people in the agricultural methods, developments and techniques used in Suffolk and the adjoining counties.

NOTES

1   Taylor, Craig. *Return to Akenfield*. London: Granta Books, 2006. p 115.
2   Charity Commission, FTCAT objective.
3   Minutes of the JF Arward committee meeting.
4   Ibid.
5   Details taken from the bid document.
6   The information for this section has been provided by Colin Smith, Trust administrator.

Appendix I

Properties donated to East Suffolk County Council by Felix Cobbold in 1910, taken from the Charity Commission Order

Extract from the will of Felix Thornley Cobbold:

I devise and bequeath my real estate at Hadleigh and Hintlesham, called Pond Hall Farm, and the Valley Farm, and the Ramsey Farm, and also my land at Sproughton, which is occupied in small holdings and allotments, and as respects the Hadleigh and Hintlesham farms, all the growing crops and stock on the farms, live and dead, and all the carts and other farming implements, and the banking account kept at the Ipswich Capital and Counties Bank, under the name of George T Harrison, Pond Hall Account, to the East Suffolk County Council, upon trust that they use the said hereditaments and personal estate, and the rents and profits arising therefrom in developing small holdings and allotments on as much of the land in Hadleigh as is not already so occupied, and on any other land that they may acquire by means of such rents and profits. And in case the East Suffolk Council refuse to accept the above devise and bequest, or are disqualified by law from accepting the same, then I direct that the said hereditaments at Hadleigh and Hintlesham and Sproughton, and the said farming stock and money at the said banking accounts shall fall into and form part of my residuary real and personal estate.

Description	Area (in acres, rods and perches)
Farm at Hadleigh and Hintlesham – Ramsey Farm	129 3 21
Farm at Hadleigh – Pond Hall Farm	289 0 16
Farm at Hadleigh – Valley Farm	216 1 32
House and land in Hadleigh and Hintlesham	12 1 28
House and land in Hadleigh	8 0 35
House and land in Hadleigh	8 0 26
Cottage in Hadleigh	
House in Hadleigh	
Cottage in Hadleigh	
Garden in Hadleigh	
House and land in Hadleigh	14 2 23
House and land in Hadleigh	14 0 0
House and land in Hadleigh	10 0 0
Pair of cottages in Hadleigh	0 1 36
House and land in Hadleigh	11 2 30
House and land in Hadleigh	0 2 27
Land in Hadleigh	35 2 17
Allotments in Hadleigh	20 2 0
Roads and fences in Hadleigh abutting on land let off	5 2 25
House and land in Sproughton	9 0 0
Land in Sproughton	10 3 8
House and land in Sproughton	17 2 0
Land in Sproughton	14 2 6
House and land in Sproughton	8 0 0
Cottage and land in Sproughton	0 1 0
Land in Sproughton	3 0 0
Land in Sproughton	1 0 0
House and land in Sproughton	4 0 0
House and land in Sproughton	10 0 0
Land in Sproughton	5 0 0

Appendix II

Chairmen of the Trust 1910–2010

George Edward John Mowbray Rous KCMG, CB, CVO, CBE, VD, TD

Third Earl of Stradbroke 1862–1947
Chairman 1910–1914

As Viscount Dunwich he was commissioned in the 1st Norfolk Artillery Volunteers in 1882, and promoted to Major in 1884. In 1888 he was made Lieutenant-Colonel and full Colonel in 1902. He finally retired from the Royal Artillery Company in 1930. After the First World War, he was made Governor of Victoria, Australia from 1921–1929 and from 1928–1929 became Parliamentary Secretary to the Ministry of Agriculture and Fisheries. He was Vice Admiral of Suffolk from 1890–1947 and Lord Lieutenant of Suffolk from 1935–1937. He succeeded his father, John Rous, to the title of third Earl of Stradbroke in 1886 when he was only 24 and still studying for an MA at Cambridge.

His family seat was Henham Hall, originally the home of the De La Pole Family, partly rebuilt by Edward M Barry in 1858, with a park improved by Henry Repton. When sold by the 'Aussie Earl' in 2001, it had an estate of 4,214 acres.

George Fiske

Chairman (1914), 1916–1917

George had been on the committee since the first negotiations and frequently took the chair in the absence of Lord Stradbroke. During the war, Lord Stradbroke sent in his resignation as he had been sent to the front, but the committee declined his resignation. However, he never returned to the committee, so George became chairman until his death in spring 1917.

George was born in 1870 at Chediston and farmed 1,600 acres in Bramford: 600 of his own and the remainder as a tenant. In 1901, he moved to Hill House, Playford, and then Thornbush Farm, Sproughton, so that his land was contiguous with Felix Cobbold's. At one point, he also owned Havergate Island. He was a county councillor, a Justice of the Peace and on the Board of Guardians.

Harry Fiske

Chairman 1917–1946

Harry took over the committee on the death of his father, George, and continued until July 1946 when he retired. Harry died in 1947. He had many vice chairmen during his time, notably H N Mason.

He lived at Runcton Hall, Bramford before taking over Thornbush Farm, Sproughton. His great grandmother had been living at Thornbush Farm after the death of his father, so he did not move into the farmhouse until after her death.

His first job was with Fison Packard Prentice Company making fertilisers; Harry was involved with several experimental stations, one on his own farm. In all, he farmed about 2,000 acres at Somersham and Alderton, as well as Flowton, Burstall and Brandon. He owned 97 Suffolk Punch horses, which were sold on his death, along with everything else on the farm. His son, Jack, inherited the land and house but nothing else. Harry, like his father, served as a Justice of the Peace.

Felix C Smith

Chairman July 1946–1949

Felix had several vice chairmen, including W Chalmers Mitchell and Lord Alastair Graham in 1949. He was born in 1900 at Trimley St Mary and farmed Searson's Farm. Felix died in 1968.

Sir Peter McClintock Greenwell

Chairman August 1949–April 1952

The vice chairmen during his time included Lord Alastair Graham.

Peter was born in 1914 and educated at Winchester and Trinity College, Cambridge. In the Second World War he served as a captain in the Royal Artillery (Territorial Army) and became a prisoner of war in Colditz Castle. On his return, he returned to farming a 3,000-acre estate at Butley and Gedgrave, living at Gedgrave Hall, having studied agriculture at Cambridge. He became a chairman of Ransomes, Sims and Jefferies, and served on the board of Anglia TV with an agricultural remit.

He was also a Justice of the Peace and became High Sheriff of Suffolk in 1966. He died in 1978.

Capt Lord Alastair Mungo Graham

Chairman 1952–April 1964

His vice chairman was R H Rash.

Lord Graham was born in 1886, youngest son of the fifth Duke of Montrose, he studied at HMS Britannia, the forerunner of Dartmouth College. In 1911, he was officer of the watch as a young lieutenant on the Canadian cruiser, *Niobe*, when it ran aground off Nova Scotia. At the court martial, his commanding officer spoke well of him, so his sword was returned the following day.

After the war, he returned to his home at Campsea Ashe and farmed his own 130 acres and 590 acres from two farms from the Glemham Estate at Farnham and Blaxhall. He became a county councillor, a Church Commissioner, and a member of the Diocesan Board of Finance. Lord Graham died in 1976.

E J W (Jack) Fiske

Chairman July 1964 until his death in 1976

He was a trustee for a total of 23 years and chairman for 12 years. J O Youngman was his vice chairman for some years and so was R R Harvey who also died in the spring of 1976.

Born in 1909 at Burstall Hall, Jack was the son of Edgar Fiske, nephew of Harry Fiske and only grandson of George. He attended Ipswich School and Wye College of Agriculture. He inherited Thornbush Farm and Fiske Farms on the death of his uncle, farming 1,000 acres. Jack was a county councillor, a Justice of the Peace, the first chairman of the governors of Otley College and a member of Samford Rural District Council and Gipping Rural District Council. He is commemorated by the Fiske Memorial Plantation on the college land.

C C Smith
Chairman July 1976 but decided to retire shortly after.
Capt R G Sheepshanks was in the chair on 29 September in his absence.

Lt Col J M H R (Mike) Tomkin
Chairman January 1977–March 1985
D R Dickson was Lt Col Tomkin's vice chairman for some time.

Mike was born in 1918 at Norton, Suffolk, and educated at Eton and Trinity College, Cambridge. He was commissioned in 1939 and posted to the second Northamptonshire Yeomanry but later seconded to the Queens Bays in Libya, where he was awarded an MC for destroying six tanks at El Alamein, despite suffering from a broken arm. He also fought in Tunisia and Italy and Korea before retiring from the army in 1963 after serving as an instructor at the National Defence College at Latimer. He became Deputy Lieutenant of Suffolk and for many years was joint Master of the Waveney Harriers Hunt. He became High Sheriff in 1978 and chairman of the Suffolk Police Authority from 1978 to 1986. He was also a governor of Halesworth Middle School, Lowestoft College, Otley College, and a council member of the University of East Anglia. He died in July 2008.

Capt Robin J Sheepshanks
Chairman 1985–1993
His vice chairmen included F Barker and H A Mitson from 1989.

Capt Robin Sheepshanks was born in 1925 and served in the army during the war in the King's Own Dragoons before returning to take over the family farm at Rendlesham. He was elected as a councillor for East Suffolk County from 1964 until its reorganisation, and then became a member of Suffolk County Council. He was leader of the council from 1978–1981, and chairman from 1982–1984. He was chairman of the Suffolk Police Authority for eight years from 1985–1993. He served as deputy Lord Lieutenant of Suffolk and High Sheriff, and was awarded a CBE for his service to local government. He died in 2007 after a long illness.

Kenneth J Doran
Chairman November 1993–1999
Kenneth Doran's vice chairmen included H A Mitson who retired after 25 years as a trustee, and died in 1999. John R Forrest was his vice chairman from 1996.

Kenneth was born in Bebington, Cheshire, and studied Modern Languages at Pembroke College, Cambridge. He

had a career in international banking in London before retiring to Woodbridge. He then served on Melton Parish Council and became the Labour councillor for Bridge Ward, Ipswich. He was chairman of Suffolk County Council from 1997 until his death in June 1999.

John R Forrest
March 1999 – until his death in 2008
During his time as chairman, his vice chairmen included B J C Moore and Bruce Hinton from 2001.

John was born in 1945 at Sandpit Farm, Bruisyard of Scottish stock, and brought up at Clamp Farm, Stowmarket. He attended St Felix Preparatory School at Felixstowe and then Gresham's. He had always wanted to farm, so went to Writtle – then called Essex Agricultural Institute – and gained a Certificate of Agriculture in 1964. In 1968, he became chairman of the local Young Farmers' Club (YFC). Shortly after he took over Mowness Hall, then a run-down farm and ran it with meticulous attention to detail. He was passionate about arable farming, and later became a keen member of the Alpha Group of arable farmers. He was a board member of Eastern Counties Farmers, and a founder member of Gipping Valley Growers. He served as a governor of Otley College and a county councillor and was involved with Morley and The Arable Group (TAG). A Memorial Fund has been set up in his name.

Robert Baker
Chairman 2008 – Acting chairman on the death of John Forrest
Robert was vice chairman when John Forrest died in April 2008, so succeeded to the chairmanship. However, he had too many other commitments, particularly with the Suffolk Agricultural Association and the National Sugar Beet Committee, so chose to revert to vice chairman at the AGM in October 2008.

Robert is a substantial and progressive arable farmer with land at Elmswell and Drinkstone.

Stephen Cobbald
Chairman 2008 – present
Stephen Cobbald was born at Acton Hall, Acton, and has lived and farmed there since the death of his father in 1968. His family have been farming in Suffolk for 450 years. Today he farms 2,200 acres in the Sudbury/Lavenham area growing arable crops with 100 acres of grass supporting a flock of sheep.

He has served in a number of positions with Suffolk Agricultural Association and has been a local chairman of the National Farmers Union (NFU) as well as a Suffolk County Deputy Delegate. He holds one ministerial position as a member of the Rural Payments Agency's independent appeals panel.

Stephen has a life-long passion for breeding sheep, and has been both national president and chairman of the Suffolk Sheep Society. He is currently chairman of the Eastern Area of the Texel Society, and has represented the sheep industry in the UK and Europe. He was governor of Otley College, and became chairman of their finance and general purpose committee. This role led on to becoming a trustee of the Felix Thornley Cobbold Trust.

Bibliography

Much of the quoted material in this book comes directly from minute books of the Felix Thornley Cobbold Agricultural Trust.

Books

Arch, Joseph. *From Ploughtail to Parliament: an autobiography of Joseph Arch*. London: The Cresset Library, 1986.

Bensusan, S L. *Latter Day Rural England*. London: Ernest Benn Ltd, 1928.

Blythe, Ronald. *Akenfield: Portrait of an English Village*. Harmondsworth: Penguin Books, 1972.

Booth, General William. *In Darkest England and the Way Out*. London: Diggory Press, 1890.

Carson, Rachel. *Silent Spring*. London: Hamish Hamilton, 1963.

Creaton, Heather J. 'Sources for the History of London 1939–1945.' London: British Records Association, 1998.

Ernle, Lord. *English Farming Past and Present*. London: Longmans Press, 1912.

Evans, George Ewart. *The Farm and the Village*. London: Faber & Faber Ltd, 1969.

Evans, George Ewart. *Where Beards Wag All – The Relevance of the Oral Tradition*. London: Faber & Faber Ltd, 1970.

Groves, Reg. *Sharpen the Sickle – the History of the Farm Workers' Union*. London: Porcupine Press, 1949.

Howkins, Alun. *Reshaping Rural England*. London: Harper-Adams Academic, 1991.

Howkins, Alun. *The Death of Rural England: A Social History of the Countryside Since 1900*. London: Routledge, 2003.

Taylor, Craig. *Return to Akenfield*. London: Granta Books, 2006.

Thomas, R. *To Suffolk with Love: the life of Felix Thornley Cobbold*. Stowmarket, Pawprint Publishing, 2009.

Wood, Anthony. *Nineteenth Century Britain: 1815–1914*. London: Longmans, 1960.

Reports and Acts of Parliament

Agricultural Act, 1947

Agricultural Holdings Act, 1948

Allotments Act, 1887

British Parliamentary Paper, 1857–8 XVII, pp 107–10

Country and Wildlife Act, 1981

European Union Statement. *Agenda 2000 – A CAP for the Future*, 1999, Brussels

Henslow, Rev J S. *Appendix to Hitcham Allotment Report for 1857* (Suffolk Record Office Document) Royal Commission on Agriculture, 1895

Industrial and Provident Societies Act, 1893

Rent Restrictions Act, 1948

Royal Commission on Agriculture, 1895

Royal Commission on Environmental Pollution, 7th Report: Agriculture and Pollution (1976) Cmnd. 7644 and 11th Report: Managing Waste: the Duty of Care (1985) Cmnd. 9675

Small Holdings and Allotments Act, 1908

Treaty of Rome, 1957

Town and Country Planning Act, 1947

Journals and Articles

Conford, Philip. 'Eve Balfour: the founder of the Soil Association.' The Soil Association's *Living Earth* magazine. 2003, Summer Edition.

East Anglian Daily Times newspaper

Flight magazine. 3 November 1927.

Huxley, R R, Lloyd, B B Goldacre, M and Neil, H A W. 'Nutritional research in World War 2: the Oxford Nutrition Survey and its research potential 50 years later.' British Journal of Nutrition. Vol 84, Issue 02. Cambridge University Press, 2000. pp 247–251

Ipswich Journal

Macrae, W D. 'The Eradication of Bovine Tuberculosis.' Paper presented at the Zoological Society Symposium. London: Zoo Society, 1961. pp 81–100

Oldershaw, A W. 'Experiments on Arable Crops at Saxmundham.' Journal of the Royal Agricultural Society of England. Vol 102. 1941.

Royal Agricultural Society Journal, 1863

Media

Mud, Sweat and Tears series. BBC Television, 2009.

Index

Bold numbers indicate an illustration and 'n' refers to a note.

About the Author

Rosalind Thomas read English at Goldsmiths and Queen Mary College in London before training as a teacher and librarian. She then worked for Southwark Libraries until she moved to Suffolk in the mid-80s.

In 1992, Rosalind joined the staff of Otley College as Librarian and since her retirement has worked as an indexer, specialising in medicine and agriculture, and as a Quaker archivist. She studied local and regional history at the University of East Anglia and the University of Essex, and in 2009 published the book *To Suffolk with Love* – a biography of Felix Thornley Cobbold.

The trustees join other guests at an open day for the STAR project in 2011.

Other Books and DVDs from Old Pond Publishing

Farm Office Handbook   Institute of Agricultural Secretaries and Administrators
A practical reference source for anyone involved in farm administration, this handbook offers comprehensive guidance on: farm office basics; setting up accounting systems; computerising a manual accounting system; VAT and Payroll; year-end procedures; management reporting and budgeting; and statutory and assurance records. *Farm Office Handbook* provides website details for legislative updates and a list of contacts for rural businesses. Paperback

Hadleigh: the portrait of a Suffolk town   David Kindred
Commercial photographer Peter Boulton recorded Hadleigh and its people in the 1940s and '50s: the town and villages; wartime work; craftsmen; carnivals; fêtes and sports days. Paperback

In a Long Day   David Kindred and Roger Smith
These 200 captioned photographs show Suffolk farm work and village life 1925–35: working horses, steam-powered threshing, rural trades and transport. Paperback

Just a Moment   David Kindred and Roger Smith
Transport scenes from around Ipswich 1925–35: motorbikes, buses, charabancs, vans and horse-drawn freight. Ipswich docks, road-building and the railways. Paperback

Farming Day by Day – the '60s   John Winter
This extensive selection of John Winter's reports from the *Daily Mail* recalls farming in the 1960s – the price reviews, push for greater output, weather and the harvests. Hardback

Ipswich: the changing face of the town   David Kindred
With over 300 photographs the author shows how Ipswich has changed over the past 100 years. He has gone quarter by quarter through the town and describes how you can still find many of the older buildings, survivors of waves of development. Change continues today with the transformation of Ipswich Dock and the building of a new university. Hardback

Brian Bell's 'Classic' archive series
These four DVD compilations of archive footage – much of it manufacturers' promotional films – constitute an unrivalled picture of the development of farm mechanisation in Britain. Compiled by Brian Bell with a clear, full narration.

Classic Tractors   **Classic Farm Machinery: 1940–1970**
Classic Combines   **Classic Farm Machinery: 1970–1995**

The Know Your . . . series
This range of pocket-sized paperbacks is designed to give an insight into what you are likely to see today in the countryside. The full-page photographs and concise informative texts are designed for novice enthusiasts of all ages. Some examples from the livestock and machinery range are:

Know Your Sheep   Jack Byard
The 41 breeds which you are most likely to see on farms today.

Know Your Tractors   Chris Lockwood
These 41 tractors include current models and one or two classics.

Free complete catalogue:
Old Pond Publishing Ltd, Dencora Business Centre
36 White House Road, Ipswich IP1 5LT, United Kingdom
Secure online ordering: **www.oldpond.com**   Phone: 01473 238200